10⁹⁵

Famous

T   E
C

This book is dedicated
with love to
Elaine and Nicholas

Library of Congress Cataloging in Publication Data

Daniels, Harvey A.
  Famous last words.

  Bibliography: p.
  Includes index.
  1. English language—United States.
2. English language—Usage. 3. English
language—Variation. I. Title.
PE2808.D3 1983   427'.973   82-10281
ISBN 0-8093-1055-4

Contents

Acknowledgments

As I have, over the past two years, slogged my way through these seemingly countless pages of dog-eared, multicolored, marked-up, misnumbered, arrow-festooned manuscript, I have always held the acknowledgments page out to myself as a reward for finshing the job. At last.

Many people helped me write this book, although most of them didn't know what they were doing at the time and now might like to disown the results. However, it's too late.

I have four colleagues whom I especially treasure and whose advice, when I had the sense to take it, has strengthened my book. Robert Gundlach, director of the Writing Program in the College of Arts and Sciences at Northwestern University, spent many long mornings with me at the Sherman Coffee Shop, pursuing the twists and turns of my arguments, pointing out connections I had missed, and trying admirably to restrain my most partisan outbursts. Bob does not agree with everything in this book—if he did, he couldn't have given me so much good advice.

Steven Zemelman, associate professor of humanities at Roosevelt University, gave me many valuable comments on chapters 8 and 9. More important, he has been my partner for the past five years in our work with public school teachers. I hope that some of his extraordinary teaching skill, as well as his knowledge of language, has rubbed off on me.

Rae A. Moses, associate professor of linguistics at Northwestern University, got me started on this whole project a decade ago when she appeared as the instructor in the first linguistics class I ever took. We sat at opposite ends of a long seminar table and, much to the amusement of the rest of the class, argued with each other throughout the rest of the term. If any errors remain in chapters 3 or 7, it is not because Rae has failed to point them out to me.

Wallace E. Douglas, professor emeritus of English and education at Northwestern has been to me, as he has to so many of his former students, a scrupulous, skeptical, and dauntingly knowledgeable editor; a comprehensive human resource center on the history of English teaching; an effective but self-effacing mentor; and, above all, a teacher who shows his immense affection for students through meticulous and frank attention to their work.

Along with such direct counsel, I have had indirect support that has been equally important. I would certainly have never written this book if I had not grown up in a family which took conscious delight in the English language and systematically exploited its resources for communication and recreation. My grandmother liked to think that the literary genes I'd allegedly inherited from her were steering me into authorship. Perhaps she was right, although the fact that my parents and my sisters are all accomplished storytellers and enthusiastic writers helped a bit, too. My parents also provided me with a wonderful and costly education which, although it certainly didn't hurt, probably did less to make me a writer than their own spirited and skillful examples.

Thanks are due to many other people for special wisdom and kindness: to Greg, Audrey, and Sarah Baldauf, who tirelessly sustained the morale of a family with a book addict in its midst; to John Harwood and Edward B. Jenkinson for their close and sympathetic readings; to Bob Boynton for being so enthusiastic when there was so little to go on; to Kenney Withers, who liked the later, larger version; to Ed Hawley of the *Chicago Tribune*, who published my articles in spite of some rather strange mail; to Rick Lane for sending me clippings on language that I'd already read and for calling me up at midnight to discuss the book; to Will Ris for his curiously uplifting letters; to Steve Dahl and Garry Meier for general moral support; to B. J. Wagner, Marilyn Wiencek, Sherrill Crivellone, Carl Sears, Ann Malone and all the members of the Illinois Writing Project who have made this past five years such a delight; and especially to my students at Westinghouse Vocational High School, Lake Forest High School, Northwestern University, and Rosary College, who have taught me much.

Finally, I realize that *Famous Last Words* would have been a quite different and less valuable book without the help of Tnuva W. Paul. She understood, often better than I did, exactly what I was trying to accomplish, and the hours we spent talking about this book made it stronger, truer, and livelier. If I had finished soon enough for her to examine the final product, she would have continued to argue with much of what I'd written. I wish we could have had that argument.

River Forest, Illinois   Harvey A. Daniels

Famous Last Words

1

Famous Last Words

The deathwatch over American English has begun again. After all the shocks and assaults of her long life, and after all of her glorious recoveries, the Mother Tongue now faces the final hour. Around the bedside cluster the mourners: Edwin Newman, John Simon, Clifton Fadiman, Tony Randall, and Ann Landers. In darkened ranks behind stand somber professors of freshman composition, a few school board members, a representative from the National Assessment of Educational Progress, and the entire usage panel of the *American Heritage Dictionary*. Like all deaths, this one evokes in the bereaved the whole range of human feeling: anger, frustration, denial, despair, confusion, and grim humor. It has been a long, degenerative disease and not pretty to watch.

Is there room for hope? Is it really, uh, terminal? The specialists leave no room for miracles—the prognosis is firm. The obituaries have been prepared and, in some cases, already published. Services will be announced. Memorials are referred to the Educational Testing Service. *Requiescat in pace* American English.

Yet, curiously, the language clings to life. She even weakly speaks from time to time, in delirium no doubt, for her words are in jargon, cant, argot, doublespeak, and various substandard dialects. She splits infinitives and dangles participles, and one of the watchers actually thought he heard her begin a sentence with *hopefully*. How can one so ill survive? It is torture to see this. It must end.

But it won't. If this is death in life, it is still the normal condition of American English and of all other human languages. As compelling as the medical metaphors may be, languages really are not very much like people, healthy or sick, and make poor candidates for personification. The illnesses, the abuses, the wounds, the sufferings of a language reside in the minds and hearts of its users, as do its glories, triumphs, and eras of progress. Our language is an essentially neutral instrument with which we communicate, more or less, and into which we pour an abundance of feeling. It is our central cultural asset and our cherished personal friend, but it is not, in many ways, what we think it is or would like it to be.

But here is another story about death which I believe does tell us something important about the present state of American English. In Chicago, during the Christmas season of 1978, twenty-six Spanish-speaking people were killed in a series of tragic fires. Many of them perished because they could not understand the instructions that firemen shouted in English. When the city promptly instituted a program to teach the firefighters a few emergency phrases in Spanish, a storm of protest arose. "This is America," proclaimed the head of the Chicago Firefighters Union, "let them speak English." A local newspaper columnist suggested, with presumably innocent irony: "Let's stop catering to the still-flickering nationalistic desires to perpetuate the Latin heritage." The city's top-rated television newscaster used his bylined editorial minute to inveigh against the Spanish-teaching program in the firehouses.

An exasperated resident wrote to the letters column of the *Chicago Tribune:* "I object to bilingual everything. It is a pretty low sort of person who wants to enjoy the benefits of this country while remaining apart from it, hiding in an ethnic ghetto." Another letter writer huffed: "What does it take to bring home to these stiff-necked Latinos that when they move to a foreign country the least they can do is learn the language? I, for one, am fed up with the ruination of the best country in the world." Still another correspondent was even more succinct: "If they can't understand two words—don't jump—they should go back where they came from." And after my own brief article on the language controversy appeared, an angry firefighter's wife wrote me to explain her husband's awful dilemma in being stationed in the Latino community. "Why should he risk his life for nothing?" she wondered.[1]

What does this story, which concerns speakers of Spanish, tell us about the current state of English? It reminds us that our attitudes about the speechways of other people are as much a part of the linguistic environment as nouns, verbs, and adjectives—and that today these attitudes appear unusually harsh and unforgiving. In the Chicago controversy, some otherwise decent people were willing to imply—and some plainly stated—that people who don't talk right can damn well take their chances in a burning building. And while the underlying hostilities that give rise to such sentiments may not begin with language, it is clear that we frequently use language as both a channel and an excuse for expressing some of our deepest prejudices. Admittedly, our unforgiving attitudes about certain kinds of language do not often decide matters of life and death. Judging by the angry reaction to the fire crisis in Chicago, it is a good thing that they don't.

It seems worth noting that this particular outpouring of linguistic intolerance occurred in the midst of a period of more general concern about the fate of the English language. For the last decade we have been increasingly hearing about the sudden and widespread corruption of our native tongue. Standard English is supposedly becoming an endangered species; jargon is rampant; the kids talk funny; politicians brutalize the language in their endless attempts to mislead us; bureaucrats pollute the environment with obfuscation and bluster; the verbal test scores of our schoolchildren are plunging; substandard dialects are often accepted or even encouraged in the schools; non-English speakers are infiltrating our cities; and no one in school or business can write a simple English sentence correctly.

We have been having a "literacy crisis"—a panic about the state of our language in all of its uses, reading and writing and speaking. Predictions of linguistic doom have become a growth industry. *Time* magazine asks: "Can't Anyone Here Speak English?" while *Newsweek* explains "Why Johnny Can't Write." *TV Guide* warns of "The New Illiteracy," *Saturday Review* bemoans "The Plight of the English Language," and even United Airline's *Mainliner Magazine* blusters "Who's Been Messing Around with Our Mother Tongue?" Pop grammarians and language critics appear in every corner of the popular media, relentlessly detailing the latest abuses of language and pillorying individual abusers.

Blue-ribbon commissions are impaneled to study the declining language skills of the young, and routinely prescribe strong doses of "The Basics" as a remedy. Astute educational publishers crank out old-fangled grammar books. English professors offer convoluted explanations of the crisis and its causes, most of which lay the blame on public school English teachers. *The New York Times Magazine* adds Spiro Agnew's former speechwriter to its roster as a weekly commentator "On Language." The president of the United States goes on record as encouraging the "back-to-basics" movement generally and the rebirth of grammar instruction in particular. Scores of books on illiteracy are published, but none outsells *Strictly Speaking*. Edwin Newman, house grammarian of the National Broadcasting Company had posed the question first, and apparently most frighteningly: "Will America be the death of English?" His answer was frightening too: "My mature, considered judgment is that it will."

It was in the midst of this ripening language panic that the Spanish courses were begun in a few Chicago firehouses. The resulting controversy and debate would surely have happened anyway, since the expression of linguistic prejudice is one of humankind's most beloved amusements. But I also believe that the dispute was broadened, extended, and made more explicitly cruel by the prevailing climate of worry about the overall deterioration of American English.

The public had repeatedly been informed that the language was in a mess, that it was time to draw the line, time to clean up the tongue, time to toughen our standards, time to quit coddling inadequate speakers. In Chicago, that line was drawn in no uncertain terms. Obviously, the connections between the "language crisis," with its mythical Mother Tongue writhing on her deathbed, and the all-too-real events of that recent Chicago winter are subtle and indirect. Yet in those subtle connections I find the motivation to write this book.

Language is changing, yes. People "misuse" language constantly—use it to lie, mislead, and conceal. Few of us write very well. Young people do talk differently from grownups. Our occupations do generate a lot of jargon. We do seem to swear more. I do not personally admire each of these phenomena. But reports of the death of the English language are greatly exaggerated.

English is not diseased, it has not been raped and ravaged, it is not in peril. A language cannot, by its very nature, suffer in such ways. In fact, it cannot suffer at all. One of the sternest of the pop grammarians, Richard Mitchell, has said in one of his calmer moments:

There is nothing wrong with English. We do not live in the twilight of a dying language. To say that our English is outmoded or corrupt makes as much sense as to say that multiplication has been outmoded by Texas Instruments and corrupted because we've all forgotten the times tables. You may say as often as you please that six times seven is forty-five, but arithmetic will not suffer.[2]

Mitchell goes on to say that the real problem we face lies not in the language itself but in the ignorance and stupidity of its users. I agree, although my definition of ignorance and stupidity is quite different from his.

At least some of the ignorance from which we suffer is ignorance of the history of language and the findings of linguistic research. History shows us that language panics, some just as fierce as our present one, are as familiar a feature of the human chronicle as wars. In fact, one of the persistent characteristics of past crises has been the inevitable sense that everything was fine until the moment at hand, 1965, or 1789, or 2500 B.C., when suddenly the language (be it American English, British English, or Sumerian) began the final plunge to oblivion. Looking at the history of prior language crises gives us a reassuring perspective for evaluating the current one.

But we need more than reassurance—we need facts, or at least the closest thing to them, about the nature of language and how it works. The study of linguistics, which has emerged only during the present century, provides just such crucial information. The fact that the sponsors of the language crisis almost unanimously condemn modern linguistics suggests the irreconcilable difference between the critic's and the linguist's views of language. The linguist's work is not to ridicule poor speakers and praise good ones; not to rank various languages according to their supposed superiority in expressing literary or scientific concepts; not to defend the Mother Tongue from real or imagined assaults. Instead, the linguist tries to understand and explain some of the wonderfully complex mechanisms which allow human beings to communicate with each other. This does not mean that linguists don't have opinions about good and bad language, or even that some of them won't cringe at a dangling *hopefully*. But their main business is not evaluative but explanatory, not prescriptive but descriptive—an orientation which is utterly alien to the work of the contemporary language critics.

One of the main tasks of this book, then, will be to offer some ideas from these two disciplines—from the history of language and from linguistic research—which can help us evaluate the nature and seriousness of the current panic. But even if such a review does tend to deflate our sense of crisis, this does not mean that the widespread fear of linguistic corruption is meaningless. Far from it. Something is indeed going on, and the wordsmiths of our society have been able to spread their concern about it quite easily to people who do not make their living by teaching, writing, or editing English. In order to understand what is at stake, we will need to look closely at the assumptions of contemporary language criticisms and the ways in which they have been shared with the public.

While this latter task will occupy several later chapters, let me summarize some of the points I will make. All this worry about a decline extends well beyond the speaking and writing of American English. It represents a much wider concern about the direction of our society, our culture, as a whole. We have displaced (to use some jargon) much of our anxiety about current cultural changes into concern for the language which of necessity reflects them. Today, as at certain other moments in the past, talking about language has become a way of talking about ourselves, and about what we mean by knowledge, learning, education, discipline, intelligence, democracy, equality, patriotism, and truth.

But there are problems, serious ones. Language itself cannot be asked to carry the weight of such grave issues alone. To the extent that we assign our problems mainly to language, and explain them mostly by reference to aspects of language, we often defeat our own purposes. The critics, in this sense, are actually compounding the problems they profess to solve. First, they are promulgating or reinforcing ideas about language that are just plain wrong. If language is as important as the critics unanimously claim, then we should at least try to tell the truth about it, even if the facts run counter to our favorite prejudices. Second, the ministrations of the critics, with their inaccurate notions about the workings of language, threaten to bring back old—or to inspire new—teaching curricula and techniques that will hinder, rather than enhance, our children's efforts to develop their reading and writing and speaking skills.

Third, the critics, ironically enough, often trivialize the study of language. Through their steadfast preoccupation with form—with spelling and punctuation and usage and adolescent jargon and bureaucratic bluster and political doublespeak—they deflect us from meaning. Of course we know that form and content are intimately related, as the study of political propaganda reveals. Yet the real study of propaganda involves penetrating beyond the surface features to the message which is being sent, to the messages unsent, and to the purposes of the senders. But much of the current scolding and fussing about language focuses on redpenciling the superficial niceties of written and spoken utterances, rather than on understanding where they come from and what they might mean.

For all their trivial obsessions, the critics do also offer a deeper, more general message. As they advise us to strengthen our democracy by cleaning up the language, they also encourage us to continue using minor differences in language as ways of identifying, classifying, avoiding, or punishing anyone whom we choose to consider our social or intellectual inferior. And this is the gravest problem which the language crisis has given us: it has reinforced and occasionally glorified some of the basest hatreds and flimsiest prejudices in our society. Surely this unfortunate side effect has been mainly inadvertent—but just as surely, it affects us all.

One thing I have learned from taking the general argument of this book before live audiences (school teachers, usually) is that some listeners begin misunderstanding me immediately. They assume that anyone who begins by asserting that literacy crises are historically routine manifestations of social prejudice can only end by endorsing permissiveness, anti-intellectualism, gutter culture, and a general lack of standards in school and society. This book will suffer from the additional problem that it delivers these apparently incendiary sentiments in a slightly nonstandard dialect. There are split infinitives here, I confess, as well as contractions, colloquialisms, puns, and sentences that begin with conjunctions. I have chosen, in other words, a level of formality that seems comfortable to me and appropriate to my topic—though I know in advance that some readers will disapprove. The rest of this volume has several important purposes; one of the smaller ones is to show why the book didn't need to be coded in a formal scholarly dialect.

2

Outlines of the Crisis

In this chapter I want to summarize, with a minimum of editorializing, the dimensions and essential contents of the current language panic. To guide the reader through the tangled underbrush of the crisis, I have divided the chapter into several sections, each headed by what seems to be a fundamental question: who's complaining? what's wrong? what are the dangers? what are the causes? what are the cures?

Who's Complaining?

Our modern language crisis is remarkable, first of all, for its apparent breadth. It is everywhere. Anyone who has recently perused drugstore reading racks, watched a television talk show, attended an educational conference, gone to a school board meeting, or read newspaper editorials has heard repeatedly and in no uncertain terms that language is in decline. But the language critics, for all their seeming variety and ubiquitousness,

11

really fall into three closely related categories. The great majority are either journalists, educators, or semi-official language "experts" (some individuals, of course, have more than one of these affiliations.) For the moment, we will not trouble ourselves with the fact that these three classes of critics often speak ill of each other.

I use the term journalist to take in all those who offer ideas about the state of language through the various popular print and electronic media. This group includes book and article-writing journalists like Edwin Newman, the *New York Time*'s genial Sunday language columnist William Safire, and *Esquire*'s poisonous ex-arbiter John Simon, as well as the whole range of newsmagazine staffers, newspaper editorialists, feature writers, lovelorn columnists, and TV commentators who, either in or beyond the call of duty, are presently airing their assessments of the condition of the English language.

Later, I will want to look more closely at a few of the better known journalists who have made it their business—made it *a* business—to promote the language crisis. But even if the Edwin Newmans and John Simons are the major purveyors of panic (as Safire might have put it in his Agnew days) it is important to recognize the extent to which ideas like theirs slosh around in the backwaters of the popular media as well. Consider, for example, this recent exchange in Ann Landers's column:

Dear Ann Landers: Have you noticed how many people, including those in radio and TV, pronounce February as Feb-yooary? Walter Cronkite, no less, is one of the principal offenders. I will be mighty glad when these so-called experts on the English language get with it. I've written to Mr. Cronkite to protest such sloppy usage but, so far, no reply. How about your trying? (signed) FEBRUARY FREAK

Dear FEB: I sent your letter to Walter Cronkite who, incidentally, is a real pussy-cat. Across the top of your letter, I wrote: "Dear Walter: The lady is right. I heard you say it. Please clean up your act or get off the air." Walter Cronkite telephoned his response. He let me know in no uncertain terms that his act doesn't need cleaning up. Moreover, he said he has no intention of getting off the air. Mr. Cronkite claims that the dictionaries are divided as to the pronunciation of February.... So Feb-roo-ary is preferred, but Feb-yoo-ary is acceptable. And that's the way it is, Monday, April 24, 1978.[1]

Or, ponder this extract from a *National Enquirer* article titled: "TV Ruining Children's Language": "TV characters who use street language, country colloquialisms, and poor grammar give children poor examples.... Just a sample of grammatical mistakes written into the scripts of top TV shows aired over one week include: 'Me and my boys, we talked it all over,' on

'Welcome Back Kotter'; 'I don't got a bad temper,' on 'Happy Days'; 'Look how I wounded up,' on 'Baretta'; and 'That there is my nephew,' on 'Laverne and Shirley.'"[2] Not about to take this sort of attack lying (laying?) down, *TV Guide's* Edith Efron placed the blame on liberal, lamebrained educators, who have given us "progressive youngsters rushing off to live in drug-soaked communes, to engage in mindless sexual promiscuity, to produce a crop of illegitimate children, and to send VD rates soaring. And, presto-magico, all about us we saw a nationfull of 'Johnnies' who could no longer *speak English*—I mean, like, wow! Y'know, man, like, y'know, heavy! *No vacabulary at all!*"[3]

The foregoing examples touch only on the presumably poisonous effects of television upon the English language, but they are enough to suggest the degree to which the correctness mania has penetrated the popular press itself. Other offhand commentaries on the sad state of language—usually someone else's language—frequently pepper the gossip columns, editorials, reviews, cartoons, and televised conversations of many journalists. I particularly remember one morning not long ago when Tom Brokaw spent several minutes of *Today Show* air time apologizing for having used *lay* for *lie* in a previous broadcast, a slip that had brought in a minor avalanche of corrective fan mail.

My second cluster of critics—educators—includes a wide range of teachers from elementary school through college, whose concerns about language occupy a good deal of the professional press and occasionally leak into the popular. Probably the most vociferous complainers are the teachers of low-level college composition courses, currently undergoing a rebirth under the somewhat pejorative moniker of "bonehead English." The director of freshman rhetoric at the University of Illinois, for example, has written:

The common language is disappearing. It is slowly being crushed to death under the weight of a verbal conglomerate, a pseudospeech at once both pretentious and feeble, that is created daily by millions of blunders and inaccuracies in grammar, syntax, idiom, metaphor, logic, and common sense.... In the history of modern English there is no period in which such victory over thought-in-speech has been so widespread. Nor in the past has the general idiom, on which we depend for our very understanding of vital matters, been so seriously distorted. And, of course, linguistic distortions help to create rhetorical ones.[4]

Many other college writing teachers seem to share these assumptions as they go about the grim business of describing their students' illiteracy. Faculty members at another institution of higher learning in Illinois were quoted in the *Chicago Tribune* as agreeing that "the majority of college freshmen can't write a complete sentence in their native language and can't organize their thoughts effectively primarily because they haven't become aware of language." One of these teachers asserted: "Most students have vocabularies of about 20 slang words."[5]

The head of freshman English at the University of California at Davis has noted: "It may well be that students now are more passive and less mentally alert and linguistically articulate than they were 15 or 20 years ago."[6] This sentiment has been echoed by local newspaper stories around the country wherein anguished instructors bemoan the writing incompetence of students at State U. Undertaking, perhaps, to provide a national summary of this prickly mood, the *Chronicle of Higher Education* has printed the sentiments of demoralized teachers under such titles as: "I Can't Teech Comp No More" and "Diary of a Mad Freshman English Teacher." The common thread of these articles seems to be the gleeful public ridicule of the speech and writing of the most unskilled students.[7]

My third group of language critics fills a category that is admittedly more convenient than actual: the Higher Authorities. Here I refer to those people generally considered by our society to be experts in the language, such as the authors of English handbooks and dictionaries. Obviously, some of these experts may also be journalists or educators, but a separate category seems justified by the common notion that there *are* some people who, even more than run-of-the-mill teachers and writers, know the truth about language.

Perhaps our most visible and familiar source of higher authority on language is the usage panel of the *American Heritage Dictionary*, a group of about 140 novelists, poets, jounalists, politicians, actors, artists, editors, and TV personalities selected on the basis of their mastery of the English language. The editors of the dictionary asked the panel to evaluate several hundred disputed usage items for the original dictionary, and continue to consult panel members concerning newly questioned items threatening to enter the language.[8] Each year the dictionary releases, with great hoopla, the panel's responses to various neologisms and infelicities, along with a sampling of the panelists' witticisms. Recently, for example, the panel was queried on the term *input* as in the sentence *The president had access to varied input.* Some of the results:

This usage brings a violent output of nausea here. (Red Smith, sports writer)
If there is output there must be input, if there is outcry there must be incry, if there is outlaw there must be inlaw. So the reasoning is junk. (Reuven Frank, TV executive)

It is the equivalent of y'know for people who don't know the right word. (Lewis
  Mumford, author)
A Watergatism—disgusting barbarism. (John Fowles, author)
I accept output but—I don't know why—input turns my stomach. Maybe it's the
  people who use such words. (Berton Rouche, author)
I don't mingle socially with people who talk this way. (Pierre Berton, author)[9]

The members of the panel do not necessarily restrict their pronouncements about the language to the official reports of the dictionary. Tony
Randall, TV actor and newly installed panelist, announced in a recent
CBS radio interview that today's young people "don't know more than 15
or 20 words." They preface all their remarks, Randall noted, with *like*, as
in *He's like 15 years old.* The language of teenagers, he says, is "stupid,
colorless, flat, and etiolated." That final, elegant lexical item is perhaps the
reason why Randall has been snapped up by the International Paper Company as spokesman for its vocabulary-building campaign, presently being
conducted in two-page advertisements in national magazines.[10]
  Another piece of freelance work by a member of the *American Heritage*
panel is this commentary on Jewish American writers by Katherine Anne
Porter:

I am an old North American. My people came to Virginia in 1648, so we have had
time to become acclimatized .... Truly, the South and the West have made and
are making American literature. We are in the direct, legitimate line; we are people based in English as our mother tongue, and when we speak a word, we know
what it means. These others have fallen into a curious kind of argot, more or less
originating in New York, a deadly mixture of academic, guttersnipe, gangster,
fake-Yiddish, and dull old worn-out dirty words—an appalling bankruptcy in
language, as if they hate English and are trying to destroy it along with all other
living things they touch.[11]

It seems fair to ask whether attitudes like these underlie the work of the
usage panel itself, and also fair to see in the quips quoted earlier more wallowing in idiosyncratic prejudices against certain kinds of people than detached observations about the language.
  Many self-appointed language authorities eschew institutional affiliations and develop independent outlets for their views. While most simply
write handbooks, Professor Richard Mitchell of Glassboro State College
has found a more direct approach. Increasingly angered over the years by
the slipshod, jargon-ridden language of his own Glassboro colleagues,
Mitchell installed an ancient printing press in his basement and began

cranking out a pamphlet called the *Underground Grammarian.* In each issue, he identifies individual teachers and administrators by their rank and salary, and proceeds to comment in biting detail on their linguistic shortcomings. Understandably, some members of the college community see Mitchell as crazed and obnoxious. But others, including some of his victims, have pronounced him amusing and even helpful. Glassboro's even-tempered president, a frequent target of Mitchell's barbs, calls the *Grammarian* "well-written and valuable to the college.... It has certainly sensitized me to the need for more careful writing." [12]

Mitchell denies that his publication has "blighted the careers of our so-called victims." In fact, he sadly notes, some of his targets have even been promoted or granted tenure after having been exposed. But undaunted, Mitchell marches on: "We will give no space to opposing points of view. They are wrong. The Underground Grammarian is at war and will give the enemy nothing but battle." Surely Richard Mitchell's hobby is not what the inventors of tenure intended to protect, but it does obliquely say something interesting about language attitudes in our society. How would the authorities at Glassboro State have reacted if Mitchell had suddenly started publishing outraged critiques of his colleagues' wardrobes or table manners? The men in the white coats, as we used to say in high school, would have come for the good professor many semesters ago. It is a testament to our undying obsequiousness toward language "experts" that someone like Mitchell can be widely viewed as merely quixotic. [13]

If thinkers from these three influential quarters—journalists, educators, and language experts—are nearly unanimous in their belief that language is in decline, it is also worth noticing who is *not* complaining. There are two sizable groups of people concerned with language which have either remained silent throughout the current debate, or have sporadically tried to refute its central claims. These are the linguists and the leaders, if not the membership, of the National Council of Teachers of English. Explaining the absence of these two constituencies from the present festival of doomsaying will occupy us later—and will, I hope, shed some light on the nature of the crisis itself.

But the existence of a few impotent dissenters has hardly detracted from the consensus. The critics have won the day. The language crisis has been marketed and bought for more than ten years. It has now become an assumption among the general public, or at least that segment of it inclined to ponder such matters, that something has gone very wrong with our national language. And as a result, public attitudes have begun to reinforce the complaints of the critics, and to themselves become another source of the crisis mentality. Businessmen increasingly complain about the sloppy speech and writing habits of their younger employees, parents assail teachers who fail to red-pencil each error on their children's themes, taxpayers ridicule the bureaucratic jargon of ever-encroaching governmental red tape, writers to the letters columns of local newspapers vigorously decry each of the press's assaults on the language, and many of our citizens have taken up pop grammar as a hobby—collecting, after the fashion of Edwin Newman, all the linguistic errors, slips, and solecisms of their friends and co-workers.

What's Wrong?

According to many of the language critics, nearly *everything* is wrong with contemporary English. As one writer has said: "People have suffered. Institutions have suffered. Laws have suffered. But no one, no thing, has suffered—has been worked over, walked on, poleaxed, stonewalled, assaulted, battered, deep-sixed, and discombobulated—as much as ... the English language."[14] While the individual critics usually specialize in certain aspects of corruption, there also seems to be a shared and overarching belief that language, in all of its uses, is swiftly deteriorating.

This conviction engenders a desperate search for adjectives drastic enough to communicate the gravity of the situation. I have lately seen the general state of American English described as disturbing, frightening, appalling, terrifying, nauseating, deadening, depressing, disastrous, ominous, brainless, mindless, impoverished, barbaric, diseased, debased, degenerated, tattered, polluted, ravished, deadly, gloomy, grave, odious, disgraceful, dangerous, malign, chaotic, unwholesome, atrocious, horrible, flabby, ghastly, bleak, execrable, abominable, abysmal, brutal, bleak, bloodless, feeble, zombielike, wretched, incoherent, and insidious. This list pretty nearly exhausts the thesaurus, not to mention the reader.

But the language crisis involves more than the hurling of epithets. The major complaints of the critics seem to fall into four main areas: blight, bloat, illiteracy, and disrespect. The first two complaints are often paired; here I am using Edwin Newman's formulation of blight and bloat, which is called "corruption from below" and "corruption from above" by John Simon. Charlene and Arn Tibbets prefer "feeble" versus "pretentious" language. Whatever the terminology, the central idea is that our language is at once becoming impoverished and overblown, simultaneously broken down and puffed up. These phenomena are often seen as both the disease and the cause, part of an ongoing interactive process. Blight makes blight seem acceptable and causes more blight; bloat produces more bloat, and so forth.

As Newman describes contemporary linguistic blight, "respect for rules has been breaking down and correct expression is considered almost a badge of dishonor."[15] This complaint spans a wide range of problems: the drift away from standardization and correctness; the loss of precision and fine distinctions; the "death" of individual words and the substitution of insidious neologisms; and the substitution of slang or even animalistic grunts for proper language. The most evident and prevalent kind of blight involves particular common errors—the use of *I* where *me* belongs, the dangling of *hopefully*, the substitution of *disinterested* for uninterested, and scores of other, similar mistakes. Such are not necessarily small matters to the critics. John Simon, for example, gave over the better part of one *Esquire* column to the *Los Angeles Time's* use of single open quotation marks instead of apostrophes in constructions like *Soup 'N' Salad*, a practice which he called "a peculiarly chilling example of ignorance coupled with moral cowardice."[16] Along similar lines, Richard Mitchell has asserted that "things like passives and prepositional phrases constitute, among other things, an implicit system of moral philosophy. . . . Those silly little mistakes always mean something important."[17]

The supposed loss of word meanings is also a symptom of blight, as Jean Staffords's *Saturday Review* commentary suggests:

Countless useful, onetime-respectable words have been so defaced and debased and deformed that those of us who look upon ourselves as custodians of the mother tongue find our vocabularies diminished. . . . One functional word I miss is *irrelevant*. *Irrelevant* has come to denote the condition of "not being with it" or "not making the scene," of not being involved in a cause, whether it is the legalization of marijuana, the right to substitue the Peace symbol for the stars in Old Glory, the renunciation of celibacy by the clergy, the decapitation of all policemen and members of the standing army, or the movement to unman sexists.[18]

Other words whose death has been mourned by other critics include *gay*, *charisma*, *ethnic*, *massive*, *man*, *lady*, and *dialogue*.

The ultimate threat of linguistic blight seems to involve the accumulation of these deceptively innocent "silly little mistakes." As the *New York Times* editorialized this view:

Youth—members of the generation that places so much importance on communication—seems to be in danger of abandoning language. Many young people now are writing a kind of code that signals, in an instant, just how high and hip the speaker is or wants to be.... The words are few, not enough to fill a dictionary page, but enough to build a vocabulary around: trip, hassle, far-out, dig, head, man, together, where I'm at, chick, dude, like (half-built bridge to a never-completed simile) and, of course, you know.[19]

While the editorial implicitly makes a social as well as a linguistic criticism, the underlying theme of blight is apparent—the essential complaint concerns loss, diminution, simplification, and the shedding of distinctions.

The corollary problem of linguistic bloat is more easily defined. Newman calls it "language used to obfuscate or conceal or dress with false dignity."[20] If blight is concerned with the loss of valuable elements from language, bloat refers to the addition of unnecessary or injurious ones. Aspects of this problem fall under such headings as jargon, puffery, euphemism, propaganda, doublespeak, and cant. Much linguistic bloat is found in occupational or organizational jargons. Richard Mitchell has discovered perhaps the single most emblematic sample of such language in the description of an environmental education program:

Project WEY—Washington Environmental Yard (1972)—is a manifestation of the intercommunal, process-oriented, interage, interdisciplinary type of change vehicle toward an environmental ethic from the school-village level to a pan-perspective. The urban focus of the project as the medium has been inestimably vital since it is generally speaking the message.... It has served evocatively as a catalyst for values confrontation, even through a soft mode of visual/physical data exchange system. Since 1971, the dramatic changes have represented a process tool for the development of environmental/educational value encounters on site/off site, indoors/outdoors, and numerous other bipolar entities and dyads.[21]

This passage certainly does attempt to dress itself in "false dignity," although it is hard to imagine who might find it dignified. Obviously, such writing raises questions about the intentions of its author, and casts a rather dark shadow of doubt over the whole environmental enterprise. Similarly, the critics argue, the jargons of doctors, lawyers, sociologists, urban planners, antiabortionists, consumerists, and fraternity members are often composed of misleading puffery and empty pomposities.

Other kinds of bloated language relate to more serious matters than the bipolar entities and dyads of the Washington Environmental Yard. The same deception by doublespeak is also practiced by political leaders. During the Vietnam War, as many of the language critics have pointed out, our official language seemed to have fulfilled George Orwell's direst prediction: it had become nothing but "the defense of the indefensible." The invasion of Cambodia (with disastrous effects that are still in evidence today) was transformed into an "incursion." Napalm raids on North Vietnamese civilians became "protective reaction strikes." One miltary leader explained that he had to "destroy the village in order to save it." Another soldier earned infamy with his protest to reporters: "Why do you always call it bombing? It's air support."[22]

Vietnam-era bloat was promptly succeeded by Watergate, offering more examples of language dressed up to deceive. There was never any subject, just "subject matter." People never ever said anything, they "indicated" it. Things were always done at some "point in time." Spokesmen did not lie, they just "misspoke themselves." Nobody threw any incriminating documents into the river, but a few were "deep-sixed." And when the whole fabric of falsehood started to unravel, the administration simply declared its previous lies "inoperative."[23]

These examples of political doublespeak clearly represent linguistic bloat in its most worrisome form. This is language designed to conceal reality, certainly from the public, and perhaps even from the speakers themselves. Historian Arthur Schlesinger has provided a convenient summary of the problem as it is typically understood by language critics:

> We owe to Vietnam and Watergate a belated recognition of the fact that we are in linguistic as well as political crisis and that the two may be connected. The military-bureaucratic jargon could be blamed on the generals. But we did not perhaps fully realize before Watergate the utter debasement of language in the mouths of our present civilian leaders.... Democracy always has the chance to redeem its language. This may be an essential step toward the redemption of its politics.[24]

In these two political crises, the language of the participants did indeed become bloated—technicalized, overadorned, impenetrable—as they attempted to make their lies more credible. So too, according to the critics, does the language of all of us become bloated when we use clotted jargon or overripe vocabulary to talk about our affairs.

If blight and bloat are two major symptoms of the corruption of language, illiteracy constitutes an overlapping but distinguishable third category. Clearly an illiterate may suffer from (or perpetuate) linguistic blight, or may produce bloated language like that of the environmental educator with his "soft mode of visual/physical data exchange system." But the problem of illiteracy also introduces a new dimension of the language crisis—the idea that our language is not just impoverished or overadorned but increasingly nonfunctional. As *Time* magazine puts it: "The argument is not between changes, linguistic innovation, new combinations on the one hand, and priggish correctness on the other. It is between meaning and meaninglessness. When language is reduced, so is civilization."[25] And the widespread complaints of American illiteracy also introduce another element central to the whole language crisis: education. For, as we shall see, our teachers, schools, and students are commonly seen as both the source and the potential solution to the new illiteracy.

Illiteracy, we are told, is everywhere around us and growing. "23 Million Called Illiterate," trumpets one newspaper headline; "Fight on Illiteracy Found to Lag Badly," reports another. An "illiterate" New York high school graduate sues his alma mater for breach of education; and John Simon excoriates those "illiterates" who misplace apostrophes. The problem, of course, lies in determining just what "illiteracy" means in each of these cases.

Until relatively recently, literacy was defined as a basic ability to read and write one's native language—about the equivalent of a fourth grade education in the American school system. By this standard, literacy in the United States has risen steadily and is now approaching 100 percent. But the newer definitions of literacy measure reading and writing skills against some standard of "successful participation" in society; hence the term *functional literacy*. It is this concept—the idea that being literate means being able to handle the language of insurance policies, employment applications, road maps, rental leases, and so forth—which has engendered much of the new literacy scare. While the National Assessment of Educational Progress has shown functional literacy to be slowly increasing among schoolchildren, other studies have revealed that many adults still have significant problems with the reading and writing skills they presumably need to "survive." Some of the public commentary on these newer findings has been rational and evenhanded, taking note of the fact that a new standard of literacy is being used, prohibiting meaningful comparison with past literacy statistics. But many of the popular articles on illiteracy take a line like that of Walter Simmons's Sunday supplement piece:

Functional illiteracy! A "disease" that is more dangerous than cancer since it takes its toll on the mind rather than the body, and its principal victims are the *young* people of our country. [He is reporting results from the Adult Performance Level study.] Functional illiteracy! It poses a greater danger to American society than all the armaments of the world. Functional illiteracy—the disease with which 115,448,556 of the 214,998,000 (the total U.S. population) are suffering—leaving only 99,539,444 unaffected.[26]

All other commentaries on this particular study set the number of functional illiterates at about 23 million, which is what the report said. But Simmons's precise body count and his exclamation points are not to be denied![27]

There are plenty of other definitions of illiteracy floating about: the one of the grade-school teacher whose students are reading below grade level; the one of the composition instructor whose students' papers are riddled with errors; the one of the businessman who finds his subordinates' memos incomprehensible; the one of the literature professor who discovers that his students have not read the Great Books. In short, the term *illiteracy* is to language as the term *busing* is to education. The word conjures up a whole range of associations, judgments, and opinions which go far beyond whatever the word denotes. Literacy means different things to different people, and various alternative definitions can be promulgated in technical language in order to advance a chosen cause. Some current definitions identify practically all of us as illiterates (surely John Simon's would), while others so label only a few of us. But definitions aside, I think that our obsession with illiteracy reflects our more general concern about the state we are in with language. It refers to the perceived, but hard to measure, decline in our ability to talk and read and write well. And this, in turn, suggests that our problem resides not in how we define *talk, read,* or *write,* but in what we mean by *well.*

The last major complaint of the language critics is rarely made as explicit, or treated in as much detail, as the cases against blight, bloat, and illiteracy. It concerns the decreasing respect for language itself, the idea that the average person (and some who are above average) no longer exhibits the proper reverence for the English language. Harvard literary critic Douglas Bush has called this disrespectful attitude "an ugly debasement of our great heritage." He notes: "Whatever may be the case in other countries, in ours efforts to establish or reestablish serious respect for the mother tongue, for the precise use of words, for clarity, simplicity, and discriminating·taste, have encountered much apathy and resistance, tacit or vocal, from average unconscious practice and, in recent decades, from very conscious academic doctrine."[28] A. Bartlett Giamatti, president of Yale University, seems to agree with his colleague in Cambridge that disrespect for language is rampant:

I believe that of all the institutions attacked in the past dozen years—governmental, legal, and educational—the one that suffered most was the institution of language itself, that massive living system of signs which on the one hand limits us and, on the other hand, allows us to decide who we are . . . Without a respect for its awesome power we can never find out who we are, and thus never have to leave the child's garden of feeling and enter the city—that is, become citizens.[29]

Bush's reference to "discriminating taste" and Giamatti's mention of "becoming citizens" suggest that something beyond mere pragmatism is at issue here. These scholars are not just arguing for "functional literacy," but for some higher order of skill, discipline, even loyalty.

Such reasoning opens the critics to charges of elitism that they often try to refute. Few critics wish to be regarded as *purists*, probably because of the lingering authoritarian connotations of that term. Yet many critics also seem to feel that there is a war on, and that the enemy is not only sloth and neglect but also a willful effort by some insidious forces to destroy the language. They are left with the problem of trying to describe how it is *us* versus *them* without sounding too self-serving and priggish. By way of summary, though, we are lucky to have John Simon, who feels no reticence about being thought a purist: "Above all, language is not just a matter of communication. It is a way of expressing one's fastidiousness, elegance, and imaginativeness; it is also a way of displaying one's control over a medium which is perhaps difficult to master but, once mastered, unites all its initiates in a common pursuit and shared beauty."[30] One begins to understand.

What Are the Dangers?

According to the critics, we have much to fear from contemporary blight, bloat, illiteracy, and disrespect for language. As Walter Simmons has revealed, the ill use of English is more dangerous than cancer or atomic bombs; John Simon says that we trifle with standard English "at the peril of our very souls." But exactly what are these dangers and perils?

While the various language critics certainly bring to the issue a wide range of personalities, points of view, and axes to grind, each of them can nevertheless be trusted to trot out either or both of two general consequences of language abuse. The first and less popular of these is the straightforward "purity of English" line: the notion that our language must be protected for aesthetic, moral, or nationalistic reasons. In this view, the English language is seen as a unique and glorious achievement of the human (or at least Western) mind, a creation so profound that it inherently requires our obeisance, awe, and conservation. As Clifton Fadiman has said, in an appeal for better composition teaching: "The case for writing, therefore, rests in part on political grounds, on the sense of duty and gratitude we feel as citizens of a free country. It is put concisely by the motto of a recent one-cent stamp: The Ability to Write—A Root of Democracy."[31] Those who, like Fadiman, attend to English with "duty and gratitude" usually view changes in the language, nonstandard usages, and other deviations from the standard as acts of linguistic vandalism, the defacing of a national monument. Obviously, the purity argument is not particularly rational; it is based on value judgments about taste, good manners, loyalty, morality, and patriotism.

The second, more favored argument about the dangers of corruption seems more logical and pragmatic. It holds that the degeneration of a language will accompany (or even cause) the corruption of the people who use it. Language, in this view, does not just reflect the nature of the culture in which it is spoken but profoundly influences the course of that culture. When we use language improperly, whether through an intent to deceive or a sloppy unwillingness to speak correctly, our lies and inaccuracies become permanent parts of the cultural-linguistic environment. We become trapped by our distorted descriptions of our affairs and are decreasingly able to use our weakening language to find out the truth. George Orwell warned that the end product of this dangerous cycle could be observed in the description of the murder of civilians as *pacification*.[32] Richard Mitchell has updated Orwell's scenario:

We may snicker and even sneer at the man who tells us that his words have now become "inoperative," but he still has a victory. He has put that tiny worm into our ears. It will eat its way into our brains and dull some power of language, so that when his successors talk to us about "enhanced radiation devices," we may snicker and sneer less. When enough of these worms have made their homes in our skulls—how long do you suppose that will take?—the day will come when we will merely nod. And from nodding we will go to dozing, and from dozing, to sleep.[33]

And this argument goes even further. Not only does the corruption of language make us vulnerable to lies and deceptions, it may even begin to erode our cognitive abilities in general. Ronald Berman, former chairman of the National Endowment for the Humanities, sees in current language "a massive regression toward the intellectually invertebrate," a gruesome if unscientific notion.[34] The final stage of this process of linguistic regression, a number of critics have warned, may be the utter disappearance of human communication.

Of these two arguments, the latter—the "practical" one—has been considerably more popular with the contemporary critics. Edwin Newman,

Richard Mitchell, Jean Stafford, Norman Cousins, Arthur Schlesinger, and the editorial staffs of *Time* and *Newsweek* are just a few of the writers employing some version of the Orwellian view. Given the alternative, this is hardly a surprising choice. To argue the case for purity in language on the basis of morality, aesthetics, or patriotism carries with it inevitable overtones of stuffiness and elitism. The practical argument, however, draws its considerable power not from blind appeals to truth and beauty but from a chillingly plausible assessment of the consequences of linguistic corruption. It also allows its proponents to counsel an essentially identical and equally wrong view of language without sounding too authoritarian, to excoriate their social inferiors "for the good of the country," and to congratulate themselves on their own elegance and taste.

What Are the Causes?

I might just as well have headed this section "Who are the causes?" since our language critics seem to take such delight in blaming linguistic decay on certain persons or groups. The list of indicted villains is a long one, and it includes such diverse language abusers as Noam Chomsky, Abbie Hoffman, Herman Hesse, Kurt Vonnegut, O. J. Simpson, Howard Cosell (and Dandy Don Meredith), Archie Bunker, John Dean, Peter Frampton, Muhammad Ali, most recent American presidents, and the Cookie Monster of "Sesame Street" ("Me want cookie!"). But for all their enthusiasm in seeking out the individual enemies of English, the critics also blame certain evil cultural trends. This list, too, is eclectic, if not all-embracing: one-parent families, modern architecture, overdoses of television, rock and roll, progressive education, English elective programs, integration, busing, teachers' unions, telephones, teenage slang, government reports, Watergate, Vietnam, linguistics, transformational grammar, structural grammar, behaviorist psychology, humanistic psychology, *Webster's Third*, books with big pictures, the disappearance of neighborhoods, and oral contraceptives.[35] While the very breadth of this blame discourages categorization, the foregoing people and events can be clustered into several discrete groupings. The leading source of linguistic decay, according to the majority of critics, is our educational system—students, teachers, administrators, and curricula from kindergarten through graduate school. As Richard Mitchell has said: "Since the schools infect everybody, it is not possible to discover a calling whose effectiveness has not been diminished by the sickness of thought and language that are spread in the schools."[36] Apparently we just don't teach reading or writing or spelling or grammar the way we used to. Our teachers are badly trained or are too stupid to train in the first place. Too many frivolous electives are allowed, and many courses are taught from textbooks which have been rewritten to make them easier. Little writing is done, and less is corrected. Students are not forced to learn standard English, and lower-class dialects are openly accepted in many classrooms. In general, there has been a widespread and cowardly abandonment of linguistic standards in our schools.

A second set of causes for the decline of English has been, in the euphemism of the Educational Testing Service, "recent disruptive events in the life of the nation," an allusion to Vietnam and Watergate and to the evasive, jargon-ridden language emanating from these upheavals. Here the bad guys are not the masses toiling in our school system, but the leaders of our country, who have been caught committing one linguistic abuse after another. The danger seems to be that our leaders' language may infect us, or that it appeals to us, or both.

The youth of the 1960s, curiously enough, were a major source of linguistic decay, according to a number of the critics. Though this distant era seems quite obscure as a place to look for the causes of present-day corruption, the critics return again and again to the "attack on language" supposedly mounted by the antiwar protestors. The general notion is that during the 1960s "there was a widespread breakdown in the enforcement of rules, and in the rules of language more than most," to use Edwin Newman's phrase.[37] For a number of the critics, the 1960s seem to serve as a symbol of the beginning of the linguistic end.

A fourth set of destructive influences on the language is the popular media and particularly television. Many of the critics believe that television's lowest-common-denominator approach to programming extends to language as well. TV, in other words, gives huge audiences and tacit approval to speakers of less-than-proper English. Clifton Fadiman has called TV talk a language "whose vulgarity, impermanence, and low-grade capacity to communicate are equalled only by its immediate power to attract." And, along with his colleague Dr. Lois DeBakey (a professor of scientific communication at Baylor College of Medicine) Fadiman bemoans the "gutter gutturals" of various ineloquent television performers and sports stars. Fadiman and DeBakey, by the way, work themselves into a real froth over that old shucker and jiver Muhammad Ali: "A prize fighter who flaunts his disregard for standard English by spouting ungrammatical, juvenile boasts and nonsensical doggerel earned $15 million last year; he has been awarded honorary degrees, has been entertained at the White House, and has been lionized the world over." It is clearly no picnic being a language critic, especially if you cannot even allow yourself to enjoy the performances of this consummately self-aware entertainer.[38]

A fifth cause of decay, often handled with a certain delicacy by the critics, has been the "democratization" of language—what Richard Mitchell calls "pathetic populism." This trend is usually defined as the overzealous attempt to treat everyone respectfully, regardless of his or her linguistic merits. Conversely, it is sometimes called "the flight from excellence"—the fear of setting high standards for one's self and others in language and in other aspects of life. Charlene and Arn Tibbets discuss how this misguided democratization injures the language: "One clear cause, certainly, can be found in the American passion for social leveling. Language is intimately bound up with social life. Consider the auto mechanic ... if he is typically American, [he] is ostentatiously a leveler. He is as good as anybody else, and nobody else is better than he .... And he uses every device at his disposal to gain such equality. The average American is never happier than when he can, through taxes, soak the rich." The Tibbetses go on to explain, "in a sad scientific spirit," how to the auto mechanic all words are equal and distinctions of meaning are uncongenial.[39] The Tibbetses and others see in contemporary society too much willingness to compromise, to make excuses, to coddle, all in order to fulfill the rhetoric of an egalitarian society. To permit the auto mechanic his sense of linguistic equality, to allow Black English in the classroom, to sponsor bilingual programs, to oppose sexist language, are to damage English in the misguided attempt to treat all its users fairly. This leveling of language goes on, then, not just in auto shops and schoolrooms, but wherever high-ranking citizens adopt folksy dialects or fail to penalize the less competent speakers under their supervision.

Jargon, much of it occupational, constitutes a sixth presumed assault on the mother tongue. In this age of specialization, everyone seems to speak a dialect related to his or her job: lawyers speak of torts and injunctions; doctors of prognoses and prophylaxis; truckers of bears and scales; psychologists of transference and repression. The critics fear that these subdialects threaten the proper language in two ways—they replace it much of the time and also influence it. This threat is all the more frustrating since it is utterly unnecessary, at least according to the Tibbetses: "Persons who operate a car wash, set women's hair, teach composition, determine economic policy, or try to keep their neighbors from going out of their minds do not in fact need a set of agglutinating technical terms to subclassify the commonplace facts and actions that make up their daily chores."[40]

And finally—seventh, for the record—many of the language critics sense that we are in the midst of a general cultural decline, of which the corruption of English is both a cause and an effect. As Mitchell puts it: "We are a culture presently in the process of disintegration, a culture that no longer cares to represent its values in its language."[41] This grave worry perhaps tells us why the critics' search for explanations ranges so widely, and why it sometimes includes such diverse and apparently nonlinguistic factors as divorce rates, sexual behavior, the role of sports stars, and assorted political scandals. More than a few of these writers seem to believe that we are living in Rome before the fall, and they see the seeds of destruction in the language of every element of our culture—in television, sports, music, literature, films, magazines, books, and family lives. The Tibbetses again provide a florid summary of this view:

> As our public rhetoric becomes more churlish and illogical; as our plays, movies, and works of fiction become more slovenly, violent, and dirty; as our scholarship becomes more pretentious and inaccurate, so our American spirit loses its magnanimity and it grows weak and mean-spirited. To abuse language is to abuse the very idea of being human. Wit, kindness, intelligence, grace, humor, love, honor—all require the right employment of language for their embodiment. In the decline of American English may also be seen the decline of the American as human being.[42]

Requiescat in pace indeed.

What Are the Cures?

The language critics, by and large, have little to say about solving the problems which they so thoroughly describe. This failure to prescribe, I think, is not so much a shortcoming of their work as an inevitable reflection of the complexity of language itself. After all, these writers are objecting to certain habits of speech which are deeply embedded in the everyday practice of millions of people, and therefore quite resistant to sudden remediation. The critics' often palpable despair over the whole business apparently mirrors their occasional awareness of their own impotence where language reform is concerned.

When the critics do take a stab at reform, they almost invariably fall back on the schools for the salvation of English. Arthur Schlesinger, after a long diatribe against the stultification of Watergate lingo, exulted: "What an opportunity for American teachers!" The silver lining in Schlesinger's dark cloud is the chance for teachers to show their students the language abuses committed by our leaders, thereby supplying them with the necessary discrimination to avoid similar pitfalls.[43] This is one of the persistent themes of school-based reform of English—that teaching children about specific abuses of the language will ultimately protect them from Orwellian authoritarianism.

But even more common than this approach is the more general notion that we should "get back to the basics," which for many of the critics means getting back to teaching the parts of speech, diagramming sentences, learning standard English, or even studying a little Latin. There is nearly universal agreement that instruction in the mother tongue has in recent years become chaotic, undisciplined, and frivolous and that a return to the firm, even harsh, standards of bygone days is in order. Beyond the simple addition or intensification of teaching in these language-related subjects, the critics nearly always urge teachers to promote respect for language as well as competence in its use. Again, it is not just skill which the critics want to see developed, but also a measure of "discriminating taste."

Outside of changes in various branches of the educational system, the critics offer few suggestions. While a few have toyed with the notion of establishing an American academy after the fashion of the French or Italian ones, they usually do so kiddingly or wistfully. The Tibbetses are an exception, proposing the establishment of an "American Society for Good English," an association of "civilized Americans" that would publish a journal, "make authoritative statements on the English curriculum at all levels," and "condemn as bad the pompous studies of the educationist and the sociologist."[44]

There is one remaining form of action which many of the critics do counsel: personal resistance to the misuse of language. They tell us to oppose sloppy, incorrect, deceptive, or nonstandard uses of language wherever and whenever we encounter them. Business executives should reject fuzzy memos from their subordinates, speakers should be interrupted and corrected if they make mistakes, newspapers and magazines should be called to task for proofreading slipups, and so forth. Many of the critics are themselves avid practitioners of such linguistic guerrilla warfare, sniping at their inferiors from every available armchair. If they have not come up with any other plans for the reform of English, the critics have at least raised this latter tactic to the level of an art form: they have shown us a rich variety of ways to demonstrate our contempt for others and to advertise our own feelings of superiority.

As chapter 1 and my occasional asides in this chapter suggest, I find the

current language crisis highly suspect. I do not accept its definitions, respect its promoters, believe its evidence, fear its dangers, or revile its villains. The reasons for my outlook are explained in the next three chapters.
Still, I do not take the crisis lightly. It is a powerful threat, not to the survival of the English language, but to our understanding of language and of
each other.

3

Something New and Ominous

As it is presented to us through the popular press and the educational system, the present language crisis appears to be a distinctly contemporary phenomenon. A dangerous combination of uniquely modern influences (television, Vietnam, Watergate, cultural permissiveness, open classroom schools, bilingual education) seems to threaten the health—even the very existence—of a tongue which has survived, if not flourished, for centuries. The sorry state of our language is described as a sign of the times, as evidence of the depths to which our ailing culture has sunk: now even the common tongue is in peril. Only, it seems, in such a depraved age, only in the last quarter of the twentieth century, could Dwight MacDonald have been forced to conclude: "[The] scientific revolution has meshed gears with a trend toward permissiveness, in the name of democracy, that is debasing our language by rendering it less precise and thus less effective as literature and less efficient as communication."[1] Only today do we face headlines like these in the *New York Times*: "Johnny Can't Read or Write, Teachers Say"; "Freshmen Found Inept in English"; and "Colleges to Fight Decay in English."[2] Only in 1983 could businessmen file these sad reports:

31

Recent graduates, including those with university degrees, seem to have no mastery of the language at all. They cannot construct a simple declarative sentence, either orally or in writing. They cannot spell common, everyday words. Punctuation is apparently no longer taught. Grammar is a complete mystery to almost all recent graduates."[3]

I have been distressed by the incompetence of many high school and college graduates. Too often, young people are handicapped by an inability to express themselves, either orally or in writing. Vocabularies are limited and many young people are uncomfortable in the use and understanding of their own language. This is a serious obstacle to advancement in an industry where communication is so important.[4]

And only at this unusually difficult moment could college English teachers be compelled to admit that their students are functionally illiterate. In the words of professors from Yale University, American University, and Adrian College:

Students at Yale ... are less competent to write an effective composition than were the students of ten years ago. There is a grave weakness in their powers of analysis and organization; even the brightest students sometimes show that they lack basic training in the ways of beginning, developing, and concluding an argument or exposition. This is a much more troubling weakness than any small errors in usage, for it shows a lack of mental discipline in the basic principles of human thought.[5]

... There is no sense of responsibility about language, no recognition of the power of words, merely a vague groping accompanied by the hope that the reader will "get what I mean." More specifically, it is apparent that most students arrive at college with little or no training in writing, and in many cases without the basic knowledge of what a sentence is, or what a paragraph is. Even such elementary matters as spelling and punctuation seem to have been neglected.[6]

One way to handle them is to force them to take "remedial" courses (often they cannot read intelligently and dislike any reading), a slow process of remedying the ills of a slothful public school life. Another is to test them, fail them, and send them home—rather heartless, but perhaps less so than to encourage the morons to go on. A third, too often done, is to accept them and work with their mediocrities; the inevitable result is the lowering of standards.[7]

As the reader may have guessed, however, all of these headlines and quotations come not from the 1983 model language crisis, but from the panic of

1957–1963. Most of our memories are sufficiently short that we have already forgotten our most recent previous bout of linguistic insecurity, which was an offshoot of the post-Sputnik educational retrenchment and the controversy surrounding the publication of *Webster's Third New International Dictionary*. During the early 1960s, it was widely argued that the English language was in decline, that the language skills of American students had taken a sudden plunge, and that only a national rededication to linguistic excellence could restore the mother tongue to its lost glory and effectiveness.

Of course, this period of breast-beating can be seen as simply the first phase of our current crisis—as the forerunner of a problem which happened to be spread over two decades. But this is not the case. The history of language is, among other things, the history of linguistic insecurity and intolerance and the periods of doomsaying which they regularly generate. These episodes have manifested themselves in different ways, depending upon the communication media and social structures of the times and places in which they occurred. But predictions of the death of language have been as regular a feature of the human chronicle as wars and, as a matter of fact, often appear to be closely related to that favorite of human pastimes. Similarly, the hobby of attacking the language used by the people of some other region, nation, occupation, race, age, class or sex has rivaled stamp collecting, bridge playing, and their antecedents throughout history. The high seriousness and grave intensity which attend debates about differences in language are apparently as old as the seemingly universal conviction that "good language" is what *I* speak.

The history of linguistic insecurity and intolerance is far too long and voluminous to review in this chapter. For the moment, it seems enough to establish the antiquity of some fears about language which we often mistakenly believe to be new. For if we can remind ourselves that language has regularly been described as imperiled, diseased, and dying in the past (and if we believe that it has more or less survived these dangers), it will help us to sensibly evaluate the diagnoses which are currently being made about the state of, and threats to, modern English.

The earliest language "crisis," or at least the earliest expression of concern, that I have been able to discover occurred in ancient Sumeria (as the Sumerians invented writing, it would be hard to imagine how, save through oral historians, evidence of any previous language problems would come down to us). It seems that among the first of the clay tablets discovered and deciphered by modern scholars was one which recorded the agonized complaints of a Sumerian teacher about the sudden drop-off in students' writing ability. Now this teacher was probably more an instructor of scribesmanship than composition, but it is at least interesting to discover that the reports from "Bonehead Sumerian" were about the same 4,500 years ago as they are from "Bonehead English" today.[8]

A story from Plutarch's *Failure of the Oracles,* translated by the nineteenth-century scholar Thomas Lounsbury, attests to the Romans' concern for the proprieties of language, if not to the existence of any particular linguistic crisis among them. Plutarch tells of a group of friends who arrived at the Great Temple of Apollo to find the people there engaged in relaxed and leisurely discussion, anointing themselves with oil and languidly observing the performance of the wrestlers. One of the new arrivals remarked to them: "It seems to me that you are not discussing any matter of great consequence, for I see you labor not under deep thought." To this observation the conversants replied that

they most assuredly were not occupied with any profound discussion. They were not, for instance, disputing whether the word *ballo* loses one of its *l*'s in the future tense; or from what positive certain superlatives, such as *cheiriston* and *beltiston,* were derived. These are the sort of questions, it is added, that make men knit their brows. About other matters, such, for illustration, as those of philosophy, discussion could go on with calmness. But questions of grammar call at once into being frowning angry looks that fill the bystanders with terror.

Plutarch, for all we can tell, may have had tongue firmly in cheek as he told this story. Yet it seems safe to assume that if he was being ironic, it was to comment upon the rabidity which presumably accompanied language debates in antiquity, as it does today.[9]

The Roman concern for correctness in language is also reflected in the writings of the rhetorician Marcus Fabius Quintillian who, in the first century A.D., served as tutor to the families of three successive emperors. Though Quintillian instructed only the male children of the tiny and generally unthreatened aristocracy of Rome, he nevertheless felt that these boys had to be protected from any unsavory linguistic influences: "Before all things else," he advised parents, "let the speech of his nurses be correct." Quintillian reasoned:

Theirs are the voices the child will hear first, theirs the words he will try to reproduce. And we are naturally most tenacious of what we have learned while our minds were still unformed: as the flavor imparted to vessels when they are new remains in them and the colors of woolen stuffs wherewith their original whiteness has been transformed cannot be washed out. And further those very impressions which are less desirable are the more enduring. Good things are easily changed for the worse, but when will you turn vices into virtues? Do not then allow the boy, even in infancy, to become familiar with a way of speaking which has afterwards to be unlearned.

If, for some reason, the family was not able to secure the services of a nurse who spoke "standard" Latin, the child should have a companion whose duty would be "to correct at once any blunders in speech made by these others in the presence of his charge and so as to prevent such blunders from taking root in his mind."[10]

Cicero, whose style for centuries was a model for writers of English as well as Latin, was involved in a small controversy that sheds some additional light on the sensitivity of language matters in Rome. In honor of Pompey's third consulate, an arch was to be erected and dedicated to his achievements. A debate arose as to whether the proper form of *third* to appear on the arch should be *tertium* or *tertio*. When Cicero was consulted as the final authority on the matter, he took the diplomatic (if nonstandard) approach of recommending simply *tert*, thus avoiding the possibility of giving offense to the partisans of either *tertio* or *tertium*. The fact that Cicero would go to such lengths to sidestep the issue suggests, perhaps, the degree to which his choice of either competing form was sure to have kicked up a fuss.[11]

While these mouldering anecdotes do remind us that language controversies occurred millennia ago, in other languages and cultures, and well in advance of the drop in Scholastic Aptitude Test scores, such knowledge is only modestly helpful. The history of similar controversies among English-speaking people is both better documented and more accessible, and can tell us a good deal about our present crisis.

From the time of the Norman invasion in 1066, French was more or less the official language of the ruling classes of England. The native tongue, which was what we now call Old English, of course continued to be used exclusively by the common people and by the aristocracy in its informal, unofficial affairs. But gradually, English began to reassert itself, and by 1400 had once again become the language not only of day-to-day business, but also of literary, scientific, legal, and governmental endeavors as well. Shortly after this important transition came the invention of the printing press, and the audience for written language quickly began to expand.

Accordingly, many Greek and Latin texts were translated into English by scholars who usually found it necessary to apologize for the "rude and symple" language which could hardly do justice to the "eloquence" of the original. In the introduction to his translation of a Latin text issued in 1545, Roger Ascham acknowledged that some readers might find the English version "vile." He admitted that: "As for the Latin or Greke tonge, euery thyng is so excellently done in them, that none can do better. In the Englysh tonge contrary, euery thinge is a manner so meanly, bothe for the matter and handelynge, that no man can do worse." [12] The widely held view that English was "rude," "gross," "barbarous," and "base" sparked a lively debate as to whether it was blasphemous to translate the Bible into the common tongue, even if the goal of such an effort was to bring the Gospel to the people. In this case at least, linguistic niceties gave way to the exigencies of religious politics; the Reformation required that the scriptures be made available to the masses. As one gloating Protestant later recalled this controversy:

There be not yet two hundred years past since the admirable art of Printing was found out, an iuention so excellent and so vseful, so much tending to the honour of God, the manifestation of the truth, propagation of the Gospell, restoration of learning, diffusion of knowledge, and consequently the discouerie and destruction of Poperie, that the Pope and Popish Politicians wish it had neuer beene, and haue bestowed many a secret curse vpon him that first reueiled it. [13]

With the rapid increase of writing, translating, and publishing in the English language, authors acquired the habit of criticizing the language of their colleagues and began issuing commentaries on the state of the language in general. William Caxton, who had set up the first printing press in England in 1478, was among the first to complain (at least in print) of the troubling diversity of speech he heard around him, and of the difficulties it presented to the printer seeking a standardized language for his books:

And certaynly our langage now vsed varyeth ferre from that whiche was vsed and spoken when I was borne. For we Englysshe men ben borne under the domynacyon of the mone, whiche is neuer stedfaste but euer wauerynge, wexynge one season, and waneth and dycreaseth another season. And that comyn Englysshe that is spoken in one shyre varyeth from a nother.

Caxton complained that "in these dayes" any man of reputation in his own region felt free to talk "in suche maners and termes that few men shall vnderstonde" him. All this "diuersite and chaunge" left Caxton, the aspiring printer, lost "between playn, rude, and curyous." [14]

Ascham, when not busy translating, apparently fancied himself something of a language critic, and was particularly distressed by persons who "make all things darke and harde" by sprinkling their language with words of "latin, french, and Italian" origin. He tells of his argument with a man—a permissivist, surely—who claimed that such borrowings actually enriched the language, asking: "Who will not prayse that feaste, where a man shall drinke at a dinner, bothe wyne, ale and beere?" Ascham dismissed this alcoholic analogy:

Truly, quod I, they be all good, euery one taken by hym selfe alone, but if you putte Maluesye and sacke, read wyne and white, ale and beere, and al in one pot, you shall make a drynke, neyther easie to be knowen, nor yet holsum for the bodye.

Ascham further insisted that too many people with an inadequate command of the English language had recently begun to publish their writing, thereby accelerating the process of "chaunge" and decay.[15]

By the middle 1500s, few English people still felt it necessary to apologize for the fact that they spoke a "rude" and "barbarous" tongue like English instead of Greek, Latin, or French. Instead, they began to apologize (perhaps having been pricked by critics like Ascham and Caxton) for the *kind* of English they spoke. There arose a demand, at least among the aristocracy, for guidance in language matters, and the English self-help industry was begun. In 1531, Sir Thomas Elyot offered this advice to those who would show themselves the masters of language:

Speke none englisshe but that which is cleane polite, perfectly and articulately pronounced, omittinge no lettre or sillable, as folisshe women often times do of a wantonnesse, whereby diuers noble men and gentilmannes chyldren (as I do at this daye knowe) have attained corrupte and foule pronunciation.

These children, Elyot argued, developed their "foule pronunciation" largely from the failure of their earliest education, and he reminded careful parents to expose their children to plenty of good Latin during the formative years.[16]

Angel Day, author of a 1586 text on rhetoric, ridiculed the writer of a medical text for his use of the terms *exasperate, egregious,* and *arcane.* "Was there ever seene from a learned man," Day wondered, "a more preposterous and confused kind of writing?" Though he claimed to be unable to fathom the "imaginatione" of so bad a writer, Day did report on the pleasure this volume gave to him and his friends: "This one thing I do know, that diuers to whom I have showed the booke have very hartily laughed in perusing the parts of his writing." Of course, Day was hardly the last (and certainly not the first) to have a good laugh among friends over the linguistic shortcomings of his inferiors.[17]

In a similar vein, George Puttenham, who in 1586 wrote a how-to book on rhyming aimed at an audience of ladies and courtiers, gave some discussion to the various "vices and deformities of speech" common at the time. Singled out for particular scorn are those who use high-flown or affected words like *audacious* or *compatible*. This kind of "fonde affectation," which Puttenham calls "mingle mangle," occurs when

we affect new words and phrases other than the good speakers and writers in any language, of then custome hath allowed, and is the common fault of young schollers not halfe well studied before they come from the Vniversitie or schooles, and when they come to their friends, or happen to get some benefice or other promotion in their countreys, will seems to coigne fine new words out of the Latin, and to vse new fangled speaches, thereby to shew themselues among the ignirant the better learned.

Puttenham's belief in the inferiority of the dialects of the hinterlands presumably underlay his subsequent announcement that the standard language of England was the speech "of the Court, and that of London and the shires lying about London within Ix miles, and not much above."[18]

A few decades later, John Locke received a letter from a friend who solicited the great man's advice about the education of his eight-year-old son. In a series of letters that were subsequently published as *Some Thoughts Concerning Education,* Locke advised his friend that correctness in language could be an important element in his son's future success. For a man of affairs, Locke noted: "the want of propriety, and grammatical exactness, is thought very misbecoming one of that rank, and usually draws on one guilty of such faults, the censure of having had a lower breeding and worse company, than suits with his quality." Since men of such position will "in the future course of their lives be judged by their handsome or awkward way of expressing themselves," Locke maintained, it was important that a gentleman be able to speak without "shocking the ears" of his listeners with "solecisms and offensive irregularities."

Elyot, Day, Puttenham, and Locke had all offered—over a century or so—their advice (solicited or not) on how to master the proprieties of English speech. Each had some sense that English was still a language under construction, in the process of acquiring new vocabulary from other tongues and working out uncertainties of grammar. Still, all four of these advisers were certain that one correct and proper style of speech existed for the mastering by people who cared to learn it. By the middle of the seventeenth century, however, a new problem had arisen. Though English was by then 300 years removed from the domination of French, and possessed of a growing literature both translated and indigenous, some experts announced that the whole language had begun to decay. The earliest English grammar books were published about this time, and most attempted to "save" the language by describing its features (with predictable difficulty) in terms of the declensions and conjugations of Latin. In 1664, a subcommittee of the Royal Society was impaneled to look into the possibility of establishing a protective English language academy modeled on the Académie Francaise. Although the committee disbanded after several profitless meetings, its cause was taken up in 1697 by Daniel Defoe, who called for a group of thirty-six experts to supervise the tongue and curtail the "impudence" of writers who coined words without his committee's sanction.[20]

Addison, whose prose later came to be viewed as the embodiment of excellence in English, was much concerned with the deleterious influence of jargon on the language. In 1711, he complained:

The present War has so Adulterated our Tongue with strange words that it would be impossible for one of our Great Grandfathers to know what his Posterity have been doing, were he to read their exploits in a Modern News Paper ... [Our soldiers] send us over Accounts of their Performances in a Jargon of Phrases, which they learn among their Conquered Enemies. They ought however to be provided with Secretaries and assisted by our Foreign Ministers, to tell their Story for them in plain English, and to let us know in our Mother-Tongue what it is our brave Country-Men are about.

Addison told an amusing if not apocryphal story about the father of an English soldier who was so distressed by the jargon in his son's letters from the front that he took them to the local vicar for a translation. The clergyman sadly commented that the boy "must either banter us or he is out of his senses." But, the worried father responded, his son was sometimes able to make sense: "When he writes for Mony he knows how to speak intelligibly enough; there is no man in England can express himself clearer, when he wants a new furniture for his horse."[21]

Probably the leading worrier about language during the early eighteenth century was Jonathan Swift, whose concern about English was manifested in both his fiction and his essays. Writing in *The Tatler* in 1710, Swift announced that the language was being threatened by three sinister trends. The first was the shortening of words, seen in the substitution of *mob* for *mobilius* and *rep* for *reputation*, as well as in the dropping of final vowels to form *disturb'd, rebuk'd,* or *fledg'd.* Swift's second concern was the use of such overblown vocabulary as *operations, ambassadors, communications,* and *preliminaries,* where simpler words would do. And finally, Swift condemned the seepage of lower-class slang (*banter, bamboozle, bully, sham*) into the speech and writing of gentility. Swift's categories of corruption seem more or less parallel to those invented 200 years later by Edwin Newman and others: blight, bloat, and illiteracy. Also like many of our modern language critics, Swift was bitterly disappointed by the evident failure of his efforts: "I have done my utmost for some years past to stop the progress of *mobb* and *banter,* but have plainly been borne down by numbers and betrayed by those who promised to assist me." [22]

Failing to achieve his ends by suasion and example, Swift in 1712 turned to legal remedies. He wrote and published an open letter to the earl of Oxford, the lord high treasurer, in which he proposed the establishment of a body of cultured gentlemen to make the necessary corrections in the language and then to "fix" it permanently. This drastic action was needed, Swift argued, because the language had been deteriorating quite rapidly since the civil war of 1642. Prior to that time, during the reign of Elizabeth, the English language had enjoyed the greatest refinement. But now a flood of corruption, emanating both from the fanatics of the commonwealth and the slovenly speakers of London society, menaced the language. If his proposal were not implemented, and if the rapid decay of the language were suffered to continue, Swift warned, future generations would not be able to read the literature produced during his lifetime. Only with the aid of patient and scholarly translators, he claimed, would the descendants of the lord high treasurer be able to learn about his life and times. The earl's concern for his personal posterity, however, was apparently not inflamed by this prediction, and Swift's proposal went unheeded. [23]

The spirit of Swift's assumptions about language was generally shared by Samuel Johnson, who in 1747 set about the task of preparing the first comprehensive dictionary of the English language. At the beginning of his enterprise, Johnson was dedicated to the reformation and "fixing" of the language, and hoped that his efforts would ultimately protect the "purity" of English. By the time the dictionary appeared eight years later, however, Johnson had been obliged to abandon "the dreams of a poet doomed at last to wake a lexicographer." He had found that language is made in "the boundless chaos of living speech," and that many of the "irregularities" commonly protested against had to be left "untouched," as "uniformity must be sacrificed to custom." Powerful though the lexicographer's judgments may appear, Johnson noted, "to enchain syllables and to lash the wind are equally undertakings of pride unwilling to measure its desires by its strength." Johnson even opposed the proposal of Swift and others for the formation of an academy for the regulation of the language: "I hope [that if] it should be established . . . the spirit of English liberty will hinder or destroy it."[24]

But the preface to Johnson's dictionary did little to stifle the enthusiastic prescriptivism of the language critics who followed Swift. In the 1750s, the crusade was taken up by Lord Orrery, who slightly revised Swift's chronology of the deterioration of English. While Swift had claimed that decay had set in following the war of 1642, Orrery argued that his predecessor had actually stemmed the tide of corruption and had moved the language closer to perfection. In Orrery's time, however, the tongue had begun to slip once again, as evidenced by the swiftly spreading expression *a few* and by the bad grammar of the Lord's Prayer.[25]

James Beattie, a minor Scottish poet with a particular aversion to the dialect of his own region, was the next to take up the cudgels for propriety. "Our language [I mean the English]," he wrote sadly in 1785, "is degenerating very fast." The evidence of corruption which Beattie (and later his son, an even more minor Scottish poet) adduced in support of their warnings tended to be more eighteenth-century versions of blight and bloat. Some words were being broken down: *reformation* changed to *reform* and *approbation* reduced to *approval*. Other plain and effective words were being supplanted by flowery neologisms: *existence* for *life; novel* for *new; capture* for *take militarily; ingurgitate* for *plunge*. The younger Beattie also identified some of the insidious catchphrases of the day, such as *netting a cool thousand, making up one's mind* and the indiscriminate attachment of the pallid intensifier *marked* to practically anything (*marked applause, marked regret,* and so forth). Despite his considerable efforts, though, Beattie, like Swift, felt that he had failed in his attempts to halt corruption: "I begin to fear that it will be impossible to check it," he wrote toward the end of his life.[26]

If eighteenth-century Englishmen were worried and discouraged about the status of their language, a curiously contradictory state of affairs obtained in the colonies. While people from many different regions of England had by this time migrated to North America (and certainly not the "better" class of people, in most cases), the English spoken across the Atlantic nevertheless began to receive admiring commentaries from British visitors. William Eddis, who toured the colonies in 1770, was surprised to find that "the language of the immediate descendents of such a promiscuous ancestry is perfectly uniform, and unadulterated; nor has it borrowed any provincial, or national accent, from its British or foreign parentage."[27] A few years later, another visitor noted: "It is a curious fact that there is perhaps no one portion of the British empire, in which two or three millions of persons are to be found, who speak their mother-tongue with greater purity, or a truer pronunciation, than the white inhabitants of the United States."[28] And even John Witherspoon, who emigrated from England in 1769 to become president of Princeton University, and who would later become a harsh critic of American language, noted in a Pennsylvania newspaper that "the vulgar in America speak much better than the vulgar in England."[29]

J. L. Dillard has suggested that these positive evaluations of American speech were the result of the colonists having created a *koiné* language—a kind of standardized dialect which often emerges among a group of emigrants speaking various dialects of one basic language. When the colonists from different regions of England came to North America and settled, they left behind their old social order, including the social rankings of dialects. In their adopted home they came in contact with a wide range of other languages: the foreign tongues of the maritime trade, the creoles of slaves, the languages of the Indians. These influences accelerated the breakdown of the colonists' English regional dialects and resulted in the formation of a naturally standardized American speech pattern, which British visitors later discovered and praised.[30]

English opinions of American speech, of course, were of relatively little interest to the colonists, who quite impolitely proceeded to separate themselves from the empire. In the aftermath of the Revolution, there was understandably even less of an urge to subscribe to English authority, in matters of language or anything else, and the Americans embarked on a period of furious growth, industry and, occasionally, romanticism. As Jefferson remarked of this period: "We have no distinct class of literati in our country. Every man is engaged in some industrious pursuit, and science is but a secondary occupation, always subordinate to the main business of life. Few, therefore, of those who are qualified have the leisure to write."[31] The relatively modest attention that language received during this era took two opposing forms: some individuals saw the regulation and study of the American language as a potential instrument of national identity; others viewed any formal study of language as a potential impediment to the freedom of expression which the people of this new country uniquely enjoyed.

No one was more vigorous in support of the former view than John Adams, who both anonymously and under his own name lobbied doggedly for the establishment of an academy for "correcting, improving, and ascertaining" the American language.[32] Adams complained of the lack of a "tolerable" dictionary of the language spoken in the United States, and perhaps his plea was heard by Noah Webster, who produced the first *American Dictionary of the English Language* in 1828. Webster seems to have shared Adams's political views about language:

As an independent nation, our honor requires us to have a system of our own, in language as well as government. Great Britain, whose children we are, and whose language we speak, should no longer be *our* standard; for the taste of her writers is already corrupted, and her language is on the decline.... We have therefore the greatest opportunity of establishing a national language and of giving it uniformity and perspicuity, in North America, that ever presented itself to mankind. Now is the time to begin the plan.[33]

A few of the founding fathers apparently felt that while the political independence of the colonies was a good thing, independence from the laws of the English language was carrying liberty a bit too far. Benjamin Franklin, who claimed that the cultivation of his writing style was his most serious lifelong endeavor, informed Webster in 1785 of his displeasure at the increased use of the verbs *to notice, to advocate, to progress,* and *to oppose* and asked the lexicographer's help in stamping them out.[34] John Witherspoon, a signer of both the Declaration of Independence and the Articles of Confederation, wrote a series of articles in 1781 bemoaning the degradation of language in the mouths of the Americans: "I have heard in this country, in the senate, at the bar, and from the pulpit, and see daily in dissertations from the press, errors in grammar, improprieties and vulgarisms which hardly any person of the same class in point of rank and literature would have fallen into in Great Britain." Though Witherspoon tried to explain, if not endorse, the development of these peculiarly American "errors," his urge to condemn overwhelmed him as he listed the offending items: *notify* for *inform; mad* for *angry; clever* for *good* and the like.[35]

The second, and generally stronger, American attitude toward language for about seventy-five years following the Revolution was a romantic, unfettered, and expansive view. Walt Whitman summarized this attitude in the 1850s when he wrote his famous lines: "The Americans are going to be the most fluent and melodious voiced people in the world—and the most perfect users of words." Though modern critics are fond of quoting Whitman ironically to chastise us for what has actually come to pass, his predictions still reveal much about the era in which they were made:

These States are rapidly supplying themselves with new words, called for by new occasions, new facts, new politics, new combinations. Far plentier additions will be needed, and, of course, will be supplied.... Many of the slang words are our best; slang words among fighting men, gamblers, thieves, are powerful words.... The appetite of the people of these States, in popular speeches and writings, is for un-hemmed latitude, coarseness, directness, live epithets, expletives, words of oppro-brium, resistance. This I understand because I have the taste myself as large, as largely, as any one.

The only authority in language to which Whitman would willingly sub-scribe, he declared, would be a dictionary of the true, common speech of Americans: "The Real Dictionary will give all the words that exist in use, the bad words as well as any. The Real Grammar will be that which de-clares itself a nucleus of the spirit of the laws, with liberty to all to carry out the spirit of the laws, even by violating them, if necessary." The only speakers who were interested in following the guidelines of British En-glish, Whitman implied, were "Bad presidents, bad judges, bad clients, bad editors, owners of slaves, the long ranks of Northern political suckers (robbers, traitors, suborned) monopolists, infidels ... shaved persons, sup-plejacks, ecclesiastics, men not fond of women, women not fond of men" and other similarly unattractive characters.[36]

Whitman's hostility toward polite language and British standards was shared, usually in milder form, by many English teachers of the early nineteenth century. An 1832 article in the *American Journal of Education* vigorously attacked the traditional forms of language instruction:

The practical truth respecting the relation of school, school boy, and grammar is, that grammar is not learned, and never can be learned, at a school, and that the attempt to teach it, the mode of teaching it, and the pretense of teaching a language through it, are insults to the common sense of mankind.... [Grammar] has been ... a stumbling block and ... a trammel, in chaining bold and free spirits.[37]

Three years later another writer in the same journal attacked the practice of parsing sentences: "The children in the United States have *parsed* themselves out of two million of years of time, and out of the power of learning language, or any other subject, understandably, and into a dis-gust for everything that bears the name of learning."[38]

What these American grammarians had discovered, and were now at-tempting to promote, was the descriptive, rather than prescriptive, view of language—an approach which would become the predominant methodology of modern linguistics a century later. In 1845 James Brown published a book called *An Appeal from the Old Theory of English Grammar,* which summarized this romantic-descriptive movement. Calling British grammar a collection of "silly rules, ridiculous notes, and nickname definitions," Brown scoffed at the traditional grammarians' fears that "disorder, dilaceration, and ruin" would result from changes in the language. What was needed, according to Brown, was a theory of language that acknowledged the actual practice of speakers and the inevitability of change in the language. Prescriptive grammar books, he argued, are so out of tune with reality that they will finally be disposed of through natural, if not human, forces: "the sea of life . . . will rise in anger, and will swallow up that compass, be it constructed by whom it may, which has been unfaithful to the mariner, in his voyage for science, art, or fame."[39]

During this era there were still, of course, plenty of traditional prescriptive grammarians plying their trade. But the tone which many of them adopted was gentler than the one of absolute certainty which characterized the pronouncements of earlier authorities. Many of these writers now took pains to dissociate themselves from hard-line prescriptivism before embarking on their own inevitably corrective commentaries. Fowle, the author of *The True English Grammar* (1829), exemplified this approach:

There was a time, before grammars were invented to clip the wings of fancy, and shackle the feet of genius, when it was considered more important to express a thought clearly and forcibly, than, as now, prettily and grammatically; when genius would as soon have stooped to accommodate itself to a rule of syntax as the eagle would to take lessons from the domestic goose; when grammarians were accustomed to note the movements of genius, not prescribe rules for them.

Just exactly when this glorious time occurred, Fowle does not say.[40]

While the Americans were enjoying, during the first half of the nineteenth century, a respite from linguistic insecurity and a flirtation with descriptive ideas about language, the British were having a language crisis of their own. While for years there had been minor complaints about the harmful effect of colonialisms on the mother tongue, the American Revolution triggered a virtual panic about the degradation of English. James Beattie, the Scot who had taken up the crusade of Jonathan Swift and Lord Orrery, noted in 1790 that English had begun to deteriorate especially quickly "during the last twenty years, especially since the breaking out of the American war." He condemned the "new-fangled phrases and barbarous idioms" in the political pamphlets, speeches, and newspapers of the day.[41] After Beattie retired, heartbroken, from the fray, his place was taken by Walter Savage Landor, who in 1824 announced that the English language had declined more precipitously in the previous fifty years than any other tongue ever spoken by man. One example of this decay was the widespread use of the phrase *under the circumstances*, which was incorrect, according to Landor, because circumstances can only be around us (*circum*) and it is therefore impossible to be *under* them.[42]

For several decades after the Revolution, British journals and newspapers heaped abuse on the language, as well as the content, of virtually all American writing which came to their attention. One of the earliest targets was Thomas Jefferson, whose *Notes on the State of Virginia* received this commentary from the *London Review:*

For shame, Mr. Jefferson! Why, after trampling upon the honour of our country, and representing it as little better than a land of barbarism—why, we say, perpetually trample also upon the very grammar of our language, and make that appear as Gothic as, from your description, our manners are rude?—Freely, good sir, we will forgive all your attacks, impotent as they are illiberal, upon our *national character;* but for the future spare—O spare, we beseech you, our mother-tongue!

This particular outburst, it is worth noting, resulted from the discovery in Jefferson's text of the verb *to belittle.*[43]

British visitors to America, needless to say, no longer praised the "purity" and "uniformity" of the language that they discovered across the Atlantic, but instead heartily condemned the "barbarisms" which they testified to be universal. Concluding a long diatribe against the linguistic offenses of the "educated and respectable class of Americans," Captain Thomas Hamilton wrote in 1833:

I will not go on with this unpleasant subject, nor should I have alluded to it, but I feel it something of a duty to express the natural feelings of an Englishman at finding the language of Shakespeare and Milton thus gratuitously degraded. Unless the present progress of change be arrested by an increase of taste and judgement . . . there can be no doubt that, in another century, the dialect of the Americans will become utterly unintelligible to an Englishman, and that the nation will be cut off from the advantages arising from their participation in British literature. If they contemplate such an event with complacency, let them go on and prosper.[44]

Another British visitor, Captain Frederick Marryat, who visited the United States in 1837-1838, later published a diary of his travels in which he underscored Hamilton's judgments. Marryat ridiculed in particular the American use of *fix* for *prepare, stoop* for *porch, great* for *splendid, right away* for *at once, strike* for *attack,* and such primitive phrases as *clear out* and *make tracks.*[45]

Even Charles Dickens, whose ear for, if not appreciation of, various dialects was well developed, unburdened himself of various inaccurate and uncomplimentary remarks about American speech following his visit in 1842. "All of the women who have been bred in the slave states," he commented, "speak more or less like Negroes." Why Dickens failed to notice the existence of a southern dialect among white men as well as women—even if he failed to detect differences between black and white speech generally—remains a mystery, though at the time it was probably his castigation of the flower of southern womanhood that raised the greatest American ire.[46] But even Dickens's slipshod linguistic judgments look sophisticated in comparison with those of the poet Samuel Taylor Coleridge, who, without even the benefit of a tour, pronounced the Americans "a people without a language."[47]

In keeping with the spirit of the age, a number of American writers quickly joined battle with their English counterparts, hurling lively linguistic insults across the Atlantic. Probably the leading resister was Edward Everett, editor of the *North American Review,* who argued in numerous columns that "on the whole, the English language is better spoken here than in England," and commented acidly upon the infelicities and neologisms he claimed to have discovered in English magazines. But perhaps Everett's ultimate attack was found in a fictitious resolution which he claimed was to be introduced into the Congress. This document began with a long list of indictments of the language spoken by the English. The dialects of Yorkshire, Somersetshire, and Cumberland are "utterly uncouth and hideous"; "barbarity and affectation" are creeping into the language of "the best educated classes of society in England"; "vulgar and cant terms are heard in what are called the best circles"; and, worst of all, Everett charged, the language of the British contained "an alarming prevalence of profane and obscene language ... which, though it is unhappily a vice too common in all countries, the House has unquestioned information prevails in England to an unparalleled and odious extent, reaching into the societies which consider themselves the most polite and best bred." Everett climaxed this piece of showmanship with a resolution that "the nobility and gentry of England be courteously invited to send their elder sons" and other potential public speakers to be educated in America, where the language "by the blessing of God, [is] quite untainted with most of the above mentioned vulgarities prevalent in the highest English circles." Upon completion of their instruction in proper speech, these students would be awarded "certificates of proficiency in the English tongue."[48]

But in spite of Everett's ironic rejoinders, and despite the fledgling efforts of the descriptive grammarians, the British attackers soon had their day. During the second half of the nineteenth century, and especially after the Civil War, there was a dramatic resurgence of American linguistic insecurity and intolerance which has continued more or less to this day. By the late 1860s, the American language was no longer seen as a reflection of the tremendous energy and opportunity of the country itself, but as a tangled mess badly needing to be straightened out, standardized, and taught in an orderly manner to children and adults alike.

This swift change of heart was undoubtedly the inevitable result of the social and economic conditions of the time. The sense of boundless opportunity had begun to diminish as the frontier was pushed to the Pacific. The cities were becoming increasingly industrialized and were filling with immigrants who were usually illiterate and often spoke no English. In an attempt to regulate this increasing social complexity, the educated classes of Americans were intently setting up what Glendon Drake has called a "genteel cultural apparatus," manifested particularly in the inauguration of many scholarly and literary publications.[49] Finally, of course, continuing sectional tensions erupted in a war which introduced new and horrifyingly effective weapons to the art of combat and very nearly destroyed the fragile Union itself.

After the Civil War, reconstruction became the major theme of American life, not just in the mending of war damage, but in the reunification and integration of the national culture in general. This cultural reconstruction paid considerable attention to language. Journals like *Galaxy*, the *Nation, Round Table, Godey's,* and others published hundreds of pages of prescriptive commentaries on language and advice on linguistic etiquette. Among these articles, there was a general recanting of the earlier view of American as a creative and autonomous variant of English. One writer in the *North American Review* (the vehicle of Everett's anti-British commentaries a generation before) bemoaned the failure of American writers to show deference to "English use and authority." The author reminded his audience that "before the English language became domecilated in this country, it had reached a point of maturity beyond which no very great and radical changes were to be expected.... [*It*] had attained a point in its development at which more was to be feared from its not being improved.... Its shape had been fixed in a sterling literature."[50] Along similar lines, the *Southern Review* in 1870 attacked the

"Americanisms" in the writings of Ralph Waldo Emerson and Walt Whitman, condemning them as "perversions of the best form of the English language,—perversions not only unlicensed, but indefensible, unseemly, and vicious." These authors had, the *Review* asserted, rendered the language "far inferior to the mother tongue in force, in flexibility, in rhythmic proportion, in precision and correctness," by turning "a cold shoulder to the precedents of good grammar."[51]

This renewed fealty to the English standard was recommended in copious detail by George Perkins Marsh, whose collected lectures given at Columbia College went through many editions during the late 1800s. Marsh was worried about the state of language in America, which he said was "affected by extraneous, alien, and discordant influences," was "overloaded with adventitious appendages," and was replete with "syntactical combinations" that were "not merely irregular, but repugnant." Somewhat coyly, Marsh announced in one lecture, "I will not here inquire whether this condition of English is an evil," and explained that his purpose was to show how English is properly learned rather than how it is typically misused. Nevertheless, Marsh's lectures were much concerned with cataloging American linguistic errors and assigning the blame for them.[52]

One of his main targets was "the periodical press," and the newspapers' "inflated diction, the straining after effect, the use of cant phrases, and of such expressions as not only fall in with, but tend to aggravate, the prevalent evil humors of the time, the hyperbolical tone in which they commend their patrons or the candidates of their party, and, in short, all the vices of exaggeration in style and language." The "mischief" of the newspapers, Marsh explained, was all the worse for their being the "agency through which man acts most powerfully upon the mind of his fellow-man." He left no doubt as to where the antidote to such corrupt language might be found: in "the study of old English writers," who exemplified "not only the most forcible terms of expression, but a marvellous affluence of the mighty thoughts out of which has grown the action that has made England and her children the wonder and envy of the world."[53]

Yet even Marsh's anglophilia was no match for the uncompromising prescriptivism of Richard Grant White, who was probably the most popular and prolific language commentator of this era. White's initial outlet for his views was the literary journal *Galaxy*, which printed dozens of his articles between 1867 and 1870. Later, White published two books based upon and expanding the ideas presented in his *Galaxy* columns. White can fairly be called the Edwin Newman of his day, not just for his considerable popularity and general lack of linguistic sophistication (he prided himself on his discovery that the English language had "no grammar"), but also for his recycling of his readers' submissions and comments in his own work.[54]

White saw around him "the degradation of language, the utter abolition of simple, clear and manly speech." Like most of the twentieth-century language critics, he maintained the distinction between linguistic blight and bloat. On the one hand he identified a "tendency to slang, to colloquial inelegances, and even vulgarities" committed by "coarse libertines," and on the other he decried the "silly bombast" and "stilted ignorance" emanating from pedants. Also like many of the modern language critics, White blamed the sudden deterioration of American English on the schools, the media, and the egalitarian ideals of the country itself:

The wide diffusion of just so much instruction as enables men to read their newspapers, write their advertisements, and keep their accounts, and the utter lack of deference to anyone, or of doubt in themselves, which political equality and material prosperity beget in people having no more than such education, and no less, combine to produce a condition in society which brings their style of speech, as well as their manners, much more to the front, not to say the top, than is the case in other countries.

This compact formulation of the threat supposedly posed to the language by free public education, the popular media, and democracy in general was to be paraphrased frequently in the century to come.[55]

When the "mass is misled by a little learning" about language, White reasoned, it is only through "criticism that our language can now be restrained from license and preserved from corruption." The goal of such criticism, he explained, was to "check bad usage and reform degraded custom." Although criticism may not always "resist the introduction of that which is debasing and enfeebling ... it may thrust out vicious words and phrases which through carelessness or perverted taste may have obtained a footing." And the standard for such criticism was not necessarily the language of educated people, or even that of respected authors. For, as White explains, "the truth is, however, that the authority of general usage, or even the usage of the great writers, is not absolute in language. There is a misuse of words which can be justified by no authority, however great, by no usage, however general." The standard which White was setting up, of course, was White. His compendia of shibboleths run for scores of pages. White was particularly aggrieved by the existence of "Words That Are Not Words." While there are persons who mistakenly employ these unreal locutions, White revealed that "Most of them are usurpers, interlopers, or vulgar pretenders; some are deformed creatures, with only half a life in them. . . . Words that are not words sometimes die spontaneously; but many linger, living a precarious existence on the outskirts of society, uncertain of their position, and a cause of great discomfort to all right thinking, straightforward people." A few of White's unwords were *reliable, telegraph, donate, jeopardize,* and *gubernatorial.*[56]

White saw words that *are* words being constantly abused. He complained of the use of *jug* for *pitcher, balance* for *remainder, caption* for the lines which identify a photograph ("laughable and absurd"), *catch* for *overtake, consider* for *think* (as opposed to study), *decimated* for *reducing* to other than one-tenth, *dirt* for *earth* ("Dirt means filth, and primarily filth of the most offensive kind"), *dock* for *wharf* (docks must be covered), *editorial* for *leading article, executed* for *killed* ("a perversion"), *lie* for *lay, like* for *as, transmit* for *send, supervise* for *oversee, repudiate* for *condemn, proceed* for *go, residence* for *home, recuperate* for *recover, locate* for *settle* ("insufferable"), *persuaded* for *convinced* ("vulgar"), *splendid* for *good* ("coarse"), *jewelery* for *jewels* ("of very low caste"), and *ice-cream* for *iced-cream* ("a real confusion of language, if not thought").[57]

White's complaints about the superficial and allegedly dangerous effects of education serve as a reminder that there was a steady expansion of school enrollments, particularly at the elementary level, during the latter half of the nineteenth century. Compulsory attendance laws were passed in many states, mostly as attempts to educate, or at least contain, the immigrant children who increasingly clogged the streets of industrialized American cities. No small part of the instruction of these children centered on teaching them—both native and foreign—the finer points of the English language, usually through exercises in grammar and the parsing of sentences.

At the pinnacle of this youthful educational apparatus, at Harvard University, dissatisfaction about the language skills of entering freshmen began to be expressed in the 1870s. President Charles William Eliot announced in 1871:

The need of some requisition which should secure on the part of young men preparing for college proper attention to their own language has long been felt. Bad spelling, incorrectness as well as inelegance of expression in writing, ignorance of the simplest rules of punctuation, and almost entire want of familiarity with English literature, are far from rare among young men of eighteen otherwise well prepared for college.[58]

Accordingly, beginning in 1873, all applicants to Harvard University, both the sons of the aristocracy and those few poor youths of demonstrated "capacity and character," were required to take an essay examination. The results of this exercise were increasingly displeasing to the faculty members burdened with reading them. Professor Adams Sherman Hill reported several years later:

I have read four to five thousand compositions written in the examination-room . . . [and] of these not more than a hundred—to make a generous estimate—were creditable to either writer or teacher. . . . . It is this tedious mediocrity which has amazed me year after year. In spelling, punctuation, and grammar some of the books are a little worse than the mass, and some a great deal better; but in other respects there is a dead-level, unvaried by a fresh thought or an individual expression. Almost all the writers use the same commonplace vocabulary—a very small one—in the same confused way.

Hill was particularly concerned by these "dreary compositions" because they were written by "the picked youth of the country," boys who came from "the best families in point of culture and breeding, and from the best schools we have." If the essays had at least been correct in spelling and mechanics, Hill noted sadly, there would have been some consolation. But not even this minimal competency was evident, and his own Harvard colleagues had "to spend much of their time in teaching the A B C of their mother-tongue to young men of twenty—work disagreeable in itself, and often barren of result." And in the end, Hill was compelled to make the most embarrassing admission of all: "Every year Harvard graduates a certain number of men—some of them high scholars—whose manuscript would disgrace a boy of twelve; and yet the college cannot be blamed, for she can hardly be expected to conduct an infant school for adults."[59]

Nor was the literacy crisis of the 1870s and 1880s confined to the Harvard-bound. E. S. Cox, speaking at the annual meeting of the National Education Association in 1886 noted:

Every practiced inspector of schools knows what dreary reading the average school essay is. Some accomplished men of letters [including Professor Hill, no doubt] have recently given us the benefit of their half-humorous but still valuable and forcible criticism on the subject . . . [the average pupil] lacks that ready and forcible use of English words and idioms which is so essential to all strong and valuable compositions.[60]

At the conference of the same body three years later, M. W. Smith underscored the deterioration: "The vocabularies of the majority of high-school pupils are amazingly small. I always try to use simple English, and yet I have talked to classes when quite a minority of the pupils did not comprehend more than half of what I said."[61]

By the turn of the century, many of the ancient worries about language which underlie our current crisis had been emphatically reaffirmed. The American language, it was agreed among the experts, was in grave and constant danger of corruption, decay, and possibly death. Most of the changes occurring in the language were changes for the worse, and only the constant solicitude of self-appointed critics was saving it from oblivion. The diversity of the American people, in their origins, occupations, and locations was an unhealthy influence on the language and worked against the desperate need for national uniformity in speech and writing. Even worse, the egalitarian notions upon which this peculiar country had been founded interfered with the preservation of the mother tongue, since the common man, filled with mistaken notions of his own equality, could not easily be brought to see the inferiority of his own dialect. Universal free public schooling had turned out to be a mixed blessing for the language. While it offered an apparent opportunity to teach all children the correct forms of speech and writing, the schools routinely bungled the job, graduating students whose crude native speech was only further degraded by a thin overlay of pomposity. Even the one generally effective effort of the schools—the teaching of reading—only served to expose young people to the vile language of the newspapers and cheap fiction of the day.

Though all of these concerns have continued more or less unabated into the present, there is one additional event from the history of linguistic insecurity and intolerance which is worth recalling here. Between about 1918 and 1928, America experienced a language panic which was remarkably similar in content and scope to the one which would develop a half century later. The historical tendency for language crises to arise after wars, usually as an element of national reintegration and cultural reconstruction, is by now apparent, and so it is perhaps not surprising that a bout of linguistic breastbeating would follow the "War to End All Wars." But other factors contributed as well, not the least of which was the considerable discomfort in some quarters about the high levels of immigration, particularly of Southern and Eastern Europeans. Many scholars and politicans who were worried about these postwar conditions joined the immigration restriction societies that were formed at the time. These groups, which enrolled professors from Harvard, Princeton, and Columbia, as well as other distinguished figures of the day, sought to stem the flow of "feeble-minded" and potentially "disloyal" peoples into America. But another outlet for some of these same concerns was commentary on, and the attempted reform of, language and language teaching.[62]

That this worry about the language arose, at least in part, from the fear and loathing of foreign "races" and "accents" is underscored by Theodore Roosevelt's stern warning in 1919: "We have room for but one language here and that is the English language, for we intend to see that the crucible turns out people as Americans and not as dwellers in a polyglot boarding house."[63] Many patriotic academics and literati were stirred to action by the spirit of Roosevelt's words. In 1923, a conference of British and American professors of English was held at Columbia University, during which most of the American representatives declared their loyalty to British standards of language, confessed the linguistic transgressions of their countrymen, and generally fawned over their trans-Atlantic colleagues. Henry van Dyke, one of the organizers of the conference, denounced the "slovenly" way in which Americans used language "not only in the streets, but also in the pulpit, on the stage, and even in the classroom." This "lazy, unintelligible, and syncopated speech," he confessed, "is like a dirty face." Professor Fred Newton Scott went even further, arguing that the impious suggestion that there was an autonomous dialect in the United States was "for Americans not a matter of ridicule, but for the hair shirt and the lash, for tears of shame and self-abasement."[64]

Whatever the indigenous reasons for such self-flagellation, Scott and van Dyke must have been painfully aware of the sudden resurgence of British attacks up on the language of Americans. As H. L. Mencken acidly observed in his book *The American Language*, the English had briefly hailed the Americans as "blood brothers, but that lasted only until the first mention of war debts. Ever since 1920 [we] have been mongrels again." In the postwar era, Mencken said, British commentaries on the American language had usually included "the objection that yielding to [it] means yielding to a miscellaneous rabble of inferior tribes, some of them, by English standards, almost savage."[65]

In 1922 the London bureau of the Associated Press sent home a dispatch which noted: "England is apprehensive lest the vocabularies of her youth become corrupted through incursions of American slang." The article cited the increasing use of Americanisms in British plays, songs, and other assorted public performances. But it was "the subtitle of the American moving picture film which, it is feared, constitutes the most menacing threat to the vaunted English purity of speech."[66] Needless to say, the addition of sound to moving pictures a few years later only made the threat more grave. As one British journalist commented: "The talkies have presented the American language in one giant meal, and we are revolted."[67] Nor did the British commentators confine themselves to attacks on American films: they criticized the language of American newspapers, novels, plays, translations, and at least one medical textbook. No special deference was shown to American leaders, and the public utterances of President Wilson were a favorite subject of British scolding. Even George Bernard Shaw took time out from his other chores to repudiate Wilson's use of *obligate* for *oblige*: "We asked ourselves if a man could become King of England if he used the word *obligate*. We said at once that it could not be done." Shaw's anger had apparently obscured his recollection of the rules of succession, which mention no linguistic prerequisites for the assumption of the throne.[68]

In the face of this British attack, most American writers, professors, and schoolteachers bowed their heads in shame, and Fred Newton Scott, at least, donned his hair shirt. But a few robust spirits fought back. Rupert Hughes, writing in *Harper's* in 1920, asserted: "Let us sign a Declaration of Literary Independence and formally begin to write, not British, but United Statesish. For there is such a language for which we have no specific name. . . . Whatever we call it, let us cease to consider it a vulgar dialect of English, to be used only with deprecation. Let us study it in its splendid efflorescence, be proud of it, and true to it."[69] Considerably less polite were the remarks of Murray Godwin, who responded in 1926 to a British article which had cited the existence of Yiddish speakers in the United States as proof that grammar had disappeared from American English. Godwin wrote:

Of course we have come to expect such tactics on the part of our British stepcousins, whose reputation for fair play has been so firmly established by tradition that it has no longer any need to be supported by example . . . Though I feel touched damn nigh to tears when I picture this noble Briton in the throes of molding and milling this length of literary leadpipe with which to bash the blinding Yank, I shall not pass up the chance to point out that his implication that English is a pure and integrated growth, while American is a nondescript tangle of underbrush, would seem to stem from a scholarly logic turned sour by contact with the viewpoint of an intestinally-constricted and malicious if unmuscular nitwit.[70]

Despite the efforts of a few vigorous defenders like Godwin, most native "experts" nevertheless pronounced the American language gravely ill.

The schools, predictably enough, were identified as both a cause of and a potential solution to the language problem. As one private-school teacher wrote in 1917:

From every college in the country goes up the cry, "Our freshmen can't spell, can't punctuate." Every high school is in disrepair because its pupils are so ignorant of the merest rudiments. A reformation is everywhere demanded. It is being brought about, and so rapidly that most textbooks are stranded in the idealism of a decade ago, and many teachers are foundering badly in the new conditions. It is hard to keep pace with swift change, hard to know what it is all about, or why our duties are preached to us in such contradictory terms. "Inspire" is still the watchcry; "drills in the rudiments" is soon to be the fact.[71]

But the predicted "reformation" apparently did not occur as swiftly as this teacher had predicted. In 1926, H. L. Mencken was still able to complain that when the average American high school student tried to put his thoughts into writing, the usual result was "confused and puerile nonsense."[72] Nor did Mencken hesitate to place the blame where he felt it belonged: "In the American colleges and high-schools there is no faculty so weak as the English faculty. It is the common catch-all for aspirants to the birch who are too lazy or too feeble in intelligence to acquire any sort of exact knowledge, and the professional incompetence of its typical ornament is matched only by his hollow cocksureness." Though Mencken was an uncompromising anglophobe and was perhaps the era's greatest proponent of an autonomous American dialect, he obviouly had little patience for students and teachers who sullied the language he had worked so hard to legitimize.[73]

These complaints, it is worth noting, were aimed at an educational system which enrolled only about one-third of the high school age population and sent fewer than 7 percent to colleges. Those relatively few students who received secondary and higher education tended to be the sons (only rarely the daughters) of wealthy, educated, presumably literate American families. Yet even among this elite group there was a "literacy crisis" (as there had been among an even more select group in the 1870s) serious enough for Princeton University to set up a remedial writing clinic for its "undergraduate illiterates."[74]

The National Council of Teachers of English, which was in its first decade of existence when this panic began, was quick to endorse and to fuel the sense of crisis. In collaboration with several other educational groups, the NCTE sponsored an event known as "Better Speech Week."[75] Patterned after other popular commemorations of the day ("Better Babies Week," "Safety-First Week," "Eat-More-Cheese Week"), this comprehensive program was designed to dramatize the importance of correct language through the use of posters, parades, contests, slogans, skits, newspaper articles, and school competitions. Among the festivities organized by some schools were "Ain't-less Week," "Final-G Week," and various

"Tag Days," during which students caught uttering such infelicities as *It's me* or *I have got* had reproving slogans hung around their necks. In California, a group of women's clubs honored "Better Speech Week" by adopting this resolution:

Whereas, we believe that if newspaper comic strips and jokes use English free from grammatical errors (except for decided character roles) they will become more attractive to many readers, and *Whereas*, we believe that this effort on the part of newspapers will be of invaluable aid in raising the standards of American speech, therefore, *Be it resolved* that we request editors of newspapers and comic writers to eliminate grammatical errors in the comic strips and jokes except for decided character roles.

This manifesto was presumably distributed to, if not nailed to the doors of, the offending newspaper editors in hope that its outraged whereases would reform the funnies. History does not record the editors' response.[76]

The standard of language by which all of these NCTE-sponsored activities were guided was not an American one, but was in fact British Received Punctuation. The early issues of *English Journal*, the first periodical inaugurated by the Council, reveal a remarkable unanimity among its contributors that mastery of the English—not the American—language should be the goal of their teaching. Instead, the main preoccupations of *English Journal* writers between 1911 and 1920 concerned the technicalities of several proposed systems for the reform of grammatical nomenclature and spelling. By the late 1920s, to be sure, the NCTE would have assumed the leadership of the battle for descriptive study of the American language and would have begun to earn for itself the enmity of purists for decades to come. But between 1917 and 1929, the Council was delighted to act as the clearinghouse for a general festival of doomsaying, prescriptivism, and anglomania.

Perhaps the single most emblematic product of the Better Speech Week campaigns and the spirit behind them was the following pledge, which students throughout the country were obliged to recite:

I love the United States of America. I love my country's flag. I love my country's language. I promise:
1. That I will not dishonor my country's speech by leaving off the last syllable of words.
2. That I will say a good American "yes" and "no" in place of an Indian grunt "um-hum" and "nup-um" or a foreign "ya" or "yeh" and "nope."
3. That I will do my best to improve American speech by avoiding loud rough

tones, by enunciating distinctly, and by speaking pleasantly, clearly and sincerely.

4. That I will learn to articulate correctly as many words as possible during the year.[77]

4

Nine Ideas About Language

Assuming we agree that the English language has in fact survived all of the predictions of doom which occupy the previous chapter, we also have reason to believe that current reports of the death of our language are similarly exaggerated. The managers of the present crisis of course disagree, and their efforts may even result in the reinstatement of the linguistic loyalty oath of the 1920s or of some updated equivalent ("I promise to use good American unsplit infinitives") in our schools. But it won't make much difference. The English language, if history is any guide at all, will remain useful and vibrant as long as it is spoken, whether we eagerly try to tend and nurture and prune its growth or if we just leave it alone.

One of the reasons why the language critics cannot understand that English needs no defense, and, perhaps, why they seem altogether unembarrassed by the quixotic history of language criticism itself, is that they know very little about language. They are able to believe that we have arrived at the linguistic apocalypse, that America *will* be the death of English, mainly because they don't know any better, don't know any other ways of looking at what seems to be a problem. They recognize that language is changing, that people use a lot of jargon, that few people consistently speak the standard dialect, that much writing done in our society is ineffective, and so forth—but they have no other way of viewing these phenomena except with alarm. But most of the uses of and apparent changes in language which worry the critics *can* be explained and understood in unalarming ways. Such explanations have been provided by linguists during the past seventy-five years.

I have said that in order to understand the errors and misrepresentations of the language critics, we need to examine not only history but also "the facts." Of course, facts about language are a somewhat elusive commodity, and we may never be able to answer all of our questions about this wonderfully complex activity. But linguists have made a good start during this century toward describing some of the basic features, structures, and operations of human speech. This chapter presents a series of nine fundamental ideas about language that form, if not exactly a list of facts, at least a fair summary of the consensus of most linguistic scholars. I have chosen to take a kind of developmental approach to the review of these principles, emphasizing not just how language works for adult speakers, but also taking note of how children learn to understand and speak their language. I hope I will be forgiven for often using as an example the one child I know best.

I present this material, these facts, for several reasons. First, although the preceding chapter has shown *that* predictions of imminent linguistic doom are always wrong, this one will explain *why*. The *that* and the *why*, taken together, should give us a fairly cheerful attitude about the future and an ability to fend off the insistent misfortune-telling of the language critics. Second, information about the basic principles of modern linguistics will be helpful when we come, in chapters five and six, to consider the varying evidence of fatal deterioration that the critics offer. Without reaching too far ahead, it is perhaps enough to say that often what the critics see as symptoms of illness are really aspects of a healthy, normal language going about its business. The critics may not wish to understand how language actually works, but we are under no obligation to share their obstinacy on this point. And finally, this material is here because it explains the assumptions about language which guide my comments in the last four chapters of the book, where I consider some *real* problems with American English.

1. Children learn their native language swiftly, efficiently, and largely without instruction.

Language is a species-specific trait of human beings. All children, unless they are severely retarded or completely deprived of exposure to speech, will acquire their oral language as naturally as they learn to walk. Many linguists even assert that the human brain is prewired for language, and some have also postulated that the underlying linguistic features which are common to all languages are present in the brain at birth. This latter theory comes from the discovery that all languages have certain procedures in common: ways of making statements, questions, and commands; ways of referring to past time; the ability to negate, and so on.[1] In spite of the underlying similarities of all languages, though, it is important to remember that children will acquire the language which they hear around them—whether that is Ukrainian, Swahili, Cantonese, or Appalachian American English.

In spite of the common-sense notions of parents, they do not "teach" their children to talk. Children *learn* to talk, using the language of their parents, siblings, friends, and others as sources and examples—and by using other speakers as testing devices for their own emerging ideas about language. When we acknowledge the complexity of adult speech, with its ability to generate an unlimited number of new, meaningful utterances, it is clear that this skill cannot be the end result of simple instruction. Parents do not explain to their children, for example, that adjectives generally precede the noun in English, nor do they lecture them on the rules governing formation of the past participle. While parents do correct some kinds of mistakes on a piecemeal basis, discovering the underlying rules which make up the language is the child's job.

From what we know, children appear to learn language partly by imitation but even more by hypothesis-testing. Consider a child who is just beginning to form past tenses. In the earliest efforts, the child is likely to produce such incorrect and unheard forms as *I goed to the store* or *I seed a dog*, along with other conventional uses of the past tense: *I walked to Grandma's.* This process reveals that the child has learned the basic, general rule about the formation of the past tense—you add *-ed* to the verb— but has not yet mastered the other rules, the exceptions and irregularities. The production of forms that the child has never heard suggests that imitation is not central in language learning and that the child's main strategy is hypothesizing—deducing from the language she hears an idea about the underlying rule, and then trying it out.

My own son, who is now two and one-half, has just been working on the

-ed problem. Until recently, he used present tense verb forms for all situations: *Daddy go work?* (for: *Did Daddy go to work?*) and *We take a bath today?* (for: *Will we take a bath today?*) Once he discovered that wonderful past tag, he attached it with gusto to any verb he could think up and produced, predictably enough, *goed, eated, flied,* and many other overgeneralizations of his initial hypothetical rule for the formation of past tenses. He was so excited about his new discovery, in fact, that he would often give extra emphasis to the marker: *Dad, I swallow-ed the cookie.* Nicky will soon learn to deemphasize the sound of *-ed* (as well as to master all those irregular past forms) by listening to more language and by revising and expanding his own internal set of language rules.

Linguists and educators sometimes debate about what percentage of adult forms is learned by a given age. A common estimate is that 90 percent of adult structures are acquired by the time a child is seven. Obviously, it is quite difficult to attach proportions to such a complex process, but the central point is clear: schoolchildren of primary age have already learned the great majority of the rules governing their native language, and can produce virtually all the kinds of sentences that it permits. With the passing years, all children will add some additional capabilities, but the main growth from this point forward will not so much be in acquiring new rules as in using new combinations of them to express increasingly sophisticated ideas, and in learning how to use language effectively in a widening variety of social settings.

It is important to reiterate that we are talking here about the child's acquisition of her native language. It may be that the child has been born into a community of standard English or French or Urdu speakers, or into a community of nonstandard English, French or Urdu speakers. But the language of the child's home and community *is* the native language, and it would be impossible for her to somehow grow up speaking a language to which she was never, or rarely, exposed.

2. Language operates by rules.

As the *-ed* saga suggests, when a child begins learning his native language, what he is doing is acquiring a vast system of mostly subconscious rules which allow him to make meaningful and increasingly complex utterances. These rules concern sounds, words, the arrangement of strings of words, and aspects of the social act of speaking. Obviously, children who grow up speaking different languages will acquire generally different sets of rules. This fact reminds us that human language is, in an important sense, arbitrary.

Except for a few onomatopoetic words (*bang, hiss, grunt*), the assignment of meanings to certain combinations of sounds is arbitrary. We English speakers might just as well call a chair a *glotz* or a *blurg*, as long as we all agreed that these combinations of sounds meant *chair*. In fact, not just the words but the individual sounds used in English have been arbitrarily selected from a much larger inventory of sounds which the human vocal organs are capable of producing. The existence of African languages employing musical tones or clicks reminds us that the forty phonemes used in English represent an arbitrary selection from hundreds of available sounds. Grammar, too, is arbitrary. We have a rule in English which requires most adjectives to appear before the noun which they modify (*the blue chair*). In French, the syntax is reversed (*la chaise bleue*), and in some languages, like Latin, either order is allowed.

Given that any language requires a complex set of arbitrary choices regarding sounds, words, and syntax, it is clear that the foundation of a language lies not in any "natural" meaning or appropriateness of its features, but in its system of rules—the implicit agreement among speakers that they will use certain sounds consistently, that certain combinations of sounds will mean the same thing over and over, and that they will observe certain grammatical patterns in order to convey messages. It takes thousands of such rules to make up a language. Many linguists believe that when each of us learned these countless rules, as very young children, we accomplished the most complex cognitive task of our lives.

Our agreement about the rules of language, of course, is only a general one. Every speaker of a language is unique; no one sounds exactly like anyone else. The language differs from region to region, between social, occupational and ethnic groups, and even from one speech situation to the next. These variations are not mistakes or deviations from some basic tongue, but are simply the rule-governed alternatives which make up any language. Still, in America our assorted variations of English are mostly mutually intelligible, reflecting the fact that most of our language rules do overlap, whatever group we belong to, or whatever situation we are in.

3. All languages have three major components: a sound system, a vocabulary, and a system of grammar.

This statement underscores what has already been suggested: that any human speaker makes meaning by manipulating sounds, words, and their order according to an internalized system of rules which other speakers of that language largely share.

The sound system of a language—its phonology—is the inventory of vocal noises, and combinations of noises, that it employs. Children learn the selected sounds of their own language in the same way they learn the other elements: by listening, hypothesizing, testing, and listening again. They do not, though it may seem logical, learn the sounds first (after all, English has only forty) and then go on to words and then to grammar. My son, for example, can say nearly anything he needs to say, in sentences of eight or ten or fourteen words, but he couldn't utter the sound of *th* to save his life.

The vocabulary, or lexicon, of a language is the individual's storehouse of words. Obviously, one of the young child's most conspicuous efforts is aimed at expanding his lexical inventory. Two and three-year-olds are notorious for asking "What's that?" a good deal more often than even the most doting parents can tolerate. And not only do children constantly and spontaneously try to enlarge their vocabularies, but they are always working to build categories, to establish classes of words, to add connotative meanings, to hone and refine their sense of the semantic properties—the meanings—of the words they are learning. My awareness of these latter processes was heightened a few months ago as we were driving home from a trip in the country during which Nicky had delighted in learning the names of various features of the rural landscape. As we drove past the Chicago skyline Nicky looked up at the tall buildings and announced "Look at those silos, Dad!" I asked him what he thought they kept in the Sears Tower, and he replied confidently, "Animal food." His parents' laughter presumably helped him to begin reevaluating his lexical hypothesis that any tall narrow structure was a silo.

The nature of the vocabulary and the phonology of a language are straightforward enough, but the term *grammar* often causes much confusion. In school, most of us have been taught that "good grammar" includes knowing the names of the parts of speech, being able to diagram sentences, practicing correct punctuation and capitalization, employing the right word usage and diction, and sometimes even spelling properly.

Linguists, who look at language descriptively rather than prescriptively, have different definitions of *grammar*—and unfortunately there are two main ones. The first, which I am using in this book, says that grammar is the system of rules we use to arrange words into meaningful English sentences. For example, my lexicon and my phonology may provide me with the appropriate strings of sounds to say the words: *eat four yesterday cat crocodile the*. It is my knowledge of grammar which allows me to arrange these elements into a sentence: *Yesterday the crocodile ate four cats*. Not only does my grammar arrange these elements in a meaningful order, it also provides me with the necessary markers of plurality, tense, and agreement. Explaining the series of rules by which I subconsciously constructed this sentence describes some of my "grammar" in this sense. But this kind of grammar is simply explanatory: if, in my dialect, plural markers are not used in such a sentence (*Yesterday the crocodile ate four cat*), a descriptive grammarian would not rebuke me, but simply try to explain the rule in my dialect that permits (or requires) this way of handling plurality.

The second definition of *grammar* often used by linguists refers to the whole system of rules which makes up a language—not just the rules for the arrangement and appropriate marking of elements in a sentence, but all of the lexical, phonological, and syntactic patterns which a language uses. In this sense, *everything* I know about my language, all the conscious and unconscious operations I can perform when speaking or listening, constitutes my grammar. It is this second definition of grammar to which linguists sometimes refer when they speak of describing a language in terms of its grammar.

4. Everyone speaks a dialect.

Among linguists the term *dialect* does not have the pejorative connotation which it retains in general use. It simply designates a variety of a particular language which has a certain set of lexical, phonological, and grammatical rules that distinguish it from other dialects. The most familiar definition of dialects in America is geographical: we recognize, for example, that some features of New England language—the dropping *r's* (*pahk the cah in Hahvahd yahd*) and the use of *bubbler* for *drinking fountain*—distinguish the speech of this region. The native speaker of Bostonian English is not making mistakes, of course; he or she simply observes systematic rules which happen to differ from those observed in other regions.

Where do these different varieties of a language come from and how are they maintained? The underlying factors are isolation and language change. Imagine a group of people which lives, works, and talks together constantly. Among them, there is a good deal of natural pressure to keep the language relatively uniform. But if one part of the group moves away to a remote location, and has no further contact with the other, the language of the two groups will gradually diverge. This will happen not just because of the differing needs of the two different environments, but also because of the inexorable and sometimes arbitrary process of language change itself. In other words, there is no likelihood that the language of these two groups, though identical at the beginning, will now change in the same ways. Ultimately, if the isolation is lengthy and complete, the two hypothetical groups will probably develop separate, mutually unintelligible languages. If the isolation is only partial, if interchange occurs between the two groups, and if they have some need to continue communicating (as with the American and British peoples) less divergence will occur.

This same principle of isolation also applies, in a less dramatic way, to contemporary American dialects. New England speakers are partially isolated from southern speakers, and so some of the differences between these two dialects are maintained. Other factors, such as travel and the mass media, bring them into contact with each other and tend to prevent drastic divergences. But the isolation that produces or maintains language differences may not be only geographical. In many American cities we find people living within miles, or even blocks of each other who speak markedly different and quite enduring dialects. Black English and midwestern English are examples of such pairs. Here, the isolation is partially spatial, but more importantly it is social, economic, occupational, educational, and political. And as long as this effective separation of speech communities persists, so will the differences in their dialects.

Many of the world's languages have a "standard" dialect. In some countries, the term *standard* refers more to a *lingua franca* than to an indigenous dialect. In Nigeria, for example, where there are more than 150 mostly mutually unintelligible languages and dialects, English was selected as the official standard. In America, we enjoy this kind of national standardization because the vast majority of us speak some mutually intelligible dialect of English. But we also have ideas about a standard English which is not just a *lingua franca* but a prestige or preferred dialect. Similarly, the British have Received Pronunciation, the Germans have High German, and the French, backed by the authority of the Académie Française, have "Le Vrai Français." These languages are typically defined as the speech of the upper, or at least educated, classes of the society, are the predominant dialect of written communication, and are commonly taught to schoolchildren. In the past, these prestige dialects have sometimes been markers which conveniently set the ruling classes apart from the rabble—as once was the case with Mandarin Chinese or in medieval times when the English aristocracy adopted Norman French. But in most modern societies the standard dialect is a mutually intelligible version of the country's common tongue which is accorded a special status.

In America we have had no end of trouble in trying to define just what our standard dialect is. It has often been said that standard English is the speech of educated people, or of the leaders of the community, or even of network newscasters. But each of these characterizations necessarily allows a fairly wide range of variation: educated people in Cambridge, Massachusetts, sound quite different from their fellow scholars in Yakima, Washington; the leaders of the Atlanta community don't talk like the members of the Anchorage Chamber of Commerce; and neither Fred Graham nor Geraldo Rivera could be mistaken for Edwin Newman. Another common (and well-worn) definition says that standard English is "reputable, national, and current." This description has all the shortcomings of the previous ones, as well as the additional problem of defining *reputable*. One result of our continuing inability to say with any precision what standard English is has been that we have concentrated on saying what it is not—a much easier, if piecemeal, form of definition. From this approach derive the hundreds of textbooks, handbooks, grammars, style manuals, and prescriptive dictionaries which try to identify the various (and often contradictory) exclusions from the standard.

Our lack of success in defining standard English does not mean that the dialect doesn't exist. As with many other aspects of language, we know it when we hear it, and we routinely judge other people on the basis of their relative mastery of this elusive pattern of speech. Still, our view of standard English must be guided by what we know about all human languages. That is, a standard dialect is not *inherently* superior to any other dialect of the same language. It may, however, confer considerable social, political, and economic power on its users, because of prevailing attitudes about the dialect's worthiness. But such considerations are the work of section 7 of this chapter.

Recently, American linguists have been working to describe some of the nonstandard dialects of English, and we now seem to have a better description of some of these dialects than of our shadowy standard. Black English is a case in point. Though there is still controversy over some of its features, there is general agreement among sociolinguists that the language spoken by many Northern urban working-class black people differs in consistently identifiable ways from other dialects of English. The differences can be described in terms of phonological rules governing sounds and combinations of sounds; syntactic rules concerning negation, possession, and verb tense markers; and lexical rules controlling word items. Some of these rules are obligatory for the speakers of Black English, others are optional, and the vast majority are identical with the rules of other American English dialects. But the most important finding of all this research has been that Black English is just as "logical" and "ordered" as any other English dialect, in spite of the fact that it is commonly viewed by white speakers as being somehow inferior, deformed, or limited (see chapter 7).

5. Speakers of all languages employ a range of styles and a set of subdialects or jargons.

Just as soon as we get past the often unappetizing notion that we all speak a dialect, it is necessary to complicate things further. We may realize that we do belong to a speech community, although we may not like to call it a dialect, but we often forget that our speech patterns vary greatly during the course of our everyday routine. In the morning, at home, communication with our spouses may consist of grumbled fragments of a private code:

Uhhh.
Yeah.
More?
Um-hmm.
You gonna ... ?
Yeah, if ...
'Kay

Yet half an hour later, we may be standing in a meeting and talking quite differently: "The cost-effectiveness curve of the Peoria facility has declined to the point at which management is compelled to consider terminating production." These two samples of speech suggest that we constantly range between formal and informal styles of speech—and this is an adjustment which speakers of all languages constantly make. Learning the sociolinguistic rules which tell us what sort of speech is appropriate in differing social situations is as much a part of language acquisition as learning how to produce the sound of /b/ or /t/. We talk differently to our acquaintances than to strangers, differently to our bosses than to our subordinates, differently to children than adults. We speak in one way on the racquetball court and in another way in the courtroom; we perhaps talk differently to stewardesses than to stewards.

The ability to adjust our language forms to the social context is something which we acquire as children, along with sounds, words, and syntax. We learn, in other words, not just to say things, but also how and when and to whom. Children discover, for example, that while the purpose of most language is to communicate meaning (if it weren't they could never learn it in the first place) we sometimes use words as mere acknowledgments (Hi. How are you doing? Fine. Bye.). Youngsters also learn that to get what you want, you have to address people as your social relation with them dictates (Miss Jones, may I please feed the hamster today?). And, of course, children learn that in some situations one doesn't use certain words at all—though such learning may sometimes seem cruelly delayed to parents whose offspring loudly announce in restaurants: "I hafta go toilet!"

Interestingly, in this connection, linguists note that these sociolinguistic rules are learned quite late in the game. While a child of seven or eight does command a remarkably sophisticated array of sentence types, for example, he has a great deal left to learn about the social regulations governing language use. This seems logical, given that children *do* learn language mostly by listening and experimenting. Only as a child grows old enough to encounter a widening range of social relationships and roles will he have the experience necessary to help him discover the sociolinguistic dimensions of them.

While there are many ways of describing the different styles, or registers, of language which all speakers learn, it is helpful to consider them in terms of levels of formality. One well-known example of such a scheme was developed by Martin Joos, who posited five basic styles, which he called *intimate, casual, consultative, formal,* and *frozen.*[2] While Joos's model is only one of many attempts to find a scale for the range of human speech styles, and is certainly not the final word on the subject, it does illuminate some of the ways in which day-to-day language varies. At the bottom of Joos's model is the *intimate* style, a kind of language which "fuses two separate personalities" and can only occur between individuals with a close personal relationship. A husband and wife, for example, may sometimes speak to each other in what sounds like a very fragmentary and clipped code that they alone understand. Such utterances are characterized by their "extraction"—the use of extracts of potentially complete sentences, made possible by an intricate, personal, shared system of private symbols. The *intimate* style, in sum, is personal, fragmentary, and implicit.

The *casual* style also depends on social groupings. When people share understandings and meanings which are not complete enough to be called intimate, they tend to employ the *casual* style. The earmarks of this pattern are ellipsis and slang. Ellipsis is the shorthand of shared meaning; slang often expresses these meanings in a way that defines the group and excludes others. The *casual* style is reserved for friends and insiders, or those whom we choose to make friends and insiders. The *consultative* style "produces cooperation without the integration, profiting from the lack of it."[3] In this style, the speaker provides more explicit background information because the listener may not understand without it. This is the style used by strangers or near-strangers in routine transactions: co-workers dealing with a problem, a buyer making a purchase from a clerk, and so forth. An important feature of this style is the participation of the listener, who uses frequent interjections such as *Yeah, Uh-huh* or *I see* to signal understanding.

This element of listener participation disappears in the *formal* style. Speech in this mode is defined by the listener's lack of participation, as well as by the speaker's opportunity to plan his utterances ahead of time and in detail. The *formal* style is most often found in speeches, lectures, sermons, television newscasts, and the like. The *frozen* style is reserved for print, and particularly for literature. This style can be densely packed and repacked with meanings by its "speaker," and it can be read and reread by its "listener." The immediacy of interaction between the participants is sacrificed in the interests of permanance, elegance, and precision.

Whether or not we accept Joos's scheme to classify the different gradations of formality, we can probably sense the truth of the basic proposition: we do make such adjustments in our speech constantly, mostly unconsciously, and in response to the social situation in which we are speaking. What we sometimes forget is that no one style can accurately be called better or worse than another, apart from the context in which it is used. Though we have much reverence for the formal and frozen styles, they can be utterly dysfunctional in certain circumstances. If I said to my wife: " Let us consider the possibility of driving our automobile into the central business district of Chicago in order to contemplate the possible purchase of denim trousers," she would certainly find my way of speaking strange, if not positively disturbing. All of us need to shift between the intimate, casual, and consultative styles in everyday life, not because one or another of these is a better way of talking, but because each is required in certain contexts. Many of us also need to master the formal style for the talking and writing demanded by our jobs. But as Joos has pointed out, few of us actually need to control the frozen style, which is reserved primarily for literature.[4]

Besides having a range of speech styles, each speaker also uses a number of jargons based upon his or her affiliation with certain groups. The most familiar of these jargons are occupational: doctors, lawyers, accountants, farmers, electricians, plumbers, truckers, and social workers each have a job-related jargon into which they can shift when the situation demands it. Sometimes these special languages are a source of amusement or consternation to outsiders, but usually the outsiders also speak jargons of their own, though they may not recognize them. Jargons may also be based on other kinds of affiliations. Teenagers, it is often remarked by bemused parents, have a language of their own. So they do, and so do other age groups. Some of the games and chants of youngsters reflect a kind of childhood dialect, and much older persons may have a jargon of their own as well, reflecting concerns with aging, illness, and finances. Sports fans obviously use and understand various abstruse athletic terms, while people interested in needlecrafts use words that are equally impenetrable to the uninitiated. For every human enterprise we can think of, there will probably be a jargon attached to it.

But simply noting that all speakers control a range of styles and a set of jargons does not tell the whole story. For every time we speak, we do so not just in a social context, but for certain purposes of our own. When talking with a dialectologist, for example, I may use linguistic jargon simply to facilitate our sharing of information, or instead to convince him that I know enough technical linguistics to be taken seriously—or both. In other words, my purposes—the functions of my language—affect the way I talk. The British linguist M.A.K. Halliday has studied children in an attempt to determine how people's varying purposes affect their speech.[5] Halliday *had* to consider children, in fact, because the purposes of any given adult utterance are usually so complex and overlapping that it is extremely difficult to isolate the individual purposes. By examining the relatively simpler language of children, he was able to discover seven main uses, functions, or purposes for talking: *instrumental, regulatory, interactional, personal, heuristic, imaginative,* and *representational.*

The *instrumental* function, Halliday explains, is for getting things done; it is the *I want* function. Close to it is the *regulatory* function, which seeks to control the actions of others around the speaker. The *interactional* function is used to define groups and relationships, to get along with others. The *personal* function allows people to express what they are and how they feel; Halliday calls this the *here I come* function. The *heuristic* function is in operation when the speaker is using language to learn, by asking questions and testing hypotheses. In the *imaginative* function, a speaker may use language to create a world just as he or she wants it, or may simply use it as a toy, making amusing combinations of sounds and words. In the *representational* function, the speaker uses language to express propositions, give information, or communicate subject matter.

Absent from Halliday's list of functions, interestingly, is one of the most common and enduring purposes of human language: lying. Perhaps lying could be included in the representational or interactional functions, in the sense that a person may deceive in order to be a more congenial companion. Or perhaps each of Halliday's seven functions could be assigned a reverse, false version. In any case, common sense, human history, and our own experience all tell us that lying—or misleading or covering up or shading the truth—is one of the main ends to which language is put. Here is Mark Twain on the subject:

Lying is universal—we *all* do it; we all *must* do it. Therefore, the wise thing is for us diligently to train ourselves to lie thoughtfully, judiciously; to lie with a good object, and not an evil one; to lie for others' advantage, and not our own; to lie healingly, charitably, humanely, not cruelly, hurtfully, maliciously; to lie gracefully and graciously, not awkwardly and clumsily; to lie firmly, frankly, squarely, with head erect, not haltingly, tortuously, with pusillanimous mien, as being ashamed of our high calling. Then shall we be rid of the rank and pestilent truth that is rotting the land; then shall we be great and good and beautiful and worthy dwellers in a world where even benign Nature habitually lies, except when she promises execrable weather.[6]

In spite of his ironic tone—and his weather forecast—Twain's description of the universality of lying rings true.

Nor is lying the exclusive vice of grownups. Even when Nicky was only eighteen months old, and had not yet progressed to two-word sentences, he was already a liar. He knew then that by pointing to the refrigerator and saying "mik" (milk) he could get his mother or me to get up, take out his bottle, and give him a drink. Shortly thereafter, he started making the same utterance when he hadn't the slightest interest in "mik." What he wanted—and usually got—was for one of us to get out of our chairs and play with him. This use of language clearly partakes of Halliday's instrumental and regulatory functions, but in some rudimentary way is lying as well.

Why is it so important that we recognize lying as one of the ordinary uses of any language? Though lying has not been a subject of much interest to linguists, it has attracted considerable attention from language critics. They commonly argue that lying—and especially political propaganda and official euphemism—are "abuses of the language." They often compare lies to pollutants, insidious elements which, once they are dumped into the environment, weaken the system itself, making it harder for us to recognize the truth or tell it. The widespread talk of "cleaning up" the American language is often based on this bit of faulty ecoscience.

The critics' mistake is that they allow their serious and appropriate concern about the *consequences* of lying to be diverted into trivial and inappropriate worry about the particular forms of language in which lies are delivered. If we admit that people routinely deceive each other, we also have to admit that language is one of the handier tools of deception. S. I. Hayakawa has said in another context: "If you scoff at the study of language, how else but in language will you scoff?" He might be paraphrased: "If you are going to lie, how else but in language will you lie?" To argue that lying abuses the language makes as much sense as to say that drowning someone "abuses the water." (See chapter 7 for a fuller discussion of these issues.)

As we look back over these three forms of language variation—styles, jargons, and functions—we may well marvel at the astounding complexity of language. For not only do all speakers master the intricate sound, lexical, and grammatical patterns of their native tongue, but they also learn countless, systematic alternative ways of applying their linguistic knowledge to varying situations and needs. We are reminded, in short, that language is as beautifully varied, and fascinating as the creatures who use it.

6. Language change is normal.

This fact, while often acknowledged by critics of contemporary English, has rarely been fully understood or accepted by them. It is easy enough to welcome into the language such innocent neologisms as *astronaut*, *transistor*, or *jet lag*. These terms serve obvious needs, responding to certain changes in society which virtually require them. But language also changes in many ways that don't seem so logical or necessary. The dreaded dangling *hopefully*, which now attaches itself to the beginning of sentences with the meaning *I hope*, appears to be driving out the connotation *full of hope*. As Jean Stafford has angrily pointed out, the word *relevant* has broadened to denote almost any kind of "with-it-ness." But these kinds of lexical changes are not new, and simply demonstrate an age-old process at work in the present. The word *dog* (actually, *dogge*), for example, used to refer to one specific breed, but now serves as a general term for a quite varied family of animals. Perhaps similarly, *dialogue* has now broadened to include exchanges of views between (or among) any number of speakers. But word meanings can also narrow over time, as the word *deer* shrank from indicating any game animal to just one specific type.

The sounds of language also change, though usually in slower and less noticeable ways than vocabulary. Perhaps fifty years ago, the majority of American speakers produced distinctly different consonant sounds in the middle of *latter* and *ladder*. Today, most younger people and many adults pronounce the two words as if they were the same. Another sound change in progress is the weakening distinction between the vowels *dawn* and *Don*, or *hawk* and *hock*. Taking the longer view, of course, we realize that modern pronunciation is the product of centuries of gradual sound changes. One of the most-studied phenomena in the history of English was the "great vowel shift." Between about 1400 and 1600, many vowels changed their position of articulation and the sound of the English language was markedly altered. The word previously pronounced *hay* became our modern *he, hoose* became *house,* and *beet* became *bite.* No one has ever discovered any useful purpose behind this complicated rearrangement of sounds, although linguists have been able to describe the pattern and sequence of the change in great detail.[7]

Shifts in grammar are more comparable to the slow process of sound change than the sometimes sudden one of lexical change. Today we find that the *shall/will* distinction, which is still maintained among some upper class Britishers, has effectively disappeared from spoken American English. A similar fate seems to await the *who/whom* contrast, which is upheld by fewer and fewer speakers. Our pronouns, as a matter of fact, seem to be a quite volatile corner of our grammar. In spite of the efforts of teachers, textbooks, style manuals, and the SAT tests, most American speakers now find nothing wrong with *Everyone should bring their books to class* or even *John and me went to the Cubs game.* And even the hoary old double negative (which is an obligatory feature of degraded tongues like French) seems to be making steady, if slow progress. We may be only a generation or two from the day when we will again say, with Shakespeare, "I will not budge for no man's pleasure."

While we may recognize that language does inexorably change, we cannot always explain the causes or the sequences of each individual change. Sometimes changes move toward simplification, as with the shedding of vowel distinctions. Other changes tend to regularize the language, as when we de-Latinize words like *medium/media* (The newspapers are one media of communication), or when we abandon *dreamt* and *burnt* in favor of the regular forms *dreamed* and *burned.* And some coinages will always reflect the need to represent new inventions, ideas, or events: *quark, simulcast, pulsar, stagflation.* Yet there is plenty of language change which seems to happen spontaneously, sporadically, and without apparent purpose. Why should *irregardless* substitute for *regardless,* meaning the same thing? Why should handy distinctions like that between *imply* and *infer* be lost? But even if we can never explain the reasons for such mysterious changes—or perhaps *because* we can't—we must accept the fact that language does change. Today, we would certainly be thought odd to call cattle *kine*, to pronounce *saw* as *saux*, or to ask about "thy health," however ordinary such language might have been centuries ago. Of course, the more recent changes, and especially the changes in progress make us most uncomfortable, though they may be just as inevitable (and nonsensical) as the great vowel shift.

But then our sense of the pace of language change is often exaggerated. When we cringe (as do so many of the language critics) at the sudden reassignment of the word *gay* to a new referent, we tend to forget that we can still read Shakespeare. In other words, even if many conspicuous (and almost invariably lexical) changes are in progress, this doesn't necessarily mean that the language as a whole is undergoing a rapid or wholesale transformation. But once you become aware of such neologisms, you tend to start noticing them everywhere and are prone to begin worrying about them. This kind of perceptual trap is somewhat akin to suddenly starting, as you drive to work, to count all the unwashed (or purple, or convertible) cars you see. Under normal circumstances, you simply drive, and pay little attention to the distinct features of the rest of the traffic. But once you begin noticing the unwashed vehicles, you are surprised to find how many there really are. "Let's see, that's six at the tollbooth and, uh, counting the four in that parking lot, that makes ten just in the last half-mile. This is really quite shocking." Next, you find yourself counting cars that aren't really dirty, but just a little smudged or dusty. Maybe you decide that beige and brown cars, clean or not, should be tallied too. And you find yourself worrying more. "Why don't these people do something about their cars? What kind of person would drive a dirty car anyway? All this grime certainly is a blight on the highways!" And so on. But then the occupants of all those dirty cars, though they may not be quite as fastidious as their observer, continue to get where they want to go.

So, in a sense (an imperfect one, I admit), it is with language change. Once we start looking for it, it seems to be everywhere, and we are sorely tempted to overestimate its importance. Sometimes we even discover changes which aren't changes at all (like the beige cars). Various language critics have propounded the notion that we are being inundated by a host of very new and particularly insidious coinages. Here are some of the most notorious ones, along with the date of their earliest citation in the *Oxford English Dictionary* for the meaning presently viewed as modern and dangerous: *you know* (1350); *anxious* for *eager* (1742); *between you and I*

(1640); *super* for *good* (1850); *decimate* for *diminish* by other than one-tenth (1663); *inoperative* for nonmechanical phenomena (1631); *near-perfect* for *nearly perfect* (1635); *host* as in *to host a gathering* (1485); *gifted,* as in *He gifted his associates* (1600); *aggravate* for *annoy* (1611).[8]

If we find ourselves being aggravated (or annoyed) by any of these crotchety old neologisms, we can always look to the Mobil Oil Corporation for a comforting discussion of the problem. In one of its self-serving public service magazine ads, Mobil intoned: "Change upsets people. Always has. Disrupts routine and habit patterns. Demands constant adaptation. But change is inevitable. And essential. Inability to change can be fatal."[9] And Mobil inadvertently gives us one last example of a language change currently in progress: the increasing use of sentence fragments in formal written English.

One other notable feature of language change is its inherent relation to childhood. If we look at any of the major changes presently occurring in English (in the pronoun system, for example), we will usually find that the common language of the future is what our young people use now. Linguists Victoria Fromkin and Robert Rodman have explained this phenomenon: "The older generation may be using 'variable' rules. For example, at certain times they may say 'It's I' and at other times 'It's me.' The less formal style is usually used with children. The next generation may use only the 'me' form of the pronoun in this construction. . . . it must be remembered that it is the children learning the language who finally incorporate the ongoing changes or create new changes in . . . the language."[10] Anyone who wishes to believe that the *who/whom* distinction is going to survive for another generation had better steer clear of the local schoolyard. Or perhaps some of the language critics *have* been hanging around the schoolyards, and this accounts for their insistence that the language of American children and adolescents is "crude," "degraded," "illiterate," and "improper."

7. Languages are intimately related to the societies and individuals who use them.

Every human language has been shaped by, and changes to meet, the needs of its speakers. In this limited sense, all human languages can be said to be both equal and perfect. Some Eskimo languages, for example, have many words for different types of snow: wet snow, powdery snow, blowing snow, and so forth. This extensive vocabulary obviously results from the importance of snow in the Eskimo environment and the need to be able to talk about it in detailed ways. In Chicago, where snow is just an occasional annoyance, we get along quite nicely with a few basic terms —snow, slush, and sleet—and a number of adjectival modifiers. Richard Mitchell has described a hypothetical primitive society where the main preoccupation is banging on tree-bark to harvest edible insects, and this particular people has developed a large, specialized vocabulary for talking about the different kinds of rocks and trees involved in this process. In each of these cases, the language in question is well adapted to the needs of its speakers. Each language allows its speakers to easily talk about whatever it is important to discuss in that society.

This does not mean, however, that any given language will work "perfectly" or be "equal" to any other in a cross-cultural setting. If I take my Chicago dialect to the tundra, I may have trouble conversing with people who distinguish, in Eskimo, ten more kinds of snow than I do. Or if one of Mitchell's tree-bangers came to Chicago, his elaborate rock-and-bark vocabulary would be of little use. Still, neither of these languages is inherently inferior or superior; inside its normal sphere of use, each is just what it needs to be.

There is a related question concerning the differences between languages. Many linguists have tried to determine the extent to which our native language conditions our thought processes. For all the talk of similarities between languages, there are also some quite remarkable differences from one language to another. The famous studies of American Indian languages by Benjamin Lee Whorf and Edward Sapir have suggested, for example, that Hopi speakers do not conceptualize time in the same way as speakers of English.[11] To the Hopi, time is a continuing process, an unfolding that cannot be segmented into chunks to be used or "wasted." The words and constructions of the Hopi language reflect this perception. Similarly, some languages do not describe the same color spectrum which we speakers of English normally regard as a given physical phenomenon. Some of these name only two, others three, and so on. Are we, then, hopelessly caught in the grasp of the language which we happen to grow up speaking? Are all our ideas about the world controlled by our language, so that our reality is what we *say* rather than what objectively, verifiably exists?

This question becomes especially important when cross-cultural differences in language serve as a basis for social, economic, or political decision making. We may believe that Indians have "no sense of time" and will therefore never make good, punctual employees, however we attempt to train them. Or we may argue that the speech patterns of Eskimos are so alien to the language of modern, industrial societies that these people can never be expected to participate in our environment. The best judgment of linguists on this subject comes down to this: we are conditioned to some degree by the language we speak, and our language does teach us habitual ways of looking at the world. But on the other hand, human adaptability enables us to transcend the limitations of a language—to learn to see the world in new ways and voice new concepts—when we must. While it is probably true that some ideas are easier to communicate in one language than another, both languages and speakers can change to meet new needs. The grip which language has on us is firm, but it does not strangle; we make language more than language makes us.

In this connection, it is sometimes objected: "Well, you could never discuss Kierkegaard's philosophy in Eskimo or Black English, and so these languages are not equal after all." The implication here, of course, is that the discussion of Kierkegaard's philosophy, or any number of other daunting intellectual topics, simply cannot be accomplished by people whose language is "too primitive" to handle them. The error in such thinking is to equate what is typically talked about in a given language with what *could* be talked about. Certainly few Eskimos, and probably few Black English speakers (or white ones, for that matter), typically discuss Kierkegaard's philosophy. And if they wished to do so, each group of speakers would have to add some new vocabulary and some new concepts to their language, which would take time, study, and adjustment. But no topic, in other words, is inherently beyond the reach of any particular human language. Conversely, when the final Ice Age arrives, standard English may very well grow enough to accommodate discussion of such a complex topic as the eternal variations of frozen precipitation.

It is also important to realize that a language is not just an asset of a culture or group, but of individual human beings. Our native language is the speech of our parents, siblings, friends, and community. It is the code we use to communicate in the most powerful and intimate experiences of our lives. It is a central part of our personality, an expression and a mirror of what we are and wish to be. Our language is as personal and as integral to each of us as our bodies and our brains, and in our own unique ways, we all treasure it. And all of us, when we are honest, have to admit that criticism of the way we talk is hard not to take personally. This reaction is nothing to be ashamed of: it is simply a reflection of the natural and profound importance of language to every individual human being.

To summarize: all human languages and the concept systems which they embody are efficient in their native speech communities. The languages of the world also vary in some important ways, so that people sometimes falsely assume that certain tongues are inherently superior to others. Yet it is marvelous that these differences exist. It is good that the Eskimo language facilitates talk about snow, that the Hopi language supports that culture's view of time, and, I suppose, that Chicago speech has ample resources for discussing drizzle, wind, and inept baseball teams.

8. Value judgments about different languages or dialects are matters of taste.

One of the things that we seem to acquire right along with our native tongue is a set of attitudes about the value of other people's language. If we think for a moment about any of the world's major languages, we will find that we usually have some idea—usually a prejudice or stereotype—about it. French is the sweet music of love. German is harsh, martial, overbearing. The language of Spain is exotic, romantic. The Spanish of Latino Americans is alien, uneducated. Scandinavian tongues have a kind of silly rhythm, as the Muppet Show's Swedish chef demonstrates weekly. British English is refined and intelligent. New York dialect (especially on Toity-Toid Street) is crude and loud. Almost all southern American speakers (especially rural sheriffs) are either cruelly crafty or just plain dumb. Oriental languages have a funny, high-pitched, singsong sound. And Black English, well, it just goes to show. None of these notions about different languages and dialects says anything about the way these tongues function in their native speech communities. By definition—by the biological and social order of things—they function efficiently. Each is a fully formed, logical, rule-governed variant of human speech.

However, the attitudes we have about other speakers do say something about our contact with them. We have a negative stereotype of German speakers, for example, as a result of the wars during the past century. So we have come to think of the German language as the "natural" sound of authoritarianism—or, sometimes, we have comforted ourselves with ironic derivatives of this stereotype, a la "Hogan's Heros." In such descriptions of German, we are obviously attaching to language our feelings about nonlinguistic matters. And it does seem generally true that we do this in both directions. For example, most Americans are irrationally impressed by any speaker of British English—often by speakers of varieties that are not particularly favored in England. We seem to think of any British English as genteel, cultured, scholarly, sensitive, dignified, and generally superior to any American dialect. In language matters at least, our colonial fealty seems to live on. Still, neither English nor German is a "better" language than the other, and neither is more likely to nurture either Hitler or Shakespeare.

It is easy enough to assert that all languages are equal and efficient in their own sphere of use. But most of us do not really believe in this idea, and certainly do not act as if we did. We constantly make judgments about other people and other nations on the basis of the language they use. Of course, some of these judgments have a basis in reality. If an American employer declines to hire a monolingual Japanese speaker to answer his telephone, he may be making a sound business decision since callers would be unable to communicate with this person. But if the same employer declines to hire an Alabama native because southern speech doesn't project the "classy" image he wants, then he is using language in a somewhat different way. The employer is saying to himself: "My customers (like me) have negative attitudes toward southern speech. I do not want to take the chance of putting them off, even in the slightest, by having this Alabaman represent the company." In each case the job applicants' natural, native, and "perfect" languages have been found inadequate. But they have been judged outside of the native context, and the employer's decision not to hire either speaker proves nothing about the inherent worth of Japanese or southern American speech.

Especially when we consider the question of mutually intelligible American dialects, we are able to see that most ideas about language differences are purely matters of taste. It isn't that we cannot understand each other—Southerners, Northerners, Californians, New Yorkers, blacks, whites, Appalachian folk—with only the slightest effort we can communicate just fine. But because of our history of experiences with each other, or perhaps just out of perversity, we have developed prejudices toward other people's language which sometimes affect our behavior. Such prejudices, however irrational, generate much pressure for speakers of disfavored dialects to abandon their native speech for some more approved pattern. But as the linguist Einar Haugen has warned:

And yet, who are we to call for linguistic genocide in the name of efficiency? Let us recall that although a language is a tool and an instrument of communication, that is not all it is. A language is also a part of one's personality, a form of behavior that has its roots in our earliest experience. Whether it is a so-called rural or ghetto dialect, or a peasant language, or a "primitive" idiom, it fulfills exactly the same needs and performs the same services in the daily lives of its speakers as does the most advanced language of culture. Every language, dialect, patois, or lingo is a structurally complete framework into which can be poured any subtlety of emotion or thought that its users are capable of experiencing. Whatever it lacks at any given time or place in the way of vocabulary and syntax can be supplied in very short order by borrowing and imitation from other languages. *Any scorn for the language of others is scorn for those who use it, and as such is a form of social discrimination.*[Emphasis mine][12]

It is not Haugen's purpose—nor is it mine—to deny that social acceptability and economic success in America may be linked in certain ways to the mastery of approved patterns of speech. Yet all of us must realize that the need for such mastery arises *only* out of the prejudices of the dominant speech community and not from any intrinsic shortcomings of nonstandard American dialects.

9. Writing is derivative of speech.

Writing systems are always based upon systems of oral language which of necessity develop first. People have been talking for at least a half million years, but the earliest known writing system appeared fewer than 5,000 years ago. Of all the world's languages, only about 5 percent have developed indigenous writing systems. In other words, wherever there are human beings, we will always find language, but not necessarily writing. If language is indeed a biologically programmed trait of the species, writing does not seem to be part of the standard equipment.

Some of the earliest writing systems—and a few still in use today—are pictographic, representing people, things, and events in a directly symbolic way. In such a writing sytem,

might mean: *The sun rises over the river.* Alphabetic writing systems, like the one we use in English, make no attempt to symbolize reality directly and represent instead the sounds of the words we use to talk about it. Thus *The sun rises over the river* symbolizes not the actual sun, rising, or the river but the sounds of the words we attach to each. Below is our conven-

ðə sʌn rayzəz ovər ðə rɪvər

tional orthographic representation of the strings of sounds as they would be noted in International Phonetic Alphabet.

Although the English writing system is essentially phonemic—an attempt to represent the sounds of language in graphic form—it is notoriously irregular and confusing. Some other languages, like Czech, Finnish, and Spanish, come close to having perfect sound-symbol correspondence: each letter in the writing system stands for one, and only one, sound. English, unfortunately, uses some 2,000 letters and combinations of letters to represent its forty or so separate sounds. This causes problems. For example, in the sentence: *Did he believe that Caesar could see the people seize the seas?* there are seven different spellings for the vowel sound /i/. The sentence: *The silly amoeba stole the key to the machine* yields four more spellings of the same vowel sound. George Bernard Shaw once noted that a reasonable spelling of the word *fish* might be *ghoti*: *gh* as in *enough*, *o* as in *women*, and *ti* as in *nation*. In spite of all its irregularities, however, the English spelling system is nevertheless phonemic at heart, as our ability to easily read and pronounce nonsense words like *mimsy* or *proat* demonstrates.

Linguists, unfortunately, have given more attention to these mechanical and historical aspects of writing than they have to more important issues. There is, in fact, a rather prevalent misapprehension among linguists that writing is a trivial offshoot of speech. Here is Leonard Bloomfield, probably one of this century's half-dozen most influential linguists, on the subject: "Writing is merely a device for recording speech. A person is much the same and looks the same, whether he has ever had his picture taken or not. Only a vain beauty who sits for many photographs and carefully studies them may end by slightly changing her pose and expressions. It is much the same with languages and their written recordings."[13] Bloomfield's view of writing as an insignificant aspect of language has been shared by many other linguists, whose preoccupations with grammar have pushed aside the serious study of writing. Another example of this outlook is provided by Paul Postal, who has observed:

Writing systems are without exception parasitic on language; they are attempts (often rather bad attempts) to represent certain aspects of linguistic structure, usually phonological aspects. . . . It is therefore neither by mistake nor by accident that we have considered language as if, in effect, writing systems did not exist. This approach recognizes that language, together with its "natural" performance medium of articulate speech, is a natural consequence of the human organism. Writing, on the other hand, is a special technique for performing the elements of language, and as such it is a clever invention like the telephone or algebra.[14]

Bloomfield's and Postal's belief that writing is an insignificant aspect of language is defensible only in a very limited sense. It is true, after all, that most people speak far more than they write, and in this strictly quantitative realm writing might fairly be called "the foam on an ocean of talk." We do also tend to use writing for quite limited purposes, whereas we employ speech in, or as an accompaniment to, almost everything we do. And, obviously, there are many subjects and occasions for which speech is clearly the better—the more appropriate—form of language. But even if we grant these points, Bloomfield and Postal are far too dismissive. In the first place, most of the historical and descriptive research which has helped us to understand the development of English and other languages has been based on written materials, since they are all that remains of past language use. Certainly the methods used in these studies have been imperfect and indirect, but this does not make them or their subject trivial.

Nor, in spite of what some uninterested linguists may have said, is writing merely speech written down. Although it derives from spoken language, writing is in some very important ways autonomous and different. In the first place, it is a fundamentally solitary activity. Though we may write in a crowded office, our audience exists only in our own heads when we compose. By contrast, in almost all spoken language situations, the presence and participation of the audience is an integral part of the event. Writing is far more conscious than speech. When we talk, we usually do so mostly unconsciously, rather effortlessly producing sentence after sentence of meaningful language. In writing, we must produce language one letter at a time, though we must also think in larger units as we go along. We have the chance, usually the obligation, to review what we have written, revising and reshaping it with our intended audience in mind. Similarly, our audience has the opportunity to study and reread individual passages as necessary. The linguistic habits of writers can even influence the spoken language in certain ways. For example, the words *hospital* and *house* had no initial *h* sound until eighteenth-century spelling reformers added one. Today, as a result of these spelling changes, most English speakers pronounce these words with *h*'s.

Most importantly, writing allows us to accomplish things we cannot do with talk. By setting pen to paper we can transcend time: we can read records of the thoughts, deeds, and inventions of our predecessors and leave ours for our successors. In writing, we can overcome distance: we can share our ideas in letters and books and telegrams and magazines—with English speakers all around the world. Using writing, we can overcome some of the limitations of the spoken language; our audience is not restricted to the number of people who can hear our voice at one place and time. Without writing, our present way of life, as mixed a blessing as it may seem, would be impossible; all science and technology depend upon the symbolic representation of reality. "Primitive" societies may or may not have writing systems, but industrialized societies could not exist without them.

It is important to repudiate the notion that writing is a mere linguistic parasite and to recognize its special qualities. Still, there are many ways in which written and oral language do overlap. Whether we are writing English or speaking English, we are drawing upon the same vast, internalized set of rules which permits us to make meaning in our native language. Beyond certain unique conventions of writing (spelling, capitalizing, indenting paragraphs) most of the rules that we employ are the same for both activities: adjectives generally precede the nouns they modify, subjects and verbs are marked for agreement, and so forth.

Writing, like speech, may be put to a whole range of often overlapping uses. We may write in a journal or diary to express our feelings, sift through experiences, or simply play with words. We can write letters to share news of our activities and bind others to us. We can use writing as a way of learning, either as an adjunct to formal study or when wrestling with a private problem. We can write reports which organize and clarify information for our co-workers. We can use writing to persuade the readers of the letters column in the newspaper to see things our way. And, of course, we can write stories or poems for selected or general audiences.

Shifts in the level of formality occur in writing just as they do in talk. An author, like a speaker, must adjust the style of her message to the audience and the occasion. A woman composing a scholarly article, for example, makes some systematically different linguistic choices than those she makes when leaving a note for her husband on the refrigerator. Both writers and speakers (even good ones) employ various jargons or specialized vocabularies that seem comfortable and convenient to the people they are addressing. Rules change with time in both writing and speech. Most obviously, changes in speech habits are reflected in writing: today we readily pen words which weren't even invented ten or a hundred years ago. And even some of the rules which are enforced in writing after they have been abandoned in speech do eventually break down. Today, for example, split infinitives and sentence fragments are increasingly accepted in writing. Our personal tastes and social prejudices, which often guide our reactions to other people's speech, can also dictate our response to other people's writing. Any given critic may prefer the spare prose of Hemingway to the intricate sentences of Faulkner. And any given teacher may prefer the writing of a rosy-cheeked, white, middle-class student to the prose of a pupil whose compositions reveal less favored origins.

Our beliefs about writing are also bound up with our literary tradition. We have come to revere certain works of literature and exposition which have "stood the test of time," which speak across the centuries to successive generations of readers. These masterpieces, like most enduring published writing, tend to employ what Joos would call formal and frozen styles of language. They were written in such language, of course, because their authors had to accommodate the subject, audience, and purpose at hand—and the making of sonnets and declarations of independence generally calls for considerable linguistic formality. Given our affection for these classics, we quite naturally admire not only their content but their form. We find ourselves feeling that only in the nineteenth or sixteenth century could writers "really use the language" correctly and beautifully. Frequently, we teach this notion in our schools, encouraging students to see the language of written literature as the only true and correct style of English. We require students not only to mimic the formal literary style in their writing, but even to transplant certain of its features into their speech—in both cases without reference to the *students'* subject, audience, or purpose. All of this is not meant to demean literature or the cultivation of its appreciation among teenagers. It simply reminds us of how the mere existence of a system of writing and a literature can be a conservative influence on the language. The study, occasionally the official worship, of language forms that are both old and formal may retard linguistic changes currently in progress, as well as reinforce our mistaken belief that one style of language is always and truly the best.

The fact that we possess a writing system suggests some further educational—and political—questions. Should all citizens be literate? To what degree? What do we mean by *literate*? How should reading and writing be taught? In America, we long ago decided that the ability to read and write is "A Root of Democracy," as the postage stamp proclaims. We insist that a true democracy depends upon the ability of each citizen to understand, evaluate, and respond to written, as well as spoken, messages. But what good is literacy if the information typically supplied to literate citizens is false or incomplete, or if that information is mainly designed to encourage the consumption of useless and wasteful commodities? Some cynics have suggested that bringing literacy to the masses of people merely opens them up to new forms of propaganda and manipulation. It is also worth noting that some of the most murderous and tyrannical societies ever known have had high rates of literacy, whereas some peace-loving, creative communities have relied solely on an oral culture.

Surely in modern America people need to write well enough to progress through school, to function in jobs, and to communicate for certain purposes of their own. But this is just another way of saying *functional literacy,* and its limits should remind us that while writing is important, our mastery of it provides no automatic guarantee of peace, freedom, justice, or beauty.

The preceding nine ideas about language are not entirely new. Many of them have been proclaimed by loud, if lonely, voices in centuries long past. It has only been in the last seventy or eighty years, however, that these ideas have begun to form a coherent picture of how language works, thanks to the work of the descriptive and historical linguists. It is their research which has been, I hope, accurately if broadly summarized here.

Our earlier look at the history of past crises offered a general kind of reassurance about the present language panic. It suggested that such spasms of insecurity and intolerance are a regular, cyclical feature of the human chronicle, and result more from social and political tensions than from actual changes in the language. The review of research presented in this chapter broadens that perspective, and deflates the urgency of the 1983-model literacy crisis in some other ways. It shows us that our language cannot "die" as long as people speak it; that language change is a healthy and inevitable process; that all human languages are rule governed, ordered, and logical; that variations between different groups of speakers are normal and predictable; that all speakers employ a variety of speech forms and styles in response to changing social settings; and that most of our attitudes about language are based upon social rather than linguistic judgments.

And so, if we are to believe the evidence of historical and linguistic research, our current language crisis seems rather curious. This is a crisis which is not critical, which does not actually pose the dangers widely attributed to it. If anything, the crisis is merely a description of linguistic business as usual, drawn by the critics in rather bizarre and hysterical strokes. It seems fair to ask at this point: What's the problem?

5

Matters of Taste

The "problem," to a great extent, is the linguistic version of the old joke: "I know I'm right. Please don't confuse me with the facts." Many educated and influential Americans, contriving somehow to repel all information to the contrary, have decided that language is going to hell in a handbasket, and there's an end to it. Since neither history nor linguistics offers much encouragement for the handbasket theory of language, the critics must necessarily fall back on two other sources of evidence for their apocalyptic views. One is the time-honored and traditional process of personal observation, of listening to the common run of talk and scrutinizing the common run of writing for tell-tale signs of decay. This is a highly personal, not to say idiosyncratic procedure, with a rich history tracing back to Richard Grant White, Jonathan Swift, and those Sumerian teachers of freshman writing.

The other, newer source of evidence, which was not available to the critics of bygone days, is the stockpile of statistical proof heaped up by the modern tests-and-measurements industry. Here, critics who sense the imminent death of language can dig up crisis-confirming evidence by the shovelful. But, as this chapter aims to show, evidence from either of these sources—from individual observation and from test scores—can be untrustworthy, inconsistent, and misleading. Further, as we survey the sources of the apocalyptic jitters, we should ask ourselves what social, political, and economic purposes are served by the doomsayers' proofs and pronouncements.

Looking first at the traditional method of diagnosing language problems, we could probably do no better than to let Edwin Newman speak for the delicate process of individual watchmanship. Since he is the dean of the critics, or at least the best-seller, it would seem appropriate to examine his methods and review some of his salient findings.

What follows might be called "The Edwin Newman Language Crisis Quiz," or, if it were to appear in a Sunday-supplement newspaper insert, it might be titled "Test Your Literacy I.Q.!" Below are twenty items (sentences, utterances, whatever) upon which Newman has commented in one of his books on the decline of American English. Study each one and decide what (if anything) is wrong: it might be blight, bloat, illiteracy, disrespect for language, misspelling, comma faults, dangling participles, or flagrant propaganda. The entire range of language abuse from the tiniest superficial error to the gravest semantic distortion is vulnerable to your red pencil, as it is to Newman's. (If you can enhance your motivation by devising some sort of scoring system, by all means devise away.) Each of these samples has been taken directly from Newman's texts or, where absolutely necessary to avoid tipping the right answer, has been judiciously recast.

1. Hopefully, this afternoon fog will lift and we can get out of there without a helicopter.
2. On December 31, 1975, the White House announced that Prime Minister Yitzhak Rabin of Israel would visit Washington on January 27 so that he and President Ford could discuss in depth the situation in the Middle East.
3. Ervin was aided by Paul Verkuil, a professor at the University of North Carolina, in gathering the evidence that convinced Congress to adopt the provision.
4. Teachers? Oh, them is my chief dread.
5. After the nature of Mr. Smith's illness was determined by a team of neurologists, he was hospitalized for an additional week of tests.
6. The government admits to more than 300 dead, giving a "body count" of 225 rebels, about 50 civilians, and only 29 of its own troops.
7. I don't believe in this mandate stuff.
8. The recent history of the Middle East has been one of outbreaks of fighting, each of them followed by an uneasy truce.
9. A high-ranking police officer was shot to death in front of his home Thursday

night in the fourth political murder since Juan D. Peron was elected President less than two weeks ago.

10. (United States ambassador responding to a question about the U-2 spy plane shot down by the Russians in 1960) It is a blown instrument.

11. There ain't gonna be no war.

12. After the new computer was installed on the second floor, it almost immediately suffered a massive breakdown, throwing the accounting department into turmoil.

13. Professor Schwartz' maieutic approach was not popular with students, who would have preferred that he simply lecture.

14. Secretary of State Henry Kissinger was believed to have played a major, although circumspect, role in the investigation of Daniel Ellsberg.

15. With frequent disdain for grammar, logic, and, often, accuracy, Hedda Hopper produced a Hollywood gossip column for 28 years.

16. There has been a gradual shift, over the past 25 years, in the balance of economic power, and even more importantly, in the attitudes governing the relationships between the United States and her neighbors in the Western Hemisphere.

17. The Kennedy Library, a memorial to a man who was President for less than three years, threatens to undo an entire neighborhood in Cambridge, Massachusetts, it is so big.

18. Take two well-known examples, one from the past—Nicholas Murray Butler, president of Columbia, 1902–45—and one from the present, Kingman Brewster, president of Yale since 1964.

19. I will not vote to stultify the Constitution of the United States.

20. "Where have you been?" she asked. "Out walking the dog," he said. "Looking for old familiar feces."

You may put down your pencils. Here are the answers.

1. This one was just a warm-up. Needless to say, the insidious dangling *hopefully* is probably Newman's most implacable foe and pettest of peeves. I might note in passing that this particular usage, despite Newman's persistent efforts, continues to be widely used in both the speech and writing of many, probably most, educated Americans.[1]

2. The problem is the term *in depth*. As Newman scoffs: "Would Ford and Rabin duck their heads beneath the surface of the White House pool and exchange signals? Snorkel? Don divers' gear and go full fathom five into the Potomac? Would each board a submarine and have the skipper pass the order, 'Take her down,' and communicate by radio?" Newman's law of usage here apparently rules out any metaphorical application of *deep* or its derivatives. One is only

permitted to go *deeply* into a bona fide liquid, perhaps only H_2O itself. It is not clear from this example and the accompanying commentary whether, for example, one could submerge *in depth* into Dr. Pepper or maple syrup.[2] The *American Heritage Dictionary*, on the other hand, resists the tide of Newman's argument and goes with the flow: "—in depth. With thorough coverage of matters likely to be overlooked: *a study in depth.*"

3. Depending upon your age, you may remember this shibboleth from your high school grammar book. "You may convince that. You may convince of. You may not convince to." Though Newman admits that this construction is probably here to stay, he does call for the censure of its chief promoter, the *New York Times*.[3]

4. Newman tells a charming story about how he met the man who made this statement in a veterans' hospital shortly after World War II. It is cited in *Strictly Speaking* not as an error but as an example of admirably pithy and direct speech: "A lifetime was summed up in those six syllables. There is no way to improve on that."[4]

5. Newman detests the infectious spread of the *-ize* suffix. He does not confine his wrath to *prioritize, personalize,* and *annualize*; even the older and seemingly more established *hospitalize* is stigmatized.[5]

6. "When—and more to the point, why—did a troop become the same thing as a soldier? A troop is a body of men."[6] Tear thoses patches off your sashes, all you Girl Scout troops. And never mind the *American Heritage Dictionary's* permissive third entry: "Military units, soldiers."

7. George Meany's comment on the election of 1974 is, to Newman, an example of "a civil tongue" in action, and is to be admired for its plainness.[7]

8. "True enough. But who ever heard of an easy truce, or a comfortable one?"

9. If you succeeded on the previous item, you may be in trouble here. The kind of logic that identifies *uneasy truce* as a hack journalistic catchphrase might similarly categorize *high-ranking police officer* or *political murder*. But the problem Newman sees in this Associated Press dispatch is the inclusion of Peron's middle initial: "The D. is there to keep you from confusing Juan D. Peron with the Juan Q. Peron also elected president of Argentina two weeks earlier.... Middle initials are thought to add authenticity and the ring of history."[9]

10. Though this may sound like typical bureaucratic jargon, Newman lauds it as exemplifying "the succinctness that is part of a civil tongue." Admiringly, he muses: "Five words. A complete answer."[10]

11. No trick here. This statement by British Prime Minister Harold MacMillan is "brilliantly effective," an example of how language can be "a marvellous servant for those who know how to use it."[11] The *American Heritage* usage panel appears to disagree: 99 percent reject *ain't*. But wait. Here in the fine print is

an escape hatch (for prime ministers, at least): *ain't* is permissible when the speaker wishes to "provide humor, shock or other special effect."

12. "*Massive* was robbed of its original meaning, which is to say forming a large mass, heavy, bulky, solid, so that it could be used to mean large..... Massive doesn't even mean large anymore. It goes by without registering. It means nothing."[12] In other words, according to Newman, a *massive* breakdown of the computer means the same thing as (or as little as) a minor, or small, or tiny breakdown of the computer. For the record, *American Heritage* records: "3. Large of imposing in quantity, scope, degree, intensity or scale."

13. Not surprisingly, *maieutic* is the focus of Newman's concern here, and he goes to some lengths to rebuke William F. Buckley (I mean William Buckley) for using such high-falutin' vocabulary. "Buckley reminds me of a character created by British comedian Spike Milligan and known as the 'pronouner.' Looting a bombed-out house during the Second World War, he came upon a dictionary, fell in love with words of many syllables, and devoted the rest of his life to pronouncing them. His wife kept the dictionary binding polished."[13] Curiously, *maieutic* is one of the very words that John Simon prides himself upon using in his continuing attempts to upgrade the vocabularies of his readers.

14. A breather. *Major* is trite and meaningless, another burden placed on the language by the *New York Times*.[14]

15. The pointy-headed eastern press has done it again. "The *Times* evidently believed that there was a difference between doing something frequently and doing it often."[15]

16. Make that more *important*, not *-ly*. This ubiquitous error prompts Newman to wonder: "What makes the incorrect more attractive than the correct? ... There is at work here the desire to be up with the latest thing."[16]

17. Was your red pencil attracted to that curious "it is so big" hanging off the end of the sentence? Mine was. But this happens to be one of Newman's own sentences (and therefore presumably beyond reproach) which stands here as an example of how often his commentaries on language drift off into general and nearly random observations on the depravity of the human race. In this section of *Strictly Speaking*, he begins by deriding the false extravagance of language used to describe our political leaders, but quickly embarks on a long series of anecdotes unrelated to language: President Nixon handing out tacky ball-point pens in Paris; huge tax deductions taken by public figures who donate their papers to libraries; the silliness of the official presidential ditty, "Hail to the Chief"; Newman's own feud with Broadway producer David Merrick; and the author's adventures reporting news stories while clad in everything from bathing trunks to tails. Of course, it is Newman's book, and he is entitled to whatever digressions amuse him. But these digressions do underscore what the

book is really about: it is a critique of certain kinds of people and their behavior, of which language is only one manifestation.[17]

18. There is quite a punctuation puzzle here. Maintaining parallels would seem to call for a hyphen rather than a comma after *present*. But then the initial hyphen would seem to fit better after *examples* than after *past*, with a comma where the post-*past* hyphen now stands. On the other hand, perhaps a colon would have been a better mark to place after *examples*, with semicolons inserted thereafter. But all of this punctillious debate is beside the point. Newman's concern here (this is one of his own sentences again) is that the names of some college presidents are funny. He spends ten full pages snickering over his discovery that some of these names sound like the British hyphenated variety (Nicholas Murray-Butler, get it?), that some of them can be reversed (Brewster Kingman, etc.), and that some of them have pretentious first initials attached (as in A. Bartlett Giamatti).[18]

19. "Eloquent," says Newman.[19]

20. No, this is not a commentary on the decline of taste in American humor or even an attack on punning. It is one of Newman's own creations, taken from the final chapter of *Strictly Speaking*, which includes a whole portfolio of word plays. "To repeat," the author explains, "I make no apology for punning, and specifically for what follows. I am proud of it." Like the one about the rabbi who says, "Do not go gentile into that good night," or the one about the mentally ill model who was "mannekin depressive."[20]

When I have showed this test to English teachers, they have rarely been able to identify more than a third of Newman's putative errors. Non-teachers find even fewer. However, many of my testees do discover other errors which Newman didn't. Some complain that *chief* is an inappropriate modifier for *dread*, while for others *this afternoon fog* seems to be missing a word (*this afternoon the fog will lift*). But most of these discoveries come from people who are looking too hard. My eager subjects, while they miss most of Newman's "errors," often continue rereading the sentences on the theory that "there must be *something* wrong here."

To be fair to Newman, I must admit that a different, less tricky test could be concocted from other injunctions in his books. Many of the slips and errors that he attacks are common fodder for grammar lessons in every school and college, and the average English teacher would have no difficulty identifying them. But it is also fair, I think, to demonstrate the extent to which popular language criticism like Newman's is the product of a highly individual and arbitrary taste—the taste of the critic himself and, often enough, hardly anyone else. Newman's idiosyncrasy is further revealed by his obsession with slips of the tongue—mistaken, confused, or bumbling utterances which, while they do not represent language at its most effective, scarcely pose a threat to it, either.

On page after page, Newman worries because Hubert Humphrey said he went at politics *hook and tong;* because someone accused the media of providing *grist for the fires;* or because Howard Cosell claimed to be *numbstruck.* Linguists have a name for curiosities of this kind: they call them "performance errors," reflecting the assumption that while all native speakers of English have the *competence* to produce grammatically correct, idiomatic, and meaningful utterances, their actual *performance* is not always perfect. Who ever said *grist for the fires,* in other words, had a little glitch in the brain, caused by fatigue or distraction or thinking too far ahead, and mixed things up. We all have this problem from time to time. But such performance errors are proof of no trend in the English language or among English-speaking people. No one I have ever run across, for example, routinely uses any of the three slips noted above; each was an isolated, individual error which did not subsequently spread to other speakers. But, if I may allow myself a brief excursion into permissiveness, I think that *numbstruck* accomplishes a rather colorful and handy fusion. If you can be struck *dumb,* why not *numb?* Perhaps Howard Cosell has actually made a contribution to the English language; slips like his are occasionally the source of new vocabulary in all human languages.

To return to the point, Newman may well discover, by way of his dogged research and his finely tuned ear, that someone has actually said: *We are condoning the concealment of a dagger of venality beneath a cloak of reform.*[21] But the fact that this person fumbled a metaphor does not prove that other English speakers are harmed by it, or that the language is somehow reduced by it.

The author of the dagger item, by the way, was the *New York Times's* language critic, William Safire. It is no accident that what to Safire was a well-crafted sentence was to Newman an example of linguistic degradation. The major critics cannot even agree on a short, clear-cut list of English errors. Newman rails that *massive* properly refers only to tangible masses, and then A. Bartlett Giamatti (he of the funny name) goes ahead and refers to language *itself* as "a massive living system of signs" at the start of an article decrying the decline of English at Yale.[22] When the critics are not unconsciously contradicting each other, they are usually doing one of two other things: either pursuing pet peeves which their colleagues ignore, or *consciously* contradicting each other.

Safire, for example, has publicly abandoned the fight against two of Newman's most cherished adversaries. As for *hopefully,* Safire notes: "The English language has been using adverbs to qualify a whole following clause or sentence for centuries; with one deft daub, an adverb can quickly and vividly color a sentence that follows, infusing the words that come after it with a meaning that otherwise would have to be evoked with a long and often awkward modifier." On *viable*, Safire has likewise run up the white flag: "of all the cliches of the 60's, this adjective alone seems capable of survival and growth. The root of the word is, of course, *life*, though the term is most often used in its nonscientific sense—as a hot possibility or a good bet for success."[23] Though John Simon has issued no ruling on *viable*, he stands shoulder to shoulder with Newman in opposing *hopefully*. Acknowledging the wide popularity of this bit of "systematized ignorance," Simon concludes: "I don't know whether it is possible *not* to follow the peasants' lead, but it is a noble experiment worth trying. Especially when you consider how unlovely the peasants are."[24]

Safire, it must be understood, is the black (or at least gray) sheep in the critics' family. Though he does grumble over many of the same locutions which trouble his more prescriptive brethren (*input, zero-based, relevant, meaningful*), he has made accepting noises about the likes of *parameter, rip-off, contact* (for *get in touch with*), and *full court press* (for *putting the pressure on*). He redeems himself from time to time by inveighing against some truly obscure language errors—*the lion's share*, he argues, means not just most but *all* of something, and one can only *be graduated* from a school (one cannot simply graduate). But time and again Safire's sense of humor and immersion in the language as it is actually used lead him to more ambivalent and humble commentaries. He intentionally titled one column "Who to Root For," because "Whom to Root For" looked *too* right, as if "the writer was straining to show he knew when to use *whom*." And, smothering under the weight of contrary advice about another disputed item, Safire closed the case by announcing: "I intend to stop bothering my head about the metaphoric difference between *farther* and *further*. Rule: Use *farther* only when you're talking about distance, otherwise use *further* allatime. Further protest will be unavailing."[25]

Richard Mitchell, for all of his bluster about giving the enemies of good English "nothing but battle," is puzzlingly permissive on a number of points. He approves of and recurrently uses, both in his book and in television interviews, the rather lame and slangy collective *stuff*. In one talk show appearance, during which he announced that the word *input* had no meaning, he used three times the tag *and stuff* to complete a series of items. Using the standard Mitchell applies to invalidate *input*—essentially that the term is too broad and inclusive to mean much—*stuff* would also seem to meet the test of meaninglessness.[26] Similarly, another language critic might strangle on some of Mitchell's own metaphors. The examples of abuse given in the first chapter of his book, Mitchell explains, "are small inklings of a whole galaxy of disorders that have coalesced out of the complicated history of language." But Mitchell always charts his own course, whatever galaxy he's in. "Forget your uneasiness about *hopefully*—it doesn't matter," he advises, and he even confides to his readers that it "really wouldn't matter much if we started dropping the *s* from our plurals." And though Mitchell does share with most of his fellow critics a distaste for jargon, he is mystifyingly selective, approving, for example, this apparent bit of bureauspeak: "A continuous and unobstructed way of exit travel from any point in a building or structure to a public way ... consists of three separate and distinct parts: the way of exit access, the exit, and the way of exit discharge."[27]

In fact, Mitchell does make some efforts to dissociate himself from the other critics, especially those who cheerily publish "collections of the pompositions and malapropisms of politicians and bureaucrats" (and we all know whose house grammarian *that* is). Such compilations of idiocy, Mitchell argues, ought not to be chuckled over, since laughter is the first step on the road to forgiveness. The inability to use English well must not be forgiven, Mitchell asserts, because careful writing makes us "men." Yet despite these quibbles with the more lighthearted (and unmanly?) of his fellow critics, Mitchell joins in the nearly general assault on *scenario*, *prioritize*, *thrust*, *module*, *facilitate*, and *interface*, and insists on vigilance with respect to spelling and typographical errors. Having caught a grade school teacher spelling *article* as *artical*, he compares her with an airplane mechanic whose sloppy work kills hundreds of people. And he is ruthless with the college president whose ill-edited memo announced: "the most notable accomplishment of the University during 1976-77 was the strides took ... "[28]

John Simon, who shares Mitchell's anger and high seriousness about language abuse—though not necessarily his specific complaints—has uncharacteristically admitted to uncertainty about one point of usage. He confesses in *Paradigms Lost* that the *further/farther* controversy that so preoccupied the readers of William Safire's column is "a fine point open to debate." But little else is, including the errors of Simon's fellow critics. He takes Newman to task for using *deprecating* in the place of *depreciating*, for saying *a bookstore which*, instead of *a bookstore that*, for committing several errors of agreement, and for allowing himself lapses of "slickness and smugness." Simon emits tsk-tsks over Safire's commencement address at Syracuse University, in which the columnist was heard to say: "We need not degenerate further from written English to verbal signals to sign language." Simon explains that "verbal means anything pertaining to words, written or spoken," and that Safire should have used *oral signals* instead. In his review of *What's Happening to American English?* Simon laments that Charlene and Arn Tibbets have "fallen prey to the linguistic anomie they seek to combat." He catches them in faulty agreement ("Everybody involved ... disclosed their illiteracy"), jargoneering ("A Warriner-type book"), redundancy ("She had been filled full of bad ideas"), and one *most importantly*.[29]

To give the Tibbetses their due (in spite of their unfortunate mistakes), they do attack many of the same fad words Simon himself deplores: *viable, concept, elitist, interface, module, gay, commitment*. And they have expanded the territory of language criticism by opening up attacks on the lingo of some heretofore unrebuked professionals, like geologists, whom they criticize for using words like *synclines, geosynclines*, and *orthogeosynclines*. On the other hand, the Tibbetses are curiously soft on some of the classic disputes. They dismiss the split infinitive, the preposition at the end of a sentence, the double negative, the use of *ain't*, and the *who/whom* snare as "pseudo-issues" best left to "Professor Grumble." Instead, the Tibbetses seem to like their language rare, if not raw. As an example of good English, they offer this: "You could not scare up an uglier set of old whores, no, not even in Mexico."[30]

But Simon still has other critics to fry. Turning his attention to a less noted but staunchly prescriptive language-is-dying volume called *Word Abuse* by Donna Woolfolk Cross, Simon redpencils *aggravate* for *annoy*, *anxious* for *eager*, *intriguingly* for *interestingly*, *not too many people* for *not very many people*, and *overly specific* for *overspecific*.[31] This last replacement, by the way, does not even appear in the *American Heritage Dictionary*.

Though Simon professes respect for this resource ("the only current American dictionary I can countenance"), he corrects it as well. The use of the word *overly* in constructions such as *overly complicated*, though approved by *AHD*, is simply "incorrect" and *overcomplicated* is right. *Masterful*, in spite of the listings in the *American Heritage*, does not mean anything like *skillful* and such definitions are "inadmissible." Finally, although the *American Heritage* allows a choice in negative comparisons ("This summer is not *so* hot as last" or "This summer is not *as* hot as last"), Simon insists that only the latter is correct.[32]

The centrality of the *American Heritage Dictionary* in contemporary language debates is an interesting subject in itself, and the rulings of its usage panel are worth a brief look. Here, instead of the judgments of individual tasteful observers of language, we have the judgments of over 140 tasteful observers. These experts, selected for their "sensitiveness to the language and their power to wield it effectively and beautifully,"[33] are polled on certain disputed usage items, and the results of the surveys are tabulated to yield rulings in the form: 58 percent of the panel approves this usage, 14 percent rejects it, and so forth. Along with the percentage votes, the *AHD* editors sometimes include a comment or two from individual panelists (on the word *balding*, Katherine Ann Porter remarks: "entirely vulgar").

The *AHD* was commissioned in the early 1960s, amid the furor surrounding the publication of *Webster's Third*, which was widely thought to be permissive in the extreme (attacks upon it have filled at least one entire book). From its inception, the *AHD* was intended to be a prescriptive volume, offering what its editor, William Morris, called "the essential element of guidance, that sensible guidance toward grace and precision which intelligent people seek in a dictionary." In facing up to this task, the editors of the *AHD* claim to have felt "a deep sense of responsibility as custodians of the American tradition in language." They apparently believed that this weighty obligation could best be discharged by a usage panel originally composed of 94 men and 11 women, with an average age of sixty-four, many of whom had been vocal critics of *Webster's Third*, and the great majority of whom were known to have quite conservative, often reactionary ideas about "the American tradition in language."

The *AHD* editors clearly got what they were after. A majority of the usage panel ruled unacceptable such common terms as *loan* for *lend, alibi* for *excuse, bus* as a verb, *in back of* for *behind, cohort* for a single person, *most* as in *most everyone agrees, negotiated* as in *we negotiated a sharp curve, outside of the house* instead of *outside the house* and *try and* for *try to.* When the judgments of the AHD panel are compared with those of other dictionaries and usage guides—a comparison which Thomas Creswell has handily provided in his book *Usage in Dictionaries and Dictionaries of Usage*—the *AHD* emerges as one of the most prescriptive available sources of information about the American language.[35]

On the use of *cohort* referring to one person, for example, eight of the nine other dictionaries studied by Creswell disagree with *AHD* and approve the usage. Two-thirds of the *AHD* panelists voted down *consequential* meaning *important*, while all nine of the other dictionaries differed. On the *further/farther* debate, 80 percent of *AHD* panelists voted to retain a distinction; yet of the nineteen other dictionaries and usage books consulted by Creswell, only five had issued a similar ruling. Eighty-four percent of the *AHD panel* condemned *taxwise*; eight of the nine other dictionaries, approved it. Eighty-five percent of the *AHD* group rejected *head up*, as in *Jones heads up the committee;* most of the other authorities ignored this alleged problem, and those which did choose were evenly divided. *Finalize* drew a ninety percent negative vote from the panelists; votes from the other arbiters come to eight approvals, three restrictions, and seven abstentions. Even the familiar quarrel over *who* and *whom* finds no consensus: the *AHD* experts voted by ninety-two percent to retain the distinction, while the other authorities who treated the problem split eight to eight.[36]

The arbitrariness of the *AHD* panel's rulings is evident even without comparison to outside authorities. Its treatment of *can* and *may*, for example, is a wriggling can of worms. Sixty percent of the group forbid *Can I have it?* but only eleven percent find fault with *Why can't I?* Twenty-eight percent reject *You can't have it*, while seventy percent stigmatize *You can have it*. Can you understand all that? I know I mayn't. The panel's struggle with split infinitives is equally tortured. The long usage note opens with this enticing double bind: "The split infinitive (as in *to readily accept*) is not a grammatical error, and it has ample precedent in literature. But it is still avoided, where possible, by many writers and editors." The note goes on to offer four specific examples, on which panel approval ranges from twenty-three percent (*to gradually, easily, and economically relieve the burden*) to sixty six percent (*to more than double*). Readers searching for that "sensible guidance toward grace and precision" which editor Morris promised must come away from this section wondering whether their own questionable infinitive construction falls into the twenty-three percent or the sixty-six percent category. The sensitive reader, in fact, may deduce that the panelists' half-hearted hair splitting simply reflects a lack of enthusiasm for the whole business and that the underlying message is: "Better not take chances by splitting *any* infinitives."[37]

Of course there are plenty of panel votes which are perfectly understandable and in which the majority endorses American English as it is actually used. But some of the *minority* votes are troubling. Forty-seven percent of the group, for example, rejects *done* as in *All work is done on the project*. (Notice the intentionally clumsy sample sentence on which the panelists were required to vote. *All work on the project is done* would have sounded more natural, but might have invited a less prescriptive response.) The sentiment favoring the word *finished* must be strong on the *AHD* panel, because twenty-five percent also rejected *through* as in *Are you through yet?* Thirty-eight percent of the judges refused to abide We *will be in Ohio next week*, preferring the British form *shall*. Many of those anglophiles doubtless were behind (not in back of) the 27 percent vote against *presently* meaning *at the present time*, again preferring the more British sense of *shortly* or *soon*. Forty-nine percent of the panel disliked *practically* when used to mean *nearly* or *almost,* and a quarter of them frowned on *The dress looked like new,* and one senses, would not accept *practically new* as a substitute.[38]

In sum, the *AHD* usage panel is a tough bunch: highly conservative, deeply opinionated, cheerfully arbitrary, unapologetically inconsistent, and often out of touch with the American language as it is used by ordinary, educated speakers and writers—which is to say that the panel is more or less the product of its 140 cranky parts.

Clearly, the rulings of language critics and usage panels are opinions and not facts. And just as clearly, these judgments are comments on certain kinds of people as well as on particular disputed word items. When John Simon criticizes certain speakers, the attack usually gets personal. When an *AHD* panelist proudly asserts: "I don't mingle socially with people who talk this way," he is revealing much about his own prejudices. Reading through the work of such authorities, it is easy enough to discover what kinds of people they happen to despise—often they dislike nearly everyone above or below them in the social hierarchy as they perceive it.

While I am fascinated by all of these prejudices, I am most interested in the loathing of education professors—those of us with the job of preparing teachers for the elementary and secondary schools. While the newsmagazines have hinted at our depravity (our theories turn classrooms into "bullpens of babble," according to *Time*), Richard Mitchell and the Tibbetses have assembled the full, shocking story. To begin with, these three writers have an even more despairing outlook on American education than the newsweeklies; in Mitchell's view, the average public school is like "a factory where this year's product is invariably sleazier than last year's but, nevertheless, better than next year's."[39] This is not a simple case of someone's letting the garden go untended, the critics make clear. There has been a willful attempt by teacher-trainers to undermine everything important, useful, exact, rigorous, and disciplined in schooling.

"A typical class in Education," Mitchell explains, "starts with a handout of materials, which provides nifty terms like 'preassessment test' and 'behavior modification.'" Then the class breaks up into small groups so that the students can "rap" and reach for themselves the conclusion that behavioral objectives are "an overall good idea." The education professor teaching this class works hard to see that his "would-be teachers spend as little time as possible in the study of any subject." In his spare time, this professor is also an inveterate and obsessive grant seeker. He sits around the faculty lounge brainstorming potentially lucrative "gimmicks" with his equally corrupt colleagues. They will eventually come up with a proposal, Mitchell says, for studying "the bagel-baking aptitudes of third graders" or they will invent some fraudulent panacea like "Enharmonic Interpersonal Dynamism Education." In order to get their project funded, they will cloak the emptiness of their ideas in bureaucratic jargon: "An Experimental Research Proposal to Study Pedagogical/Instrumental Outcomes/Behaviors as Related to the Unconscious Symbolism of Traditional and Non-Traditional Spatial Placement of Individualized Learning Stations within the Primary Learning-Facility Location."

The professors will take the money they get from the government and buy "whole wardrobes of polyester double-knit leisure suits." These grantsmen, Mitchell insists, are hardly different from common criminals: "The Professor of Education seeking a grant and the neighborhood lout looking for a score simply go and do as their predecessors have done. The one litanizes about carefully unspecified developments in philosophy, psychology, and communications theory, and the other sticks up the candy store."[41]

But these professors don't construct their grant proposals only to get money; they also aim to "reduce the power of language" among the children their projects will eventually affect. Therefore, any project they propose will scrupulously avoid "details like spelling and the agreement of subjects and verbs." Instead, their projects will promote "self-indulgent wallowing in ignorance." Perhaps they will invite "Avon ladies to rap with third graders about their career objectives" or devise a program to engender "a profound respect for the folkways of migrant workers and the peculiarities of octogenarians." Or maybe they will promote "values clarification," lessons in which students are asked, for example, whether they "identify" more with a Cadillac or a Volkswagen. Such an activity, however fancy its title or polysyllabic its rationale, is bound to stupefy students—which, Mitchell reminds us, is exactly what is intended. Professors of education, he explains, have taken the role of "dentists handing out lollipops to ensure that there will be no falling off of customers." Naturally, when their programs fail to accomplish much, it will then be "time for a new round of grants, projects, experimental proposals, expensive consultants, packets of materials, instruction booklets, sets of visual aids, more teachers, carpeted classrooms, air conditioning, just about anything you can imagine."[42]

While Mitchell has described education professors in general, the Tibbetses confine their attention to one particular subspecies: professors of English education, the people who train teachers of reading and writing. The permissive ideal burns in these demons' hearts, and they take every available opportunity to undercut attempts to teach the basics in English. They try to persuade teachers to replace their writing and literature courses with courses on film study and media ecology. These "jackass" authorities maintain a lucrative practice conducting in-service workshops for English teachers, during which they unload briefcases of "weird" ideas and then fly away, leaving everyone in confusion. Such an individual is always essentially "a politician in disguise," spreading a malignant gospel of democratization, the abandonment of linguistic standards, and reverence for "poverty-stricken usage." The efforts of these jackass professors, as well as other lamentable factors, have by now created a situation in which six out of seven English teachers do not do "a satisfactory job."[43]

The itinerant professor of permissiveness gets most of his doctrine from the National Council of Teachers of English, the wellspring of "bad ideas about English." From its headquarters in Urbana, Illinois, comes a "never-ending stream of publicity and propaganda" aimed at undermining English instruction in America. The NCTE's leaders—"a relatively small group of theorists and college professors"—travel from place to place "delivering their latest notions of right thinking," which usually include seditious notions borrowed from linguists. One such blasphemy, the Tibbetses disclose, is this "pentalogue": "(1) language changes constantly, (2) change is normal, (3) spoken language is the language, (4) correctness rests on usage, (5) all usage is relative." The leaders of the NCTE, the Tibbetses disgustedly report, have even made statements like this one: "In the name of basic skills and literacy, we see a revival of methods and routines that the profession abandoned because they DID NOT WORK—because they were, for many or most of our students, wrongly based, counter-productive, pervasively negative in their whole orientation." And not only has the NCTE issued a proclamation in support of "Students' Right to Their Own Language," arguing that social dialects are actually real human language, but it has even passed a resolution opposing discrimination against "gay men and lesbians." The Tibbetses appear to believe that this last action has considerable explanatory power where the decline of American English is concerned. The descriptions of education professors offered by Mitchell and the Tibbetses, if I may draw on my personal experience, are about as accurate as Edwin Newman's lexicography—and they are equally revealing of the prejudices of their authors.

The work of all the language critics and experts reviewed so far in this chapter tends to suggest that the tasteful observation of other people's language, whether it is practiced individually or in packs, yields little helpful or accurate information about speech or writing. About all that these tasteful observers have in common is the leftover lore of their schooling in grammar, the sense that they are worthier than almost everyone else, and the conviction that something must be wrong out there. Personal tastes being what they are, this method of amassing information is bound to produce inconsistencies and contradictions, and to offer complicated, if not mystifying, advice to its intended beneficiaries.

What is the learner, the good-hearted, open-minded, self-improvement-oriented reader of all these commentaries supposed to do? Follow Newman and avoid dangling *hopefully,* or go with Safire and Mitchell and use it freely? Should we drop *viable* from our vocabularies or embrace it? Shun *prioritize* but utilize *hospitalize?* Refer to *massive* things in the abstract or only in the measurable? Make *verbal* signals or just *oral* ones? Be a real man like Mitchell and write slashing prose about *maieutics?* Respect English teachers or fret over their sexual proclivities? Split this infinitive, or that one, or some of them, or do it 54 percent of the time, or 13 percent of the time? Conceal a dagger of venality beneath a cloak of reform? Or maybe, in the face of all these mutually excluding absolute rules, gradually lose confidence in our ability to speak our native tongue. Or even, perhaps, to throw up our hands in despair and say: "Language critics? Them is my chief dread."

There is one other suspicious fact about the tasteful policing of other people's language. It is so damned easy. Because of the wide range of dialects in America, because of the naturally varying levels of formality in talk and writing, because of the performance errors all of us make, because the tastes of the language critics and most of the rest of us differ—because of a whole host of factors—filling up a book with examples of someone else's mistakes is much easier than the noncritic might imagine. I proved to myself how effortless such tasteful observation can be when, a couple of years ago, I appointed myself language critic for a day, and set out to record on my legal pad every fluff, abusage, fad word, inelegancy, typo, and double negative that crossed my aural or visual path over twenty-four hours. And a long day it was, though certainly not a taxing one.

The first half hour was uneventful. I couldn't catch my wife making any errors because she was still asleep, and my son couldn't produce any mistakes because he wasn't born yet. When I got in the car and turned on the local "newsradio" station, things started to pick up. Before I had even turned out of the driveway, I heard an ad for a store advertising itself as "Chicagoland's most progressive appliance dealer." I immediately envisioned the salesmen stalking through the aisles of dishwashers, wearing red armbands and carrying placards reading: "DEATH TO CAPITALIST EXPLOITERS OF KITCHEN WORKERS!" At the first stoplight, I heard that March had been "designed as Inoculation Month." Waiting for the green, I gazed at the bumper sticker ahead of me: "WMAQ is gonna make me rich," it proclaimed. The adjacent truck had a sticker saying "Savenergy" with one *e* missing, presumably "saved."

Out on the tollway, I heard a contractor being interviewed about a house he had built and then later had to move twenty feet to satisfy some local ordinance. The relocation had ruined all the electrical and plumbing connections, and the reporter wondered if the contractor expected to have any trouble selling a house with such a history. "Oh, well, I don't really think so," he replied, "we're just gonna hafta kinda try to represent the house for, you know, for what it is." Less than a mile down the road, an official at O'Hare airport (which I happened to be passing) complimented the Federal Aviation Administration for scheduling the arrival of planes "in incremental steps, so to speak," instead of all at the same time. Considering the alternative, this seemed faint praise. But with the difficulty of writing while driving (and the possibility that the FAA might suddenly revise its incremental arrival policy to the detriment of those of us passing by) I decided to suspend collections until I got to work.

Picking up my mail and a cup of coffee, I strolled toward my office, checking bulletin boards as I went. On the Social Commission board was a flyer from a local nightclub, which read in part:

LOOKOUT!

Ron Fabiani's
Charade Lounge
Presents

Live on Stage——Lucy and the Pulsations

SEE THIS 10 PIECE DYNAMITE ENTERTAINMENT PACKAGE THIS FRIDAY 11TH AND SATUR-
DAY 12TH ONLY.

FIVE VERSATILE SINGERS AND FIVE INSTRUMENTS A TOTAL OF 10 PEOPLE DAZZELING
YOUR EARS AND EYESIGHT WITH A NIGHT YOU WON'T EASILY FORGET.

ORIGINALITY AND PERFECTION IS OF UTMOST IMPORTANCE TO THIS GROUP. THEREFORE
WHEN ENTERTAINING, EACH PORTRAYS A UNIQUE INDIVIDUALISM MAKING LUCY AND
THE PULSATIONS A PHENOMENAL UNIT.

IF YOU'VE CAUGHT ANY OF OUR SHOWS YOU KNOW WHAT WE'RE TALKING ABOUT IF YOU
HAV'NT YOU' BETTER BLAME DESENEX!

By the time I had finished copying down this goldmine of illiteracy, my coffee was cold. But the Placement Center bulletin board made me stop, too. An announcement from a California law school hung there, informing me:

Today, the need to go beyond their initial degree is so widely recognized that students are seeking secondary support credentials which will enable them to move ahead more quickly in their careers. The advantage of a law degree is of inestimable value in accelerating a student's progress in a chosen profession. Wherever they go, whatever they do, the addition of a Juris Doctor degree to their academic qualifications and the training that is acquired in law school is significantly helpful in achieving career goals.... Our whole person admission philosophy permits us to penetrate beyond the traditional numerical evaluations of LSAT and GPA scores and grades and consider applicants on a more perceptive and enlightened basis.

I had an inescapable feeling that while this law school might have a "whole person" admissions philosophy, it would nevertheless be willing to settle for any parts of the whole that decided to apply.

Settling down with my iced coffee and the morning paper, I promptly collected three more items. "Works of the Romantics Is Music to President's Ears" read (or should that be readed?) the headline of a feature story. Then there was the news item about a shoot-out in a nearby suburb. Under the headline "Skokie Cops Slay Texas Man in Gun Battle after Robbery," I read: "Police opened fire, killing him several times, and again Martinez returned the fire, they said. Another police blast finally cut him down in a driveway at 8531 McCormick Blvd., but as he lay there, Martinez fired still another shot, officers said. Police fired again. When Martinez's body was examined, police said, it was discovered that at least nine shots had struck him." Back in the business section was an advertisement for the impending sale of assorted vehicles and equipment: "AUCTION IN seal enveloped bitting," it trumpeted. "Repossess articles.... Acceptable bit will be notified within 72 hours." I suppose this meant that if your seal performed the cutest bit with an envelope (not just the old ball-on-the-nose routine) either you or your seal could possess the articles of your choice within three days. Finally nearing the back of the *Tribune,* I found a confidence-building ad for a "plant care seminar" given by a local nursery. "You can grown Bonsai," it promised. "Bonsai, Bonsai," I growned to myself. They were right. You can.

My legal pad was filling up nicely now, and it was still only 9:15. I began opening my mail but realized immediately that I would have to stop every minute or two to jot down each error I was discovering. Compromising my standards, I recorded the following and then took a break. The brochure announcing a new book for school administrators guaranteed prospective readers, among other things, that "Chapter 7-9 are filled with practical guidelines and examples for using PPBS language, allocating budgets with respect to conflicting value systems, communicating with personnel from a human perspective, surviving as a female administrator, and turning operational evaluation into personal respect!" There were many funny, or at least perplexing, ways to read all this. Perhaps in PPBS language we use a different numbering system for the chapters of a book: we have Chapter 1-3, Chapter 4-6, Chapter 7-9, and so on. Anyhow, it is clearly a tough world out there in the principalities of principals. You've got those gosh-darned value systems out there arguing and conflicting in the halls, and you never know when an operational evaluation might pop up. You may have to try to survive as a female administrator when all your masculine superiors are pressuring you to have the operation. Hey, but what a good idea that communication from a human perspective is. We really should jolt ourselves out of our comfortable old reptilian perspective once in a while.

Having exhausted all the ways of misreading and criticizing the language of this silly flyer, I had also exhausted myself. I declared my Newman-for-a-day project inoperative and terminated it "with extreme prejudice," as they used to say in the CIA. I was sure that I had proved my point, though my brain was so clogged with all these verbal/oral misdemeanors that I couldn't remember what it was.

Recollected in tranquillity, my point returns. It is this: being a tasteful collector of language errors is pitifully easy. This can mean only one of two things. Either the English language is in truly desperate shape, worse even than the most anguished critic has dared to claim. Or, much more likely, I (and the full-time language critics) have merely recorded parts of language business as usual—language, now as always, full of slips and gaffes and variations and jargon and, most of the time, getting the job done.

Of course the language of daily commerce among the common folk is a well-worn instrument, carrying the scars and bruises of continuous rough handling. But even if we accept such rough-and-tumble language from the average citizen, we still expect something different from the language critics themselves. When the subject of some language is propriety in language, in other words, we expect the expert to be purer than Caesar's wife, or Caesar's grammarian at least. Needless to say (as this transparent introduction forecasts) such expectations cannot be relied upon.

My favorite, if trivial, example of this genre was the first sentence of an Associated Press interview with our nation's youngest college president. "Leon Botstein," the article commenced, "think the English language is dying." In a similar vein was an angry editorial in a Chicago newspaper: "Reporter Bob Schnet and many others have gone into the paradox that youngsters growing up amidst the world's greatest assembly of communi-

cations apparatus overwhelmingly are failing to learn to communicate."
How, one wonders, do you go into a paradox? Probably through a para-
dors. The editorial goes on to explain why today's college graduates don't
know "a verb from a Flugelhorn," which has to do with a lot of "aspects
of the post–World War II era, which produced new circumstances and
new ideas too rapidly to allow for a careful assortment of what was good
and what was worthless or harmful."[45] Perhaps a *sorting* of the good and
the harmful would have been even more productive than an assortment,
which could be handled by any reputable florist.

America's newspaper of record, the *New York Times*, ran a long article
about the "aprarent sllppage" in the "wrltfng" abilities of high school students. It noted that the College Board was already administering an "experimental writing te&t wfth some of fts examinations" and was sending
off "sample co fes of it" to the students' prospective colleges.[46]

But then one could not reasonably expect the *New York Times* to be
chasing around the composing room after minor mistakes like these; much
of the staff has apparently been working on a more important project. "Is
there a writing crisis at your school?" wondered a full-page house ad in a
Times Sunday edition. If so, then: "Here's an easy way to solve it." The
solution is *A Writer's Guide to the New York Times*, a volume guaranteed
to turn "ordinary students into good writers." Yes, the newspaper that has
editorialized furiously about the deterioration of student literacy for the
past twenty years ("Watch Your Language," "The Decline in Literacy is
No Illusion," and so forth) also happens to have a simple and economical
answer to this enduring problem. "The basis of the program is student in-
volvement with the daily *New York Times*. The *Times* is available to any
school or college at a discount price. . . . drop the coupon in the mail." The
"basis of the program," actually appears to be not so much student *in-
volvement with* as student *purchase of* the *New York Times*.[47]

But if you don't want *all* the news that's fit to print, perhaps you and
your class should try the Newsweek Language Arts Program. You will remember *Newsweek's* juicy stories on the decline of American English and
education—most notably "Why Johnny Can't Write" and "Why Schools
Flunk." And though its own past issues have helped to build the market,
Newsweek's flyer announcing the new "Program" takes no chances. It
opens with a quotation from one of the magazine's periodic exposés:
"Many students enter high school with language deficiencies so severe
that desperate teachers inform them that they are about to be taught a
foreign language—standard English." Richard N. Burch, director of
Newsweek's Educational Division and purported author of the flyer,
asserts at the outset that while this statement may frighten readers, it is

nevertheless "absolutely true." He goes on to confide that "at Newsweek, where language is literally our life, we're concerned, too." Burch implies that the fellows down at the Educational Division have sworn off the kind of work done on the editorial side: "instead of producing still more doleful surveys or conducting educational witch hunts" they've spent their time "perfecting" the Newsweek Language Arts Program. "The Program has been tested," Burch bravely announces. "It has been proven. It works." Teachers who act now—who require each of their students to subscribe to *Newsweek*—will receive a "FREE DOUBLE BONUS." Included in this FREE DOUBLE BONUS are "relevant features," "hands-on packages," sequenced exercises," "pre-test and post-test activities," "supplementary resource materials," and a "sturdy storage container."[48]

Although I suppose I am accusing the *Times* and *Newsweek* of exploiting a problem which they have at least partially invented, there is another business which has been mining this same vein of linguistic insecurity for at least as long, if not as noisily, as the media heavyweights. I refer to Don Bolander, whose modest ads ("Shamed by Your English?" "Why Aren't You a Good Talker?") sporadically appear in major newspapers and in magazines like *Ebony*. In many of these ads, there is a photograph of Don professorialy gesturing with his glasses, and under his visage stands the reassuring legend: "BS University of Chicago, MA Northwestern University." His Career Institute promises to mend the inadequate language of those who find their social or professional progress impeded by poor speech habits. In the spirit of scholarly research, I once sent off a request for Don's free pamphlet, neatly typed on college stationary. This was a mistake. After waiting for three months to hear from the Career Institute, I took out a plain piece of paper and a number two pencil and simply scrawled, in my own naturally unimpressive hand: "Please send me your booklet on good English."

A few days later, Don's first pitch landed in my mailbox. He was, not surprisingly, selling books. Three hardback handbooks and six slim little pamphlets on good English, for the low low price of $87.50. When I did not reply, Don sent a rather stern query asking whether I was simply disorganized or just didn't care enough to improve myself. Was I satisfied with my pathetic little slot in the social and economic hierarchy, or did I have the gumption to pull myself up by my bootstraps? The flyer's offer was pretty hard to pass up, because it showed drawings of people (many of them from minority groups) winning respect, leading meetings, giving speeches, and addressing generally rapt audiences.

My failure to respond to even this multicultural appeal brought a third, and curiously gentler missive from the Career Institute. Perhaps money is the problem after all, Don speculated. Perhaps we can make a deal. Would you be willing to make this crucial investment in your future if we dropped the payments to $5.00 per month? Still, I had to admit that my scholarly mission to investigate linguistic insecurity wherever its source was being stymied by Don's awesome price tag. I even briefly considered seeking a grant to underwrite my researches into the Career Institute, but I couldn't imagine what agency might finance such a project. (Perhaps Richard Mitchell could have helped me find funding.) Finally, my dilemma was resolved when I discovered the full set of Career Institute materials at a used book sale, where the asking price was $6.50 for the lot. Presumably, one of Don's satisfied customers had finished the course, remitted the final payment, received his or her handsome certificate of achievement and, tapping into some of the increased wit and perception gained from the course itself, had the good sense to recoup part of the investment by selling off those well-thumbed volumes.

I weighed the pros and cons: the purchase would be tax deductible as a research expense, effectively lowering the price to about $5.00. Still, as I leafed through the books, it was hard to determine what this purchase might accomplish. They contained an endless series of tired, outdated, and mercilessly boring socially graded usage exercises, spelling lists, tips on speech-making, little self-scoring diction quizzes, and so forth. The only significant attraction in the whole package was the promise that your enrollment in the course qualified you to correspond personally with the members of the faculty back at the main campus of the Career Institute. (The campus had recently been moved from Mundelein, Illinois, to Danbury, Connecticut, probably for the most innocent of reasons—perhaps to accommodate the tremendous growth of the Institute. My most recent evidence confirms that CI has since moved again, this time to Little Falls, New Jersey, and has sprouted a branch called the Conversation Studies Department.)

Anyhow, I was interested in the faculty because, judging from the photographs—or tintypes—in the brochure, I was absolutely certain that every one of them was dead. I deduced this not only from the turn-of-the-century clothing and hairdos but also from the antique ring of the blurbs describing each. Thelma A. Farison, the booklet proudly noted, was the holder of a Ph.B. degree from the University of Michigan. This statement drove me to my beloved *American Heritage Dictionary*, where I discovered that *Ph.B.* is an anachronistic, but in this case conveniently misleading, designation for a bachelor's degree. W. Lane Schulze, another Ph.B., was somewhat tautologically noted for his role as "director of the English Language Clinics which were held at the school to analyze and answer English and speech problems presented by the students in the course." And Walter W. Kester from Iowa, it turned out, had been recruited from La Salle Extension University (of matchbook fame), presumably to add a little gloss and respectability to the faculty roster.

Still, in the end, even the powerful lure of communicating with the dead faculty was outweighed by the $5.00 ticket on the set of books, and I bravely turned by back on the social mobility, public respect, and fatter paychecks that those materials might have earned me.

But to return to more familiar campuses. Even when the academic press takes on the problem of illiteracy, illiteracy often seems to win. *Change* magazine which, despite its misleading title, is a journal about higher education, devoted a whole issue to the crisis in language. Introducing their special articles, the editors intoned: "The eroding communicating skills of America's young prompt us to take an in-depth [sorry, Edwin] if selective view of this phenomenon. . . . The articles in the following pages provide some intimation of the complexity of the problem." Now, speaking for myself, I prefer communication skills to communicating skills, and I would rather have my articles on pages than in them—but I'm always glad to be offered some intimation of the complexity of a problem, if not a paradox. And I am stirred by the editors' conclusion: "clearly American academics can no longer sweep illiteracy under the carpet [Please! Not the rug!] as not really being any of their business." There's just no room left under that lumpy carpet anymore.[49]

Alas, even when a handpicked group of academics assembles to write about writing, illiteracy can still spill out in crumbs and globs from under the rug and/or carpet. At the University of Illinois (where Arn Tibbets recently served as director of freshman rhetoric), a committee was appointed in 1975 to study the decline of writing skill among students in the College of Liberal Arts and Sciences. Dean Robert W. Rogers drafted seven faculty members to serve on this panel; his memo of invitation called for strong remedies and steps to be "undertaken" (not just taken) toward "an appropriate overall strategy to remove or to ameliorate the problem." In Champaign's Freudian-Slip-of-the-Year, Dean Rogers simultaneously announced: "I believe that the Committee should not be as thorough and comprehensive in its review as time permits." Taking up the dean's challenge to work courageously toward predetermined recommendations, the committee's report notes: "it would be folly, in the face of the accumulated evidence, to prove that general writing skills have improved." You certainly would not want to *prove* something like this to Dean Rogers, after all, because he has already explained that student talk and writing are deteriorating because public schools have "abandoned the effort."

Following this same line of reasoning, the committee announces that it is considering all of these problems "de novo": the members were not "biased, nor were its members prejudiced regarding the issues, the facts, or the outcomes." A few pages later, the report notes, "one cannot live in the United States in 1976 without feeling some anguish for the general erosion of the quality of life and particularly for the lack of linguistic values." It may be, the committee sadly notes, that "the worst fears of George Orwell forty years ago are even now being realized." De novo.[50]

Describing its methodology, the committee explains that it first "determined to ascertain" student and faculty opinions on "the more apparent issues" by way of a questionnaire that could be "tabulated and analyzed ... from a statistical point of view." The result of this effort, "from a psychometric point of view," was that students didn't write very well. Next, the committee turned its attention to the "placement and proficiency vehicle" then in use, driving it around the campus a few times. Some alternative "devices" are considered, both ones that test for mechanics and others that ask students to write "regarding literature," but none is wholly satisfactory. Even the history of prior committees comes under scrutiny, and the forerunner "Committee to Explore Coordination of Campus Services Dealing with Language Problems" is lambasted because it "appears not to have provided functional ties between these units nor to make them very visible as independent services or as a group of remedial efforts." The downfall of the CECCSDLP, according to the new panel, was its unwillingness to handle writing problems "from a broader base," and any replacement committee should "have oversight of the many issues and concerns regarding student English"—not to mention a shorter name.[51]

To make a long and increasingly dull story short, this sixty-two-page document, which was distributed both on and off campus, suffers from many of the same flaws that University of Illinois professors undoubtedly punish in their own students' writing. It is full of jargon: things don't exist, they're "extant." We don't have tests, we have "vehicles." We always look for "the viable central position." Whenever we're puzzled, we institute "assiduous scholarship." There are also many odd word choices: there is an "incremental loss" in students' writing abilities; we have commitments "toward" things, not "to" them; we try to "infuse a better sense of continuity into the program"; we approach statistics from "a psychometric point of view" but always with "some degree of circumspection." There are dozen of typos and spelling errors ("becomce," "depattments," "thsse," "frequenty".) Nowhere in this document, so far as I can tell, are there any split infinitives—although the contortions necessary to avoid them often result in sentences that are slightly off-kilter: "We would propose that departments ... offer periodic competitions, especially to commend projects of special merit," and "It will not do simply to relegate this task to a single department." Perhaps the most serious "misuse of language," though, is the committee's clumsy, ill-disguised posturing about objectivity, the piling on of vacuous academic pieties as the panel rushes headlong to serve the dean exactly what he ordered up, no more and no less. [52]

At Fordham University in New York, they are also trying to do something about the deplorable writing of college students, and one of its Ph.D. candidates has begun a nationwide study of concerned faculty members. My own invitation to participate in this project opened on a flattering note: "You have been identified as an *expert* in one of the following categories: (1) A college supervisor of teaching composition courses for a total of two or more years. (2) A college teacher of composition for two or more years, You have also been identified as an educator who would be willing to actively participate in my study, a doctoral dissertation research at Fordham University."

I had also been identified, according to the letter, as someone who might have information "regarding the opinion of importance of certain teaching behaviors as essential criteria for supervisors to use in evaluating the effectiveness of what college writing teachers do or should do in teaching students to write." All of us in the study were going to use the *Delphi Technique* to reach a "concensus" about whether we preferred to use "encountering behaviors" and "social interacting teaching models" or whether we leaned more toward "didactic behaviors" and the "accumulation of information, concepts, and skill building."

All of this made me suspect that the survey letter was a trick designed to reveal how many writing "experts" would ignore, in the prose of a colleague, errors that they would certainly red-pencil in a student paper. I wrote back to the survey director, calling his bluff. A few days later, I received a long and in places anguished response explaining that the letter had been no hoax: "If it was your purpose to hurt me," he wrote, "you have succeeded." He went on to describe the problems that had caused his error-ridden missive, including intense and conflicting advice from various advisers, urgent time pressure, and sloppy typing. In three long pages of nearly flawless prose, the graduate student rebuked me for my arrogance, offered some explanations, confessed that the errors were in fact there, rebuked me again, and closed with the promise to keep me informed on the progress of his work in spite of my attitude.

In his original letter, my sad friend in New York had written poorly for certain reasons, and regardless of how much credence one gives to his explanation, he also showed in his second letter that he could write very well when he was on his own and cared enough. Similarly, the other authors of "bad English" I've quoted in this chapter could doubtless explain why their errors crept in, or why they used so much jargon, or why their bosses forced them to write in this way. Perhaps what all of these quotations most clearly show is that once you enter the critic's frame of mind, once you attune your ear to a certain wavelength, you can find mistakes everywhere—even in the writing of self-conscious, well-trained writing experts who are writing about writing itself.

Of course, being a temporary language critic, I have tried to make all of these writers sound as stupid and slipshod as I could. In each document I've quoted there are many other passages which are written in clear, uncluttered standard English and which make perfect sense. But I did not mention these passages because they did not serve my purpose, which was to scold and complain. When I remove my critic's cap, however, I find that the assorted chunks of language quoted in this chapter roughly represent the normal range of writing done in our society; some is relatively clear, some quite opaque; some is pretentious, some humble; some is riddled with mechanical errors, some just sprinkled with them. No, none of it is perfect. But then writing (like speaking) is complex work, and seems almost unpreventably vulnerable to small errors of many kinds. That such errors are not always spotted, resisted, or eliminated is not evidence of the depths to which we have sunk in language—but at the worst, it is evidence of the "depths" at which we *always* operate in language.

This realization does not make me a defeatist, a relativist, or a permissivist. One can acknowledge reality, recognize the durability of certain human imperfections without necessarily applauding them. Some of the writing I've quoted here does trouble me, and whatever excuses its authors may have, it is clear that they should have (and most could have) done better. But I cheerfully admit that my concerns are mostly matters of taste. Some readers of this very book may, in fact, have complaints about *my* writing—and may even have been keeping a tally of my split infinitives and failures of agreement. I might agree with some of these criticisms and I might disagree with others. But as long as we recognize that tastes, as well as "facts," are involved, we could probably have a pleasant and even useful discussion.

I was strikingly reminded of this need for civility during my impersonation of a language critic. When I shifted from being "Newman-for-a-Day," a harmless imaginary drudge, and actually wrote that smug letter to the man at Fordham, I succeeded in hurting someone. All of the linguists' theoretical speculations about language being central to the identity of a person were painfully confirmed in that long letter I got back. It made me wonder again what purpose is served when self-appointed experts ridicule all dialects but their own. It made me wonder why it seems so important to divide the world into "the illiterates" and "us." It made me wonder why the cheap and effortless hobby of criticizing other people's language always seems so popular. It made me wonder what kind of person would enjoy hurting others in this small but efficient way.

Why do the critics do it? Undoubtedly, one motive for writing language criticism is self-congratulation. Many commentators apparently find it pleasant to lord their own superiority over others who happen not to have been born into circumstances which virtually guaranteed the acquisition of a "better" style of speech. When someone like John Simon sprinkles his columns with words like *tergiversator, propaedeutic, caducity, batrachians, maieutics, peccant, sesquipedality, tonitrous,* and *golgotha,* he is just showing off; when he dismisses certain huge groups of fellow English-speakers as "boobs," "cretins," and "ignoramuses," he is patting himself on the back; and when he describes himself in consultation with his language-loving colleagues, we get an embarrassing glimpse of the language critic as social climber:

In Rome, I was having lunch with Lina Wertmuller, the marvelous director, and her husband, Enrico Job, the artist and art director of Lina's films. Candice Bergen and Giancarlo Giannini, the stars of Lina's first English-language film, *A Night Full of Rain,* were also with us. Lina was saying how much she loved Art Nouveau, called Liberty in Italian, and wondered, along with Enrico and Giancarlo, why the word "liberty" seemed to be on the decline in English. [53]

Such self-congratulation obviously cannot explain why the arguments of Simon and his more modest colleagues have been so widely and thoroughly accepted. The sense of linguistic crisis which they have helped create has proven quite broad and durable—a phenomenon too powerful to have been engendered only by the urge for self-aggrandizement among a few commentators. Though the language reformers may occasionally be tempted to explain why they are better than the rest of us, they also have some less obviously self-serving points to make.

The critics' nobler purposes—and their stronger arguments—are related to fears not just about the English language itself, but about the society that uses it. As I noted earlier, the critics have been using language, sometimes explicitly and sometimes implicitly, as an instrument for measuring the health of the social, cultural, political, and economic order. It goes without saying that most of the critics find both language and society to be sick. Perhaps less apparent is the similarity of the diagnoses made by the various critics. The fundamental illness they claim to have discovered in American English, and in American society generally, is "democratization"—the misguided and overzealous implementation of egalitarian ideals. This supposed epidemic of democracy has by now affected nearly every aspect of our national life. Instead of enforcing traditional standards of authority, we have given in to a brand of spineless cultural relativism that shrinks from judging in its hopeless effort to be fair to all. Instead of maintaining an orderly hierarchy based on ability, we have subscribed to a pluralistic credo which accords power and respect to everyone, regardless of merit. The American public, and especially its schools, are now asked not only to overlook, but to celebrate the cultural differences of blacks, Hispanics, Indians, the poor, the uneducated, and the young. And the perceived deterioration of language, it is argued, stands not just as a symbol of these sinister developments, but as an unavoidable by-product and reflection of them.

This presumed mutually causal relationship between "democratization" and the decline of language and culture is nowhere more vigorously outlined than in John Simon's *Paradigms Lost.* "Democracy," he writes, "encourages the majority to decide things about which the majority is blissfully ignorant. Of course, matters of social, political, and economic well-being are for the majority to determine; cultural, artistic, scientific, and intellectual matters are not." Simon elaborates this dichotomy:

I am willing to give two cheers for democracy, and, on occasion, one for pragmatism, but for maintaining good and useful English words I'll give three cheers at any time, along with my lifeblood. Neither the New York hackie nor the upper-crust ignoramus who graduated from Groton and Harvard nor yet the black-English-speaking hordes shall dictate what good English is to those of us who adhere to an enlightened and serviceable tradition—though, in the end, they may prevail over our dead bodies.

Simon is happy to confirm that "those of us" is a pretty small group. "Contrary to popular misconception, language does not belong to the people, or at least not in the sense in which belong is usually construed. For things can rightfully belong only to those who invent or earn them." And those who have "earned" the English language, according to Simon, are the "sensitive, concerned, and discriminating" people united with him in "a common pursuit and a shared beauty."[54]

This select group realizes that "some people are simply not bright enough to become fully literate and articulate, no matter how good the instruction they receive." For the remainder of humankind—for those who stand on the borderline of educability—the disposition is clear: "it behooves us to try to educate the ignorant up to our level rather than to stultify ourselves down to theirs." And how is this elevation of the ignorant to be accomplished? In the schools, naturally, but also in the streets:

Whenever we hear someone say "between you and I" or one of the related horrors, and whoever the offender may be, we go into action. To strangers in the street, we may have to be polite; to superiors (in position, evidently, not in knowledge) we may even have to be somewhat humble. But correct them we must. To all others we may be as sharp, forceful, tonitrous as the circumstances permit or demand: let family, friends, and neighbors hear us correct them loudly and clearly.[55]

Anyone following Simon's do-it-yourself instructions, of course, will be viewed as a stuck-up crank by practically anyone he accosts. But that is *exactly* the point. When the would-be tonitrous correcter cannot get others to shamefacedly reform their ways, his own sense of lonely nobility simply increases, along with his conviction that he is one of the linguistic elect fighting the good fight against unspeakable depravity.

At the beginning of this chapter I suggested that we should ask what social, political, and economic causes are advanced by language criticism. Now, I hope, the question is more sharply focused. What ends, other than the immediate gratification of individual critics, are served by these persistent, often vicious and hypocritical attacks on other people's language? By the direct testimony of Simon and others, we have our answer if we wish to hear it. In their loathing references to equality, leveling, and democracy, the critics have revealed the rest of their agenda. Language criticism endorses the existing social order and offers not apologies for its inequalities, but the celebration of them. The "slobs" and "ignoramuses," whose speech reveals their origins, are shown to deserve their lowly status; the refined and wealthier classes, whose speech reveals their origins, have "earned" the comforts they enjoy. Thus are justified the powers and privileges of the powerful and privileged; thus are perpetuated, among other things, poverty, powerlessness, and hate.

I am not much of a believer in conspiracies, and certainly do not envision some secret committee of politicians, industrialists, and language critics meeting to plot the continuing oppression of the American underclasses. On the other hand, I can't help noticing that we have managed to repoduce our stratified social, political, and economic order essentially unchanged over many generations. This feat has been accomplished through a complex interaction of many phenomena, both accidental and contrived. But one element in this perpetual renewal of the *status quo* has been the unjust classification and punishment of certain people on the basis of their language.

6

Tests and Measurements

Another, seemingly more reliable source of information about language and literacy in America is our ever-increasing stockpile of standardized test results. To hear the tasteful observers' interpretations of this data, the language skills of schoolchildren and college entrants have shown a drastic and unrelieved slide over the past fifteen years. Without question, scores on some of the most familiar national tests have indeed gone down, though some other test scores have been rising. Most important to the current sense of crisis have been the recent results of the college entrance examinations (the Scholastic Aptitude Test and the American College Testing program) and the National Assessment of Educational Progress, which has evaluated the writing skills of nine-, thirteen-, and seventeen-year olds for the past decade.

To find out what such test scores may say about the state of our language, I want to focus in this chapter on the verbal section of the SATs and the NAEP high school writing assessments.[1] A close study of these two revered tests shows that our ability to measure language skill is still at a very primitive stage, and that we are nevertheless irresistibly tempted to misread and misinterpret whatever meager information such tests do provide.

More than any other single piece of apparent information about language, the fact that the SAT scores of college-bound high school seniors have been steadily dropping since 1964 has helped critics to persuade the general public that both American English and the public schools are in a bad way. Typical of the many headlines announcing this connection was the *Chicago Tribune*'s banner: "Test Scores Dip as Standards Skid." Along with its news reports, the *Tribune* also ran an editorial which noted: "The S.A.T. has proved a very good predictor of how well students will do in college, and as such it is an indicator whose readings must be taken seriously. We can't afford to waste any of the intelligence and learning ability of our young people through trivializing of the schools and the increasing mindlessness of much of the environment. We have no alternatives but to keep studying this worrisome trend until we figure out how to reverse it."[2] Virtually every current article or book on the decline of language perfunctorily refers to—or whimpers at length about—the SAT decline. These notorious scores, in short, have become the cornerstone of the literacy crisis.

Before taking a look at the tests and their score patterns, it is worth acknowledging the growing irony of the whole furor over the SATs. Today, unlike in 1963 when average scores were at their peak, college entrance test results are a relatively minor factor in determining the educational future of most students. In 1979, 91 percent of all college applicants were accepted by the college of their first choice. While some self-selection occurs (students with very low SATs tend not to apply to Harvard), this percentage of admission is quite remarkable, as is the College Board's own finding that four-fifths of colleges now accept more than 70 percent of all applicants.[3] Higher education has changed considerably over the past twenty years in America—a shift not yet fully understood and certainly not welcomed by many of the people working in it. But the fact remains that today almost any high school graduate who wishes to attend *some* college may do so, virtually regardless of his or her standardized test scores. The lingering power of the SATs in college admissions now primarily affects two groups: students applying to highly selective colleges and students (often from poor or minority backgrounds) whose scores place them on the borderline of admission to the college of their choice—or to *any* college. While the way the tests treat each of these groups is certainly important, it is an illusion to believe, as most writers in the popular press appear to, that college entrance exams constitute a thorough, across-the-board sorting device for the whole body of college-bound students. There are other illusions abroad about the SATs too, but one thing at a time.

The Scholastic Aptitude Test, taken each year by more than a million high school seniors, is a two-and-a-half-hour test designed to measure verbal and mathematical abilities "developed over a lifetime."[4] The verbal section of the test, which most concerns us here (and which has suffered the larger decline in scores), consists of about eighty-five multiple-choice questions to each of which the examinee will have somewhat less than one minute to respond. The verbal section has four kinds of questions, and a sample of each type appears below:[5]

Antonyms
Choose the word or phrase that is most nearly *opposite* in meaning to the word in capital letters.

1. RECTITUDE: (A) deliberation (B) laziness (C) prejudice (D) laxity of morals (E) weakness of intellect

Sentence Completion
Each question below has one or two blank spaces, each blank indicating that something has been omitted. Beneath the sentence are five lettered words or sets of words. Choose the word or set of words that *best* fits the meaning of the sentence as a whole.

2. From the first the islanders, despite an outward_____, did what they could to _____ the ruthless occupying power.
   (A) harmony . . assist
   (B) enmity . . embarrass
   (C) rebellion . . foil
   (D) resistance . . destroy
   (E) acquiescence . . thwart

Analogies
Select the lettered pair that *best* expresses a relationship similar to that expressed in the original pair.

3. CHOIR:SINGERS:: (A) victory:soldiers (B) class:teachers (C) crowd:protestors (D) challenge: duelists (E) orchestra:musicians

Reading Passages
Read the following passage and then answer the questions on the basis of what is *stated* or *implied* in the passage.

The behavioral sciences are making rapid strides in the understanding, prediction, and control of behavior. In important ways we know how to select individuals who will exhibit certain behaviors and to establish conditions in groups which will lead to various predictable group behaviors; in animals our ability to understand, predict, and control goes even further, possibly foreshadowing future steps in relation to man.

If your reaction is the same as mine, then you will have found that the potentials of this young science are somewhat frightening. For all its present immaturity, behavioral science may contain awesome possibilities. If some individual or group had the power to exploit this science, it would be a nightmare of manipulation. Potential troublemakers could be discovered and dealt with before they became such. Morale could be improved or lowered and behavior could be influenced by appeals to motives of which the individual was unconscious. Admittedly this is wild fantasy, but it is not an impossible fantasy.

Some of you may point out that only a few of the findings I have mentioned have actually been put to use in any way that significantly affects society, and that for the most part these studies are important only to the behavioral scientist but have no serious impact on our culture. I agree with this point. The behavioral sciences at the present time are at somewhat the same stage as the physical sciences were several generations ago. For instance in 1900, the public believed the science of aeronautics to be of little importance and did not anticipate the significant effects that aeronautics would have on culture. They preferred to use their common sense, which told them that man could not possibly fly in a contraption which was heavier than air.

However, the public attitude toward physical science is quite different today. The public is ready to believe any prediction the physical scientist might make. When science predicted a satellite would be launched into space, very few voices were raised in disbelief.

There is every reason to believe that the same sequence of events will occur in the behavioral sciences. First, the public ignores or views with disbelief; then, as it discovers that the findings of a science are more dependable than theories based on common sense, it begins to use them; eventually, the widespread use of these findings creates a tremendous demand. Finally, the development of the science spirals upward at an ever-increasing rate. Consequently, even though the findings of the behavioral sciences are not widely used today, there is every likelihood that they will be widely used tomorrow.

4. The author suggests that the next change in the public's attitude toward behavioral science will lead the public to
   (A) ignore the findings
   (B) increase the use of the findings
   (C) disbelieve the findings
   (D) use these findings against each other
   (E) lose interest in the findings

5. The tone of this passage can best be described as
   (A) condescending (B) humble (C) insipid (D) admonitory (E) inspiring

6. According to the passage, present behavioral studies involving animals may
   eventually produce
   (A) a breakdown in social control
   (B) undesirable repercussions for man
   (C) an increased awareness of man's limitations
   (D) disillusionment in regard to the ability of scientists
   (E) new kinds of animals beneficial to man

7. Which of the following best states the author's main point?
   (A) In the behavioral sciences lies the hope for mankind.
   (B) The influence of the behavioral sciences is decreasing.
   (C) The behavioral sciences are more important today than the physical
   sciences.
   (D) Research in the behavioral sciences should be re-evaluated and curtailed.
   (E) The findings of the behavioral sciences have potentially harmful implica-
   tions.

8. The author recognizes that some readers may accuse him of
   (A) exploitation
   (B) exaggeration
   (C) omitting supporting evidence
   (D) failing to consult authorities
   (E) taking the subject too lightly

After each student's answer sheet has been turned in with the chosen
boxes blackened, the test papers are forwarded under tight security to the
Princeton, New Jersey, headquarters of the Educational Testing Service,
where they are scored by high-speed reading machines. With certain adjustments, the student's score on these eighty-five items is then trans-
posed onto a scale of 200 to 800 points (some of these adjustments include
removing as many as 20 percent of the items, which are experimental and
do not count).

In 1963, the average score on the SAT Verbal was 478; by 1979 it had
dropped to 427, a decline of about 8.5 percent. Since success on the
eighty-five questions is reported on a 600-point scale, each item is worth
about 7 points. The decline in SAT Verbal scores thus represents the in-

ability of the average contemporary test taker to answer correctly seven questions that a 1963 student could have handled. Since the SAT test is specifically designed to predict the student's first-year performance in college, the verdict seems to be that the average college-bound student today has about 8.5 percent less aptitude for college level work than a similar student of two decades ago.[6]

It is certainly reasonable to wonder why such a drop-off might have occurred. But any assessment of the decline's causes must begin with an understanding of the scope and procedures of the SAT testing program itself—and exactly this sort of background has been lacking in much of the popular press's (and the language critics') treatment of the score declines.

In the first place, the SAT Verbal test is taken by only about one-quarter of each year's high school seniors—a group, naturally, that intends to go to college. Nor, as their makers and administrators constantly point out, are the SATs supposed to be "achievement tests," measuring what students have learned only in school. Instead, they aim to reveal deeper "aptitudes" involving the testee's entire intellectual development, learning that has occurred throughout life. As the head of the Educational Testing Service's College Board Division explains, the SAT is a "prospective measure," meant to tell how well a student is likely to do in a specific future situation (the freshman year of college) and not a "retrospective measure," which would find out what a student had learned in some past courses or series of courses.[7] Because the SAT aims to predict success in college, it is in no way a test of basic literacy, of whether the student has a functional command of the reading and writing skills necessary for day-to-day survival in a literate society. Rather, the testers look for higher-order skills: a relatively sophisticated, largely literary vocabulary; the ability to draw subtle inferences from reading passages; a familiarity with standard English and a detailed understanding of grammar rules; and the ability to cope with a test which offers finely shaded answer choices, none of which may be entirely correct. While students who do well on such a test are unquestionably literate, others who do poorly or who do not even take the test cannot, as an automatic corollary, be called *illiterate*. I know of one student at a nearby high school, for example, who scored 200—the lowest possible score, equivalent to 0—on the SAT Verbal test, who is also quite literate and is carrying a B- average in his studies.

Though the apparent precision of any given student's SAT Verbal score, which may fall anywhere within the 600-point range, suggests quite meticulous measurement, the three-digit number reported to testees and their prospective colleges is really only a rough guess at the student's "true score." According to ETS guidelines for the interpretation of score results, a difference of sixty-two points between two students' scores on this test is insignificant and should be ignored. An individual's reported score—say, 400—means that there is a two in three chance that this student's exact scholastic aptitude (if such a thing could be measured perfectly) would be somewhere between 369 and 431, and a one in three chance that the reported score will miss the "true score" by an even greater margin.[8] At least one SAT official has admitted that the range, for many students, may be as much as 100 points in either direction.[9] Not incidentally, an "insignificant" 62-point difference in the SAT Verbal scores of two marginal candidates for admission to a college can, and sometimes does, influence admissions decisions. If a particular college maintains a "cutoff score" (400, for example) below which it will consider no one, a student whose reported score happens to fall into the low end of the band of error (a 395 representing a "true score" of 426) may promptly be rejected. Naturally, any standardized test will have such errors of measurement, and results are always more reliable for groups than for individuals. Yet it still seems odd that the whole crisis regarding SAT scores has arisen from two decades of score declines that, when added up, are still less than the sixty-two-point difference which ETS instructs us to disregard when comparing two student scores.

An even more important drawback to the SATs is the fact that they do their fundamental job—which is forecasting freshman-year college grades—rather poorly. The correlation between SAT scores and freshman grade-point averages is about 0.43, a rate of prediction only about 12 percent better than rolling dice. High school grades, on the other hand, make this prediction about twice as well, showing a correlation of about 0.58 with freshman grade-point averages. One study at the University of Southern California, in fact, found high school grades to be not twice but four times better than SATs at predicting freshman grades. And some other research indicates that the only reason SATs show *any* correlation with freshman grades is because of the prevalence in introductory college courses of ETS-type multiple-choice, machine-scored examinations.[10]

My own awareness of this unreliability factor has been heightened by my experience as a member of the admissions committee at the selective college where I work. Every week we see the files of several students who fall below our baseline criterion on college entrance exams. Luckily, we do not have an absolute cutoff and are free to consider marginal candidates as we see fit. A pattern we commonly see is the student with a respectable grade-point average, high class rank, and test scores below the national average. Last year we admitted twenty-six students in this category. A year later, twenty-four of them are in good standing, and their cumulative grade-point average is only two-tenths of a point lower than the college-wide average. As a matter of fact, for this special group the high school record was an astoundingly direct predictor of college performance: the mean college grade-point average of these students was exactly one-hundredth of a point lower than their high school average.

Still, first-year grades have their limits, too. As a forecast of later achievement in college, and beyond college, the SATs have almost no predictive value at all. In college, the correlation between a student's SATs and the grades actually earned is initially modest and deteriorates steadily from one semester to the next throughout the four years. Even if we turn to persistence in college—the completion of requirements for the degree—as a crude measure of success, the SAT still demonstrates little usefulness: 97 percent of the time, a dice-roll would predict this persistence as well as the entrance exams.[11] Some colleges have taken note of the discrepancy between test scores and actual performance in school. At Bowdoin College, cum laude graduates were studied to see whether their SAT scores could have predicted their superior performance. Of these honors graduates, a plurality had average SATs, while 31 percent had scored significantly above the college average and 24 percent well *below* it. Following this discovery, Bowdoin dropped the SAT as a requirement for admission.[12]

Beyond college, SAT scores really mean nothing. As one Harvard researcher summed up the investigations in this area: "No consistent relationships exist between scholastic aptitude scores in college students and their actual accomplishments in social leadership, the arts, science, music, writing, speech, and drama." Nor do the tests, by predicting an intermediate performance—early grades in college—somehow forecast, indirectly, eventual achievement in life. There *isn't* much correlation between college grades and actual achievement. As one researcher for the American College Testing program reported, after reviewing the data: "college grades bear little or no relationship to any measures of adult accomplishment." The best predictor of future success, in fact, is past success. Students' own unauthenticated accounts of their past accomplishments forecast future accomplishments better than any standardized test. Even college freshmen's predictions of their own subsequent grade-point averages are more accurate than the ETS tests.[13]

All this evidence—much of it from the testers' own internal studies—suggests that the SAT acts as one small and semi-efficient cog in a largely imaginary meritocratic machine. The tests, in other words, weakly predict certain phenomena that are sometimes true for a moment, but promptly change—and in the end don't matter anyway. If we wish to use some test to allocate places in higher education to people showing some promise of accomplishment and contribution to society, we should use some other measure than the SATs.

But none of this necessarily means that the SATs don't measure some other things. There is, for example, a relationship between a student's scholastic aptitude scores and her parents' income:[14]

SAT average	Parents' mean income
750–800	$24,124
700–749	21,980
650–699	21,292
600–649	20,330
550–599	19,481
500–549	18,824
450–499	18,122
400–449	17,387
350–399	16,182
300–349	14,355
250–299	11,428
200–249	8,639

If these family income figures seem modest, that is because the year covered in the table is 1974. ETS has not, understandably, released these statistics recently.

Note that the link between income and test score is consistent at each step: the higher the score, the higher the income. Naturally, these statistics describe groups; some rich kids will score poorly on the SATs and some poorer ones will do well. But, on average, SAT tests can "predict" the social class of a student about as well as they predict his freshman average. Of course there are a couple of ways of looking at these figures. In one view, we might say that the SAT-income correlation merely reflects the smooth functioning of our competitive society. The rich are rich because they are smarter and the poor are poor because they are dumber. On the other hand, these statistics may make us wonder whether the American meritocracy has really achieved such awesome efficiency, whether the numbers mainly reflect the superior schooling offered to the children of the wealthy, whether talent and intelligence may actually be distributed more evenly in the population than the SATs suggest.

Obviously, these income figures call to mind the lingering and much-discussed suspicion that many standardized tests are "culturally biased" in ways which give an unfair advantage to students from wealthy, white families. Why there should be any debate on this question is a mystery to me. The average black student's score on the SATs is about 100–130 points lower than that of the average white test-taker. Both the contents and the linguistic style of the tests are less familiar to poor and minority students than to suburban white teenagers. As early as 1970, the ETS commission on tests was willing to admit that "the Board's tests ... do not tend to reduce the competitive disadvantages of being other than white and middle class; in fact they seem to almost perfectly reflect the bias against disadvantaged groups that results in their relatively depressed scholastic attainment."[15]

The saving grace in this general pattern of bias, the commission allowed, was that the tests could be used "to identify the disproportionately few students in such groups who can successfully compete with the white and middle-class students on their own terms." But in an internal memo written one year later, the ETS vice president in charge of the SATs admitted that the commission's latter assertion was "untenable." The vice president's own information had simply confirmed the charges of a number of outside researchers (including Junius Davis, George Temp, and Roy Goldman): that minority students were being systematically denied admission to college on the basis of low SAT scores that did not accurately measure their scholastic promise.[16] Still, in spite of all the evidence and all the accusations, the ETS made no fundamental changes in its testing program, and simply issued fine-print warnings to its score users about "the desirability of establishing separate prediction equations that might increase the accuracy of test data for minority groups in the admissions process."[17]

Though the SATs are a poor predictor of freshman grades, a nonpredictor of actual achievement, and an unreliable predictor of anything concerning poor or minority students, the question does remain: do they, in spite of these other problems, actually reveal something about the language facility of American young people? In the literacy crisis, it seems worth repeating, the SATs are continually seen as the "leading indicator" of the deterioration in American speech and writing.

Certainly the SAT Verbal test questions are written in a rather formal register of standard English and to some extent measure the student's familiarity with and ability to manipulate this code—or at least its component parts. One heavy emphasis in all of the subtests is on vocabulary of a quite literary, or at least scholarly, sort. To score well even on the pamphlet of sample questions distributed to students a few weeks before the test, one needs to know the meanings of *plethora, dilettante, malediction, enervate, naivete, irremediably, cessation, paucity, winnow, risqué, entreaty, pacification, ballast, seethe, perambulator, impressionistic, cull, reticence, diminutive, effusiveness, indelibly, fathom,* and *inebriated.*[18]

The antonym questions are the most direct measure of such vocabulary, and they contain terms both common and obscure. Students who come from schools or homes where British literary vocabulary is in consistent use will score quite well on this section. But the antonyms are not just a straightforward test of such a lexicon; they don't simply ask "What does *gelid* mean?" The student is instead required to find a "most nearly opposite" definition on a list of often imperfect antonyms. So the student must first know the meaning of the target word, try to think of its opposite, and then try to match up that possible opposite with a list of alternatives that often includes other obscure words, several tempting "distractors," and a "correct" answer that is only nearly, rather than exactly, its antonym.

Such questions become measures not just of vocabulary, but of test-taking strategy as well. Consider the first of the sample questions given above. Is the opposite of *rectitude* (A) deliberation; (B) laziness; (C) prejudice; (D) laxity of morals; or (E) weakness of intellect? According to the *American Heritage Dictionary*, *rectitude* has three meanings: "1. Moral uprightness 2. Rightness, as of intellectual judgment. 3. Straightness." Assuming for a moment that a student is fully familiar with these three definitions, which answer is she supposed to choose? Answers (D) and (E) seem to be "nearly opposite" to the *AHD* definitions 1 and 2, respectively. And then we have *laziness* and *prejudice*, which are pretty good symptoms of a lack of *rectitude;* rectitudinous folk are never lazy. And *prejudice* is a wonderfully effective "distractor," given the fact that in present usage *rectitude* usually connotes a kind of stuffy, righteous, hypocritical, covertly *prejudiced* attitude. Finally there is *deliberation*, which might sound like a perfectly respectable choice to a student sufficiently deprived of culture as to not know what *rectitude* means in the first place. But, of course, the key to the right answer is that the student know the meaning of another fairly rare word: *laxity.*

The sentence-completion item I have cited above illustrates, along with the general construction of such questions, the problem of cultural bias in some SAT items. The purpose in this section of the test is to check the student's ability to make correct fits of both sense and syntax into the available slots. But this sample question also tests the student's world view. The correct answer is (E): "From the first the islanders, despite an outward *acquiescence*, did what they could to *thwart* the ruthless occupying power." But one researcher noticed a curious pattern in the responses on this item. While white test-takers generally had little trouble with it, a disproportionately large number of minority students chose the "wrong" answer (D). These students had apparently failed to see the situation through the eyes of the "ruthless occupying power," and didn't automatically assume that the natives would dissemble. They preferred: "From the first the islanders, despite an outward *resistance*, did what they could to *destroy* the ruthless occupying power." The "occupying power" is putting up the resistance, despite which the islanders continue trying to destroy the occupiers.[19] Clearly this question is freighted with sociocultural assumptions (in such a situation, "natives" will grin and roll their eyes until they get a chance to stab you in the back) that one must share in order to demonstrate grammatical and lexical knowledge.

The analogy question included here, which, by the way, the *Chicago Tribune* called one of the "easy" questions on the test, illustrates the difficulty of choosing the "best" answer. While the "right" answer may seem fairly evident—*musicians* make up an *orchestra* just as *singers* make up a *choir*—the choice *crowd:protestors* seems equally logical, at least to me. *Singers,* when they act as a group, may form a *choir; musicians,* when they act as a group, may form an *orchestra;* and *protestors,* when they act as a group, may form a *crowd.* The similarity of subjects, in this case music, is a clue to the correct response.

But in many other SAT analogy questions, such subject-matter similarity is irrelevant to the comparison at hand—or is used to distract students from the correct answer. Consider:

AESTHETE:BEAUTY:: (A) enthusiast:cause (B) hunter:nature (C) administrator:government (D) advocate:legality (E) philanthropist:money

Here the only possible answer with somewhat overlapping content is (B), but the beauty of nature has nothing to do with the correct answer, (A). The underlying analogy concerns excessive dedication to an interest. Here is another:

BARREN:PRODUCTIVITY:: (A) torrid:warmth (B) innocuous:harm (C) aberrant:change (D) prodigal:reform (E) random:originality.

A student who was still back in the *choir:orchestra,* still looking for subject-matter connections, might be taken in by a line of thinking, for example: warmth—torrid—drought—barren. But the correct answer here is (B), and the relationship is essentially opposition—although it is effectively disguised by the use of the adjective-noun pairs. The skills which the successful student will show on these questions include: an extensive vocabulary, including a good awareness of connotations and secondary definitions; a willingness to forget each question once it has been answered and not look for any overall logic or continuity in the test; and the wit to do it all fast.

The reading passage questions that I have reproduced are, like the other three types, partially tests of vocabulary. In order to answer question 5 correctly, for example, the student must know the meaning of *admonitory*—or at least use the meanings of *condescending, humble, insipid,* and *inspiring* in order to eliminate them. But more important here is the test-taker's ability to determine what is "stated or implied" by the text at hand, mostly by judging the accuracy of short paraphrases and summaries. In its structure at least, this would appear to be the most searching, perhaps most meaningful assessment of the student's language skills (and potential for college-level work) among the four subtests offered.

But what a strange piece of writing this is, obviously concocted for the test and not taken from anywhere in the real world of prose. It begins in what must be to students a familiar, authorless, textbook style: "The behavioral sciences are making rapid strides in the understanding, prediction, and control of behavior." Then, in the second paragraph, the author abruptly decides to address the reader personally ("If your reaction is the same as mine") about how frightening all of this is. Since the preceding paragraph has given no specific examples of the problem at hand, the reader is probably not yet very scared. Next we get assertions that "troublemakers" might be "dealt with" or all of our "morale" manipulated, without any suggestion of what techniques might be used to accomplish these goals. Up to this point, we are apparently supposed to be afraid of the general malevolence of "behavioral science," which on many college campuses simply designates psychology, sociology, and other similarly benign disciplines.

Then there is a strange rhetorical shift in which the author briefly appears to reverse himself ("Some of you may point out . . . I agree with this point") in response to unasked questions from an unseen but oddly palpable audience. Returning to his original argument, the writer next claims that because scientists invented airplanes (which they in fact didn't) the general public now believes everything they say—an admirably compact distortion. Having revealed his single, half-relevant piece of mistaken evidence ("For instance, in 1900"), the author is happy to begin wrapping things up: "There is every reason to believe that the same sequence of events will occur in the behavioral sciences." This still-unspecified discipline promises to spiral "upward at an ever increasing rate" until its findings (whatever they are) "will be widely used tomorrow."

Many of the problems with this passage—its shifting authorial voice, its

awkward treatment of the audience, its utter lack of detail and conse-
quent reliance on flimsy generalities—make it sound more like an essay
written *by* a high school student than one designed to test him. I find it
moderately amusing that one of these flaws, "omitting supporting evidence," is listed as a possible (and wrong) answer to question 8: "The author recognizes that some readers may accuse him of . . . "

While the ETS has a perfect right to measure students' understanding
of poor writing (this may in fact be a good predictor of success in reading
some introductory college textbooks), the inclusion of such odd passages
does cloud the issue. A sophisticated student, for example, might decide
on question 5 that the tone of this passage is just as *insipid* (incorrect) as
it is *admonitory* (correct). And the test-taker looking, as instructed, for
implications in the essay might decide on question 7 that the author's
implied point is that "Research in the behavioral sciences should be re-
evaluated and curtailed," and not just the insipid "The findings of the behavioral sciences have potentially harmful implications." In spite of these
quibbles, however, the reading passages are clearly the best of the four
subtests, at least in the sense that they try to measure language skill in
some kind of context, some kind of nearly actual use, rather than in artificial, game-like exercises.

Do any of these kinds of questions yield an accurate or appropriate or
meaningful appraisal of language skill? Perhaps in a gross way they do. A
student who scores 750 on the SAT verbal is probably more facile with
standard English than one who scores 250. In order to score well, one
simply must speak the standard dialect, be a close, critical reader, know a
great many words, and be able to discriminate quickly among varying,
often trivial, semantic relationships. The SAT is certainly a superb measure of the student's ability to cope with timed multiple-choice tests. This
may be a tautology, but it could be a useful one when beginning college
students are required to take just such tests in general psychology,
introduction to political science, Western civilization, or, God help us,
freshman English. Nevertheless, the information which these test scores
purport to offer about language is sufficiently doubtful, and the results so
thoroughly conditioned by the individual's ability to cope with the mentality of the test itself, that small score differences—on the order of 150 or
250 points—are probably not a reliable indicator of what a student knows
about, or can do with, the English language.

Even if we suspect that the SAT is a crude and highly discriminatory
measure of the language skills of seventeen-year-olds, we are still perfectly
free to wonder why average scores on this overly respected test have been
declining for two decades. Such wondering, in fact, has already been done

quite thoroughly by a blue-ribbon panel of experts appointed by the College Entrance Examination Board and the Educational Testing Service. In 1978, this body released its findings in a pamphlet called: *On Further Examination: Report of the Advisory Panel on the Scholastic Aptitude Test Score Decline*. The earliest sections of the report offered some interesting and persuasive explanations of the slippage, which the panel believed to have occurred in two distinct stages. The drop between 1963 and 1970 was attributed by the commission primarily to the dramatic changes in the population taking the tests during this period. Not only did the number of test-takers triple in the 1960s, but "traditionally low-scoring groups" —blacks, other ethnic minorities, women—were increasingly represented in the pool, reducing the average scores. The nice thing about this early section of the report is that it is based upon some facts: statistics about how many students of what kinds of backgrounds took the SATs during one year as compared with another, and so on. The panel's interpretation of all this data leaves only about one-half of the score decline unaccounted for. In other words, the panel's remaining job is to explain why test-takers in the late 1970s missed three or four questions that their 1963 predecessors had answered correctly.[20]

Unfortunately, this other half of the score decline—the part which occurred between 1970 and 1977—presented the commission with a puzzle clearly beyond its ability to solve. The panelists confessed that they could not figure out why scores had continued to decline after the population of test-takers stabilized. But even more unfortunately, the commissioners' taste for conjecture was not in the least inhibited by their lack of information. The report went bravely on to speculate about six "pervasive" factors that *might* have sustained the decline: (1) changes in high school courses of study; (2) changes in learning standards in school and society; (3) changes in the role of the family in the teaching and learning process; (4) television; (5) recent disruptive events in the life of the nation; and (6) various motivational developments.[21]

These alleged causes, of course, were already familiar to everyone who had read the dozens of newspaper and magazine commentaries on the SAT crisis, and the panel's willingness to reiterate them shed little additional light on the problem. In fact, the undisciplined contents of this long-awaited report simply gave rise to another round of shrill and inaccurate press reports and editorials which were, predictably, even less helpful than the report itself. The *Chicago Daily News*, for example, boiled down the panel's explanations into this headline: "Studies KO'd by TV; Kids Down for Count." Under the subhead, "Test Score Decline Explained," the story's lead ran: "Television is winning the battle over homework in American homes ... And the growth of two-income families is making it more difficult for parents to limit TV-watching by their youngsters. This has been singled out as a major reason for declining test scores among college bound students." Not until the seventh paragraph do we hear anything about the one certain and single largest cause identified by the panel—the changing pool of test-takers—but this central factor is simply listed in a series of "other" causes including "wars, assassinations, riots, and political corruption." Along about the thirteenth paragraph, more is revealed about the demographic factors, but it is far too late to erase the impression that TV is the main culprit.[22]

The panel's sponsors and funders hardly seemed troubled by the media's sometimes ludicrous distortions of the report. A few weeks after its release, the ETS mailed out a handsome flyer announcing that the report was available (84 pages, $4.00), and employing a backdrop of newspaper clippings ("Our Failing Schools" and so on) to highlight the legend: "*On Further Examination* Makes the News!" And, to be fair to the now-deceased *Daily News*, I should note that the panel report, for all of its claims of objectivity, tentativeness, and scrupulous methodology, abounded in just the kind of seductive exaggerations and random prejudices which make for juicy copy.

In its introduction, the panel casually announced that many American students had "barely a speaking acquaintance with the English language and no writing facility at all." Later, it described a slice of life in the average American home: "Children come home from school, without homework, to sit passively hour after hour and day after day in front of television sets." The sinister box, noted the report, is not just over-popular with children—it is "surrogate parent, substitute teacher." Today's kids do not simply need help with learning to write, they suffer from "juvenile writing delinquency." Their teachers, "who used to train students to write, now advise them about the advantages of using soft tip pens and pencils" instead. Practically every contemporary social phenomenon, arrangement, or trend comes in for blame in the report. Working mothers (meaning more than half the mothers in America) are accused of eroding SAT scores, as are single-parent families and deserting fathers. Former President Nixon is awarded a share of the responsibility, as is the Vietnam War and our continuing series of political assassinations. The panel's meandering but all-embracing speculations also indict cowardly teachers, irresponsible principals, uninvolved parents, large families, sexism, absenteeism, "corridor crime," grade inflation, automatic promotion of students, multiple choice tests [sic], boredom, drugs, the pill, and textbooks with big pictures. This tangle of explanations, which are really only guesses, is quite evidently too broad and unfocused to have any explanatory power at all.[23]

But if the panel is startlingly promiscuous in its embrace of causes for the score decline, one particularly tempting possibility—the test itself—is promptly and firmly excluded from consideration. The report explains that the ETS staff has been *very* careful to be sure that no changes in the test could possibly affect score averages and that there are several truckloads of persuasive in-house studies available for perusal by anyone silly enough to question the test-makers. It is made clear that to blame the tests for the decline is simply to indulge in the old "kill the messenger who brings the bad news" gambit. But ETS is no mere messenger, unless we define a messenger as one who largely decides what the form and content of the message will be. And while the ETSs emphasis has been on proving that it has *prevented* alterations in the tests, the fact that considerable changes have recently occurred in the English curriculum (to be taken up again in chapter 9) suggests that perhaps the tests *should* have been changed. In other words, it seems altogether possible that over the past twenty years the content and language of the SATs may have increasingly lagged behind the subject matter actually being studied by its takers, as well as departing further and further from the standards of educated language actually being used in school and society.[24]

But back to the panel's hunt for causes. The report does note that changes in school programs may have had some effect on the test scores. In this connection, the panel refers mainly to the development of elective English courses in the high schools, which have in many cases replaced the traditional, test-oriented grammar and literature programs most college-bound students took in the early 1960s. The panel's ill-concealed disapproval of this development at least does not descend to the usual scholarlier-than-thou name-calling about the wanton substitution of Science Fiction for Shakespeare or Media for Milton.

Anyone who has been an English teacher, or has worked with teachers, during the past fifteen years, knows that the focus of high school courses has indeed shifted considerably. Formal grammar is no longer emphasized in many classrooms, and many students now choose from a range of alternative courses, some of which may altogether ignore the skills necessary for success on the SATs. In chapter 9 I will try to show why this has happened and how it may reflect something other than spinelessness on the part of English teachers. But for now, it is enough to say that college-bound students no longer take (as I did in the early 1960s) one course after another designed to teach the meaning of *aesthete, dilettante, emanation, espouse, commensurate,* and *panegyric.*

But there has been an even more revealing—and more reliably measurable—development in high school English programs which appears to
have a rather obvious connection with the decline in SAT scores. Today's
graduate has, on average, taken a lot less English of *any* kind than
graduates of fifteen years ago. Enrollments in high school English courses
have dropped by at least 11 percent nationally, according to the most
thorough study of this subject— and there are strong indications that the
actual enrollment decline may be twice as great.[25] Many high schools
which used to require four full years of English have lowered the requirement to three years—which, as we have already seen, might consist of six
semester elective courses, few of which have high SAT scores as their
primary "instructional objective." Given this rather sudden change in the
kind and amount of language study pursued by adolescents, it seems
remarkable that SAT scores have dropped as little as they have. But wait.
We must remember that the SATs are supposed to be invulnerable to such
trivial influences as high school course offerings, since they purportedly
measure a "lifetime" of language learning. Why, then, does the panel
itself mention this enrollment change as a possible cause of the score
decline? Probably the SAT is not nearly so much an "aptitude test" as its
title insists, and even the advisory panel recognizes this fact.

I don't happen to believe that the decline in high school English enrollments is the only cause of the SAT decline. Another fundamental "problem" might even be that today's kids are *not* stupid. They know perfectly
well that the college admissions picture has changed and that low SAT
scores will not prevent most of them from attending college. The pressure,
in other words, is off. You don't really need to bone up in your classes, in
guide books, in cram courses. When you arrive on that once-fateful Saturday morning to face the examiners (DO NOT BREAK THE SEAL UNTIL
YOU ARE INSTRUCTED TO DO SO) you don't have to take the whole
business as seriously as the previous generation did. Scores may have
dropped not only because of this more lackadaisical (and realistic) attitude
toward the test-taking situation, but also because of a rather specific
interaction between this attitude and the test itself. The SAT is what
educators call a "speed test," and anyone who has taken it knows what
that means. You get *exactly* twenty minutes to work on this section, thirty-
five minutes for that one—and if you happen to get done early you read:
"STOP! DO NOT GO ON TO THE NEXT PAGE." On such a speed test
it is vital to work as quickly as you can, answering every question you can
handle. And, as most test-takers in the glory days of the SATs knew, you
should also guess at every question you can't anwer with certainty.

But here comes Joe Doakes, the 1983-model high school senior, knowing perfectly well that he can still go to Millard Fillmore Community College even if he really muffs the test. If Joe happens to have been a fairly good student in school *and* his parents can afford to pay his full tuition, he also knows that he can walk into all but a handful of selective private colleges *whatever* his SAT scores turn out to be. But also floating around in Joe's head may be some questions about the value of going to college at all. While his counterpart in 1963 accurately saw college as the gateway to a high paying, respect-earning job, Joe knows that a mere sheepskin no longer guarantees such benefits. Today, plenty of college graduates are looking for work or working cheaply, and perhaps Joe wonders about his own prospects. With all this information in mind, Joe breaks the seal of the SAT test booklet. To be sure, once that seal is broken he works hard—he tries to answer the questions and move along promptly. Still, he probably doesn't attack the test with quite the fervor and careful pacing of the 1963 teenager, and he is probably a lot less likely to bother with guessing. In fact, Joe may be even more prone to being distracted by a question—he may spend more than his fifty-five-second allotment wondering, "Now what the hell does *gelid* mean? I know I saw that someplace. Jello?"

All told, Joe doesn't really have to behave much differently from his higher scoring predecessors to help drag the average score down. All he has to do is miss three or four extra questions. A couple of these questions he will miss because of the fourth English course he didn't take, or because of the year he spent studying Heinlein instead of Hamlet. The other couple of questions he may miss because he goes at the test less demonically, neglects to make those last few desperate guesses, or fails to suppress his anger over the intentionally confusing answer choices. The final results of all this won't necessarily mean that Joe and his contemporaries are dim. On the contrary, their lower scores may reflect (among other things) a solid understanding of the realities of college entrance testing in a buyer's market, when the students are buying and the colleges are selling.

Although the SAT score decline actually looks, on further examination, to provide only trivial information about some language skills of one-quarter of our high school seniors, we have been asked to view it as a linguistic and educational tragedy of the first order. Never mind the warnings of the test-makers themselves (half-hearted, to be sure) that the SATs do not measure the "scholastic aptitude" of all seniors, the state of the English language, the performance of particular high schools or the condition of American education in general. Managers of the media know that crisis sells, gloom sizzles. Never mind the steady rise in reading achievement at all grade levels since such data has been collected. Disregard the studies which show that the good old days weren't invariably better than the present.[26]

Forget to mention, for example, the 1976 experiment in which Indiana sixth graders were given the same reading test that had been administered to similar sixth graders in 1944, and were found to score higher on every subskill measured, as well as on the total score.[27] Omit, while you are at it, the Ohio study which compared modern twelve-year-olds with children in 1917, and found today's students to be significantly better readers.[28] Skip the report that showed Iowa third graders to be "dramatically" better at reading than their counterparts in 1940.[29] And please don't bring up the experiment in which the reading, writing, and arithmetic skills of California tenth graders were tested against those of a group of adults (half of whom had college degrees) and the kids outperformed the grownups on every skill.[30]

And let's just keep the lid on the contradictory evidence even ETS has produced. During the whole period of SAT declines studied by the panel, the Achievement Tests given to some college-bound students, which measure actual learning in particular school subjects, have stayed even overall. And those "norming tests." What a can of worms they are. You go out and give an SAT-like test to a cross section of *all* high school juniors to provide a basis for scoring the real SATs, and what do you find? No drop-off at all. Think of all the uncomfortable questions *that* could raise: Do juniors know more than seniors? Does including non-college-bound students in the testing population drag the average *up*? Are the wrong people going to college? No, better we just go easy on all those statistics.[31]

As I have said earlier, I am not much of a conspiracy buff, and doubt that anyone in Princeton, New Jersey, or anywhere else has sat down and thought about test results in the way I've just impersonated. But we do seem to rather consistently ignore the substantial body of reassuring, or at least unfrightening, information about the state of American education and the degree of its success. The preference for "hot copy" apparently afflicts not just the news media but the faculty lounge, the PTA, and the public at large.

Probably the most interesting and useful sets of test data paralleling the SAT decline are the student writing tests conducted by the National Assessment of Educational Progress between 1969 and 1979. This long-term research effort of the Education Commission of the States has sampled the compositions of nine-, thirteen- and seventeen-year-olds at staggered intervals for a decade. Unlike ETS, NAEP tried to measure the applied language skills of students by collecting and scoring actual samples of their writing, rather than by subjecting them to sets of isolated multiple-choice questions with doubtful connections to real language use. High school students, for example, wrote on five different kinds of topics (descriptive, narrative, persuasive, explanatory, and expressive) over the course of the ten-year study. Their writing samples were subsequently evaluated in several ways: for general effectiveness; for rhetorical skill; for coherence and cohesion; and for grammar, spelling, punctuation, and other mechanics. The scores reported from NAEP's comprehensive study of student writing do not plot the same steep downward course as the SAT scores. In fact, the results show a remarkable stability in writing ability, with upward and downward fluctuations that the NAEP staff calls "undramatic." The NAEP writing tests are complex and their findings occasionally ambiguous, but for all their shortcomings, they tell us much more about the language skills of American schoolchildren than the SATs.

The National Assessment first came to wide public attention in 1974, when it released the results of its second assessment of student writing. The baseline assessment in 1969 had generated little publicity, since there was nothing with which to compare its results. But the 1974 scores showed some declines. Thirteen-and seventeen-year-olds, for example, wrote more awkward, simple, and incoherent sentences than their counterparts in 1969. The assessment staff noted that, as a whole, the writing of these older students had shown "an overall decline between 1969 and 1974." On the other hand, the writing ability of nine-year-olds had improved, and "the vast majority" of students at all ages, according to NAEP, handled the mechanics of writing—grammar, spelling, and punctuation—adequately on both assessments; no age group had shown an appreciable deterioration in this aspect of writing.[32]

These results, although not entirely negative, engendered a wave of worried press reports which neatly dovetailed with the concurrent concern about the SAT decline. The tenor of these interpretations ranged from the *New York Times's* sober article, "Writing Ability Found Slipping," to the more typical renderings by the *Chicago Sun-Times* ("U.S. Education on the Skids") and the *Los Angeles Times* ("Three R's Take a Beating"). Most extreme was the cover story printed by *Newsweek* in its December 9, 1975, issue. "Why Johnny Can't Write" used the NAEP results (as well as the SAT decline and the testimony of various experts) to buttress its contention that "willy-nilly, the U.S. educational system is spawning a generation of semi-literates." Not satisfied merely to quote the parts of the NAEP assessment that actually were negative, *Newsweek* heaped on summaries of findings the testing had *not* discovered: "It [NAEP] found that 9-year-olds showed almost no mastery of basic writing mechanics." *Newsweek* called the writing problem an example of cultural "rot" and endorsed the notion that, in the words of National Endowment for the Humanities chairman Ronald Berman, it signaled "a massive regression toward the intellectually invertebrate." Dire consequences threatened if things proceeded along the current path, *Newsweek* warned: human communication might not even "remain decipherable" when we "find ourselves back in Babel."[33]

Television, the all-purpose whipping boy of the print media, naturally came in for much of *Newsweek's* wrath, delivered by such impressive surrogates as E. B. White and Jacques Barzun (White said that the only cure for bad writing was "throwing away all the television sets").[34] But then *Newsweek* could have gotten the television notion from NAEP itself, which had speculated in its own report that some of the observed changes in student writing—the increased use of run-on sentences and sentence fragments, for example—might have reflected the influence of television. One NAEP consultant, in fact, had noted: "What worries me, and what I think ought to worry all of us who are concerned about communication, is the strong evidence in the NAEP survey that coherence is changing ... evaporating perhaps. There apparently has been a decline in the ability to develop ideas."[35] Given such gloomy interpretations from the test-makers not to mention the gloomier reports from the news media, the NAEP writing assessments predictably took their place alongside the SAT decline as co-cornerstone of the late-1970s literacy crisis.

But then something embarrassing happened. In the next round of tests, many of the measures of student writing ability went right back up—to or above the levels of the first assessment in 1969. Even the measure of coherence and cohesion among seventeen-year-olds, which had knitted more expert brows than any other single finding, reached an all-time high in the 1979 tests. What had been confidently identified in 1974 as "a massive regression toward the intellectually invertebrate" had suddenly developed some spine; whatever had "evaporated" five years earlier was now reprecipitating; that revolting pile of cultural "rot" was smelling a little sweeter; the insidious influence of television (though kids still watched it) was mysteriously on the wane; and Babel, instead of being just around the corner, turned out to be a bit further down the street, or maybe somewhere in the next county. Reviewing its data for the entire decade of testing, NAEP concluded that "changes in overall writing quality are basically undramatic for any particular age group" and it urged "caution in making global statements about writing." The popular press, seeing no potential headlines or cover stories in this mild summary of the once-dreaded "writing crisis," accorded the 1979 assessment only a fraction of the coverage devoted to the score patterns of 1974.[36]

Looking back at the infamous 1974 assessments (an exercise which few public commentators have bothered with), one finds that few of the downward changes so widely bewailed had even been statistically significant—meaning that NAEP was never able to say with 95 percent certainty that *anything* had actually changed. The writing samples of high school students provide a good case in point. The comparisons made between 1969 and 1974 concerned six major sets of scores. Although four went down and two stayed even, only two of these changes were statistically significant: the drop in narrative writing and the decline in paragraph coherence. For the longer period 1969–1979, on these same six tests, three went up, one went down, and two stayed even—and the only two significant changes were improvements. One of the significant improvements over the whole decade occurred in narrative writing skill, a measure that had actually shown a significant decline between 1969 and 1974. Paragraph coherence, which showed the only other significant drop in 1974, improved overall for the decade. The overwhelming reminder of all these figures is that writing skill seems to change very little over long periods of time.[37]

Still, there does appear to have been a modest rebound in the scores of high school students between 1974 and 1979 (a period during which, as we know, SATs continued to fall). Either this rise in writing scores reflects meaningless fluctuation caused by the assessment's inherent errors of measurement—which is entirely possible—or else some change in the schools may have caused students' writing to improve slightly. Looking back over the fuss over the 1974 results, it is certainly tempting to think that teachers simply buckled down in response to all the pressure and began to teach writing better. But there are some problems with this explanation. In the first place, if writing is indeed a complex skill, deeply embedded in a student's whole lifetime of language-learning, we would not expect to see the oldest students benefiting much from improved or increased instruction in the last few years of their schooling. These students would presumably have a weak foundation upon which to build, and would have developed the kinds of bad habits and negative attitudes about writing that make remediation an uphill struggle. Even less would we expect to see such instruction (if it did occur) affecting cohesion and coherence, which are among the most sophisticated and hardest to teach of writing skills. As NAEP points out, these skills require "a thorough program with considerable writing, diagnosis, modelling, and as much attention to the deep structure as to the surface features of student writing." Such instruction, according to NAEP, is presently being offered to only about 7 percent of high school students.[38]

Perhaps most confounding of all, NAEP studies show that teachers in 1979 were actually assigning *less* writing than they did in the precrisis days of 1974. In fact, the majority of high school students still write a paper no more frequently than once every two weeks—in all of their subjects combined—and nearly a quarter write only once every six weeks. In spite of the call for more remedial writing courses in the high schools, there was only a tiny increase in enrollments (1.9 percent) between 1974 and 1979. Nor has the average student volunteered or been pressured to take extra writing courses in school: in 1974, 26 percent of nonremedial students elected an additional writing course; in 1979, only 24 percent did so.[39]

On the other hand, NAEP did find that teachers were spending more classroom time on writing and that they were more scrupulously marking students' papers. While it is encouraging to hear that teachers are spending more time on composition, the fact that no more actual writing is being done makes one wonder exactly how that increased classroom time is being spent. The NAEP results imply that much of this extra time is being devoted to the consideration, if not the actual drafting, of narrative (that is, "creative") writing, since this kind of writing showed by far the greatest growth between 1974 and 1979.[40] But creative writing is, if anything, being downplayed and discouraged in most high schools. During the flap over the 1974 scores, teachers were roundly criticized for assigning *too much* creative writing, too many personal, undisciplined, gee-this-makes-me-feel-good stories. Teachers were warned, in effect, to dispense with such frivolity and get down to the presumably more serious kinds of writing.

My own experience with writing teachers in several dozen schools suggests that teachers are spending this increased instructional time in tremendously varied ways: some are indeed bucking the trends and assigning much personal, creative writing; others are trying to teach their students certain models and structures and formulas for different kinds of writing; and many are giving extra drills on punctuation, grammar, usage, and spelling. Almost all teachers, whatever else they may be doing, are indeed more diligent in the marking of student papers, though *how* they mark them varies considerably. While a greater number of corrections sometimes reflects an intensified attempt to instruct, it often results mainly from the teacher's fear of being upbraided by crisis-conscious parents or principals for failing to circle every error in each home-bound piece of student writing. In sum, the assorted information about teaching practices, both from NAEP background studies and from the observation of working teachers, presents an inconclusive picture. Some things may have changed in English classes—a little more emphasis here, a few more drills there, a little less of that—but in general, writing instruction, like the writing performance of students, remains about the same.

The NAEP writing assessment results, along with their ancillary data and interpretations, provide a useful contrast with the SAT scores. The ETS statistics suggest a continuing decline in the language skills of American seventeen-year-olds; NAEP finds overall stability. These tests differ in just two essential respects. NAEP examines the actual language skill of writing, whereas ETS uses multiple-choice questions to probe "verbal scholastic aptitude." And NAEP has tested a cross-section of all high school students, while the SATs sample only a fraction of the college-bound. If we—and *Newsweek* and the rest of the media—are in the market for a barometer of students' language skills and the general performance of the schools, then the NAEP tests would seem to be the better indicator. Of course, it is also helpful if we report and discuss the results of *any* such test with a modicum of skepticism and restraint. Massive regressions toward the intellectually invertebrate are really quite rare, and we should guard against announcing devolution every time school kids write a few extra sentence fragments.

Obviously, I could go on for many pages reviewing statistics and percentages which purport to reveal either the failures or the successes of American public education. There is indeed a large body of data showing that the performance of high school students has deteriorated in certain subjects over the past few decades. But the population of the high schools has also changed and nationwide efforts at dropout prevention have kept more low-achieving teenagers in school. Nevertheless, the performance of the 80 percent of American teenagers who finish high school compares favorably with the much smaller percentage of European students who are offered the same sort of secondary schooling.[41] About all that any such arguments would show, finally, is that any realistic appraisal of American public education yields mixed results: neither a portrait of wholesale failure nor a saga of unending triumph, but a hodgepodge of successes, failures, puzzles, anomalies, quirks, and mysteries. Given all of the information available to us, we have no compelling reason for either complacency or panic. But, of course, panic is what we have had. And to a very large extent, that panic has originated in the grotesquely mistaken use of the SAT scores as our primary measure of educational achievement.

Questions remain, needless to say, about the powers and responsibilities of the testers themselves. It is only fair to point out that the recent crisis in test scores has been a real boon to the test-makers, in spite of their coy, occasional cautions that the rest of us shouldn't make too much out of it. ETS, for example, is in the curious position of having uncovered a decline in academic skills for which it believes it happens to have the cure: more tests. Bad test scores, in other words, if they sufficiently arouse educators and the public, can only result in demands for further, more detailed testing—to check up, naturally, on whether the previously revealed deficiencies are being effectively remediated. Nor does the ETS sit quietly by waiting to see if someone will ask them to make up and administer such additional tests. On the contrary, there is a constant, on-going effort in Princeton to create markets for new tests, to devise them, to promote them, and to sell them. While one arm of ETS is issuing sober, scholarly qualifications about the generalizability of test score results, another apparently more robust appendage of the company is out churning up new business.

Sometimes these two subsidiaries join forces, with ludicrously transparent results. Among ETS's recurrent publications is a journal called *FOCUS*, which the company describes as a "series of occasional papers," each of which discusses "a critical aspect of education today and the work the Educational Testing Service is doing to cope with it." The masthead downplays the organization's testing activities, noting instead that ETS is "the nation's largest nonprofit educational research organization" and that its "2,000 staffers apply the tools of the social sciences to the problems of minority students, school finance, access to higher education, human development, occupational certification, and a host of other areas that demand attention."[42]

The 1978 edition of this journal opens with an editor's note announcing: "FOCUS 5 describes efforts to improve students' and others'—command of an ability that is among the most difficult to master yet essential to a highly complex society—writing." The issue does indeed begin in the detached and erudite tone which all of these noble pledges would predict, with bows to James Thurber and E. B. White. But then it goes on to confide that there are signs of a "writing crisis" about, signs like the decline in SAT scores; "Although these scores say nothing directly about writing ability, they do reflect students' facility with language, which is fundamental to writing." Undeterred by his own admission that the SAT is not directly relevant, the unnamed author promptly and confidently enumerates the causes of the "writing crisis." Students at Berkeley, the City Colleges of New York, Harvard, Yale, Cornell, and Brown are writing poorly and being forced to take more English classes. The Council for Basic Education (surprise!) is deeply concerned. "Television debases the language." Politicians obfuscate. Advertising language "short-circuits rational thought." "Many a self-serving profession uses jargon to exaggerate its claims of special knowledge." Instead of composition, our schools are teaching "film criticism, journalism, theater, and what have you." The only writing today's teachers assign is "uninhibited free form" prose, which is "heedless of conventional grammar" and amounts to nothing more than "self-gratification." Even if all this is merely an intemperate rehash of the ETS panel report on the SAT score declines, at least we get an idea, over the magazine's first six pages, of what the writing problem looks like when viewed from Princeton, New Jersey. But what about the other part of the editor's pledge—the promise to describe "efforts to improve.... writing," the things that those 2,000 helpful ETS staffers have to offer?[43]

Not surprisingly, what *FOCUS* 5 has to offer, over the last nine of its sixteen pages, is a series of advertisements for various writing *tests* invented by and available for purchase from the Educational Testing Service. Students can't write? Give them a test. Want to use a writing sample? No problem, we can score 85,000 papers in a week. Want a multiple choice writing test? You should see the one we did for the California State University and College system. Want to place your freshmen in different levels of writing classes? Try our brand-new battery called the "Descriptive Tests of Language Skills." Need a minimum competency test in reading, writing, and/or math for your whole *state?* How about our "Basic Skills Assessment" program? (I love the parenthesis which appears here: "See FOCUS 4, Learning to Read.") Or do you just want to join with the rest of us and be concerned about the deterioration of writing? Send your inquiries to the new ETS concern center called "Programs for the Assessment of Writing."[44]

Am I implying that the ETS is intentionally exploiting the results of its own tests to expand the market for others and ultimately to make more money? Certainly. But, one might object, ETS is a "nonprofit educational research organization." It certainly is, and a quite profitable one at that. Last year ETS made a profit of more than 10 percent on its SAT testing program, funds that it plowed right back into the development of more tests and the dissemination of self-serving literature like *FOCUS*. As Alan Nairn has shown in his book *The Reign of ETS: The Corporation That Makes Up Minds*, ETS operates like any other large corporation in most ways, and consequently one of its main goals is its own growth. The altogether staggering success of ETS in this effort deserves scrutiny—and soon, because this utterly unregulated agency is rapidly taking over control of entry into scores of schools and occupations in America and around the world. Today, if you want to be a policeman or a fireman in Philadelphia; if you want to sell insurance in Illinois; if you want to get your high school diploma as an adult; if you want to study for a Ph. D. in

English, French, history, sociology, psychology, art, geography, Italian, political science, Spanish, or linguistics; if you want to receive a college scholarship from Union Carbide, the Brotherhood of Steamfitters, the Lutheran Church, Getty Oil, Minnesota Mining and Manufacturing, Sunshine Biscuits, or the states of Kansas, California, Maryland, New Jersey, or Georgia; if you want any of the $12,000,000 of National Merit Scholarship money; if you want to go to Andover, Groton, the Dhahran Aramco School, or any of 450 other exclusive preparatory schools around the world; if you want to be a school teacher in Chicago, New York, Boston, Los Angeles, or rural Louisisana; if you want to attend the Institut pour l'Étude des Méthodes de Direction de l'Enterprise in Switzerland or the University of Petroleum and Minerals in Saudi Arabia; if you want to become an officer in the Liberian merchant marine; if you want to advance into certain specialties in auto mechanics, beauty care, or gynecology; if you want to go to any American law school or practice law in any of forty-two states; if you want to attend high school in Trinidad; if you want to do any of these things, you will have to take an ETS test. A test which is probably just as trustworthy as the SAT.[45]

Here is one example of the problem which this awesome list represents. My wife has recently been tutoring a thirty-seven-year-old man who works as a respiration therapist in a large hospital near Chicago. About twelve years ago he took the standard college course given to respiratory therapists, received his degree, and found a job, which he has held ever since. He is supporting a wife and five children. His evaluations from supervisors at work have always been good, so good that he was promoted to be the supervisor of the ten other respiratory therapists in his department. He knows his business well—knows how to take care of patients with breathing problems, and he is justifiably proud of his clinical expertise. Now however, in order to protect his job, this man must take an ETS test to become a "registered" respiratory therapist. The pressure is on at the hospital for all staff to be registered; those who do not become registered will be dismissed. This man has now taken the test four times and has failed it four times. He is trying to figure out a way to pass the test, but right now his reading skill is simply too weak for him to cope with the intricately tangled multiple choices on the test forms. Since he is willing to study, read, and find himself a tutor, and since scores on all ETS tests improve with cramming, he may eventually pass. Or, the test may win, and he will eventually lose his job.

Now, I know nothing about respiration therapy and cannot begin to judge whether this particular ETS test is a good predictor of clinical performance—which, it seems to me, is the only valid thing for a test of this kind to try to measure. But it does make me wonder. Is this test better than rolling dice? How much better? What is the significance of inflicting this test on someone with a decade of highly successful clinical practice? And how exactly does this test reflect the professed concern of ETS for "human development" and opportunities for members of minority groups, when it threatens, either through its own errors of measurement, cultural bias, or sheer stupidity, to cost a competent, experienced black breadwinner his job?

7

Jive

In the first six chapters of this book I have tried to give a general summary of contemporary language criticism: to review the assorted arguments, accusations, and fears; to describe the historical tradition of which the critics' gloomy predictions are a part; to contrast the critics' assumptions about language with the findings of linguistic research; to show how meager, contradictory, and trivial much of the evidence of deterioration is; and to review some of the critics' more idiosyncratic and mean-spirited prescriptions. The cumulative impact of these efforts, I hope, has been both reassurance and skepticism: reassurance that the English language is surviving, and will continue to survive, all manner of changes, deviations, and apparent assaults; and skepticism about the thinking of those who, despite abundant evidence to the contrary, continue to insist that a crisis does exist.

The rest of the book is concerned with three issues involving American English—black dialects, political propaganda, and the teaching of writing—which, unlike the "crisis" itself, are real, substantive, and important. Each of these problems has, of course, been mentioned amid the general furor over the "death of English" and the "decline of standards." But none of them, so far as I can discover, has received from any language critic the detailed, balanced consideration it deserves. I'll begin, in each case, by reviewing the ways in which these issues are ordinarily discussed, and go on, hopefully (full of hope), to offer some alternative views.

All of the language critics, whatever their peculiar specialties may be, have at one time or another taken a whack at the language of black Americans—what one professor-critic catchily dubbed "the shuffling speech of slavery."[1] For it is in the recent controversy over Black English (BE) that all of the critics' concerns about standards, authority, democratization, and permissiveness collide in a grinding, unsightly, but apparently irresistible mess. The fundamental problem, the critics contend, is not just that so many black people speak incorrectly, but that in this age of malignant egalitarianism, the black style of speech has come to be accepted—even admired or adopted—by people who should know better.

Richard Mitchell's summary of the problem is direct and typical. "It is only sentimental populism," he argues, "that can pronounce Black English a language just as rich and useful as standard Anglo-American or any other tongue." Black English, Mitchell explains, is not really a language at all but a mere collection of slang which does not show "the same linguistic complexity" as a true language. People who speak such nonstandard dialects "don't think at all. To think, we must devise connected chains of predications, which, in turn, require fluency in language. Those who are fluent in no language just don't have the means for thinking about things. They may remember and recite whatever predictions experience provides them, but they cannot manipulate them and derive new ones." It follows, then, that Black English "will not serve us when we want to explain or understand the rationalistic epistemology that informs constitutional democracy or how birds fly."[2]

But what *is* Black English, if it is not a real language? Mitchell allows that it is "the private talk of the oppressed" and that it "provides countless words and expressions with sexual meanings." It can sometimes be "jaunty and rambunctious and pleasing to the ear. Its metaphors can be subtle and penetrating, and its blithe disregard for standard grammatical forms is as crafty as it is cocky." This rambunctious little nonlanguage does have its uses for ghetto folk, whose lives Mitchell outlines:

Every year, without fail, they will consume just so much junk, just so many TV dinners, and just so many pay-by-the-week burial expense insurance policies. They will invest a predictable proportion of what little they have in lottery tickets and patent medicines.... They will support prodigiously the enormous illegal drug industry and contribute vast sums all along the line to the people who profit from it, very few of whom are to be seen in the streets of the ghettos. They will buy couches and lamps and refrigerators of the sleaziest quality on the never never plan at fantastic rates of interest.

The language which such people use, however jaunty it may be, is still only a grab bag of synonyms that lacks the "fine distinctions" of standard English.[3]

Mitchell is convinced, in fact, that the whole idea of Black English itself—with the capital letters implicitly legitimizing a separate dialect—is a fraud which amounts to "a vaccine against black literacy." This "gimmick," he warns, may prevent black children from learning to read and write "for decades and perhaps forever." He attacks those irresponsible educators who lack the spine to hold minority children to the standards of correct English, and instead flatter them by applauding their degraded speech patterns. This kind of pandering—allowing Black English to be spoken and accepted in schools—Mitchell insists, is "a concept about as sensible as Black Arithmetic or Black Botany."[4]

But here Mitchell parts company with some of the other critics of Black English. For he believes that the failure to teach standard English to black students results from a conspiracy among the white teachers and social workers who profit from the poverty and ignorance of their clients. If black students learned standard English, Mitchell explains, they would then be "capable of logical thought." Then the white parasites would be out of work, and the society would have to deal with a sudden infusion of fluent thinkers: "You think *they're* going to buy those lottery tickets and lamps in the shape of Porky Pig?" Not for a moment retreating from his conspiracy theory, Mitchell concludes: "When we look around the country and see that schoolchildren are more ignorant that ever, and that black schoolchildren are ordinarily the most ignorant, we are inclined to think that something has failed. That is a naive conclusion. In fact, something has succeeded."[5]

John Simon's view of Black English is essentially parallel to Mitchell's. He acknowledges that most linguists have asserted ("in their democratic, egalitarian frenzy") that all dialects are equally good. But, Simon argues, while the structures of nonstandard dialects "may indeed be comprehensible, they go against all accepted classical and modern grammars and are the product not of a language with roots in history but of ignorance of how language works. It may be a regrettable ignorance, innocent and touching, one that unjust past social conditions cruelly imposed on people. But it *is* ignorance, and bowing down to it, accepting it as correct and perhaps even better than established usage, is not going to help matters. On the

contrary, that way lies chaos." Simon complains that the defenders of
Black English, when faced with attacks like his, invariably drag out "that
bugbear of the gutter radicals, the three-headed monster Snob-Elitist-
Racist." He is not intimidated by such labels. Not only must we continue
to use language as a measure of the individual's "fastidiousness," but we
must also maintain our link with the "giants of the English tongue who
preceded us.... We do not wish to dissociate ourselves from them, lose
familiarity with their mode of utterance on account of ignorant,
misguided, or merely lazy creatures for whom making distinctions is an
unnecessary effort."⁶

Unlike most of the other critics, Simon at least offers some program for
the salvation of substandard speakers. Propriety, he reasons, begins at
home. Even though most moms and dads "do not speak very good English, many of them can at least manage an English that is good enough to
correct a very young child's mistakes; in other words, most adults can
speak a good enough four-year-old's idiom." This facility, sadly, belongs
only to white parents. "The problem is what to do in the most underprivileged homes: those of blacks, Hispanics, immigrants from various
Asian and European countries. This is where day care centers could come
in." While such parents are sent off to work, Simon suggests that their
children be sent to standard English day camps, where they would have
"good English inculcated in them."⁷

Even Edwin Newman, whose books contain more examples of language
abuse than explanations of it, does offer an occasional comment on the
Black English problem. He traces the modern prevalence of the phrase
y'know ("one of the most far-reaching and depressing developments of
our time") to the black subculture: "There is some reason to believe that
in this country it began among poor blacks who, because of various
disabilities imposed on them, often did not speak well and for whom
y'know was a request for assurance they had been understood. From that
sad beginning it spread among people who wanted to show themselves
sympathetic to blacks, and among those who saw it as the latest thing and
either could not resist or did not want to be left out." This willful adoption
by the better class of people of "a lower order of speech" especially trou-
bles Newman. Incoherence has become so chic, he complains, that "you
are likely to be told that you are a pedant, an elitist, and behind the times"
if you observe that such talk implies a "certain scorn for organized, grammatical, and precise expression."⁸

As he surveys the "larger causes" of the deterioration of English,
Newman is happy to ascribe part of the blame to the "black revolt." He

claims that when "people who felt oppressed by society organized to enforce their demands," the rules of language began to break down. Modestly, Newman hypothesizes: "If you are a member of a group that has been rejected, or at any rate not favored, it is natural to respond by insisting that the group is good, and then you take pride in it, and then you make a virtue of necessity.... It is understandable, and it is not for me to tell people who have suffered because of their name or their skin color how they should react." Despite this nonpartisan pledge, Newman does conclude his comments on nonstandard English by asserting: "I cannot see that it makes any sense to encourage the ethnic outlook."[9]

Even genial old Andy Rooney, of "60 Minutes" fame, who is not usually noted for his language criticism, has joined the fray with a cranky newspaper column attacking both bilingualism and bidialectalism. Spanish, he admits, is a "magnificent language with a great literary tradition and a sound to it that is better than English, and I can understand anyone's reluctance to give it up" (though he does say that they should). Black English, however, is another matter: "It is not a language at all. Some great words and expressions come from it and they'll be taken into standard English along with so many other good words English has adopted. After that, it should be rejected and abandoned as soon as possible—just as anything called Black Arithmetic would be if it claimed that 2 times 2 equals 5."[10]

It is worth noting that criticisms of Black English are not exclusively the hobby of white commentators. In fact, many black scholars and politicians have spoken out against legitimizing the dialect or even acknowledging its existence. As early as 1971, Bayard Rustin condemned the "cult" of Black English, arguing that "reinforcing this consequence of poverty will only perpetuate poverty since it will prevent black children from mastering the means of communication in an advanced technological society with a highly educated population."[11] In the same year, a publication of the National Association for the Advancement of Colored People editorialized: "Black parents throughout this nation should rise up in unanimous condemnation of this insidious conspiracy to cripple their children permanently.... Let the black voice of protest resound thunderously throughout the land!"[12] Years later, Roy Wilkins, president of the NAACP, was still fighting Black English: "I think it is a lot of nonsense.... This pretense that you can somehow teach English by *not* teaching English is a lot of baloney."[13] And in a recent issue of the *Chronicle of Higher Education*, one black college president wrote that the study and acceptance of Black English amounted to "a modern version of pater-

nalism," and that "academic excellence cannot be achieved without first
mastering Standard English—not black or any other kind of nonstandard
English."[14]

Syndicated columnist Carl Rowan has long struggled against the
legitimization of Black English, which he has called "the mumbo-jumbo
of ignorance." He argues that "the current campaign to classify the bad
English of ghetto blacks as a separate language is one of the silliest and
potentially most destructive of all the terrible things done in the name of
racial pride by any race of man." As Jim Quinn has noted in *American
Tongue and Cheek,* Rowan's description of the gravity of the Black
English problem seems a bit hyperbolic when one actually reviews some of
the other "things done in the name of racial pride" (pogroms, lynchings,
genocide), but Rowan will not compromise.[15] The acceptance of Black
English would be "a tragedy," he says, that would "consign millions of
black children to a *linguistic separation* that would guarantee they will
never 'make it' in the larger U.S. society." Instead, we need "a massive al-
location of teachers and resources to remedial programs to teach black
children to speak, read and write the language of their native land."[15]

The assertions of Mitchell, Simon, and Newman, as well as those of the
black commentators, have several themes in common. First, of course,
there is some uncertainty about whether Black English in fact exists or, if
it does, whether it deserves to be called a language or even a dialect. But
beyond definitions, there is a general view of black speech as a crude,
error-ridden, and inadequate imitation of standard English that, though
the sympathetic ear may find it "jaunty" or "touching," cannot serve the
cognitive, educational, social, or occupational needs of its users. Further,
for schools or other social institutions to accept such language constitutes a
kind of "reverse racism," causing further deprivation in the name of
justice and understanding and democracy.

However congruent the critics' views may be with each other, and no
matter how widespread their acceptance by the standard-speaking public,
these ideas about Black English are nevertheless wrong on most counts.
While I am happy to agree at the outset that the mastery of some form of
standard may be an economic asset to many black people in this society, I
also believe that organized attempts to change the language of black people (and especially black schoolchildren) have had, and will continue to
have, largely counterproductive results. Though it will take considerable
time and space to explain this point, it seems worth the effort. For the
controversy over Black English not only raises some important educational
issues—it also provides a telling example of how linguistic prejudices are
reinforced and sustained.

The critics' difficulty in describing Black English strongly hints that any useful consideration of this issue must begin with definitions. To begin with, does Black English exist? Of course it does, as almost all American speakers intuitively know. When someone calls on the telephone to inquire about an apartment that has been advertised for rent, the landlord can *usually* determine whether the caller is black or white. When we hear people talking in the next classroom, we can *usually* tell black and white students apart. When linguists play tape recordings of various American dialect speakers to groups of listeners, the hearers are *usually* able to distinguish black from white speakers and, in fact, are quite willing to make judgments about the personal character of these taped speakers on the basis of their language alone.[17] Common sense, then, as much as formal academic research, reminds us that most black Americans speak in a way that is distinctive, recognizable, and remarkably alike in various regions of the country. One major book on this subject, J. L. Dillard's *Black English*, suggests that about four-fifths of American blacks share this dialect.[18]

Does this mean that 80 percent of blacks speak the language described by Mitchell, Simon, and the others—a chaotic slang full of fractured syntax and sexual synonyms? Of course not. For one of the greatest problems with the attacks on Black English has been the critics' insistence on drawing their "examples" of the dialect from the speech of alienated adolescents in inner-city ghettos—from street talk. To say that the language of a black sixteen-year-old gang member from the south side of Chicago typifies Black English makes as much sense as saying that the language of a white sixteen-year-old gang member from the southwest side of Chicago typifies standard English.

To be sure, street talk does exist, and while it cannot be described as linguistically deprived (or depraved), it does resemble adolescent dialects in other languages and cultures. It is the talk of young people who wish to separate themselves from the adult world, to manifest their defiance of authority, and to disguise their conversation from unwelcome listeners. That poor black teenagers would develop such a subdialect, and that its form as well as its content might be shocking to outsiders, is hardly surprising. What *is* surprising is the willingness of both black and white experts to let this narrow sample of black speech stand for the whole range of language that black people use.

But there is more to this. Even the archetypal, angry, underprivileged, and perhaps criminal black teenager is not completely restricted to street talk. With his parents and his teachers, he is able (though perhaps rarely willing) to adopt a different style of language which is more deferential, more "proper," more accessible to his listeners. And this youth has other speech styles which he uses with brothers and sisters or with his girlfriend or when he is looking for a job. In other words, though he may be a master of street talk, and at this stage of his life may generally prefer it, he shares with all other speakers of a human language the ability to shift from one register to another as circumstances change.

So, if not street talk, what is Black English? Like any other language, Black English is primarily composed of three elements: lexicon, syntax, and phonology. Also like any other language, the black dialect operates by rules: it is not a random, sloppy imitation of some other dialect, but the manifestation of a set of systematically contrasting, equally logical language rules. Before we consider some of its distinctive rules, it is important to understand that Black English, in its lexicon, syntax, and phonology, is very similar to white, or standard, English. When the critics describe BE as a nonlanguage or as a "collection of slang" that virtually prohibits thought, we tend to believe that BE must be quite radically different from the more prestigious forms of English. But this is not the case; in fact, most of its rules overlap with those of what we call standard. This is why black and standard English are mutually intelligible dialects; that is why black and white folks can understand each other, when they wish to.

The differences between BE and SE are on about the same order of magnitude as those between an SE speaker and a speaker of standard British English. The British speaker shows a modest number of lexical differences from his American cousin: he may *knock you up* instead of *waking you up*, he may look under the *bonnet* instead of the *hood*, he may go to the *loo* instead of the *john*, and he may ride a *lift* rather than an *elevator*. The Britisher's grammar also differs in a few ways from the American's: instead of treating collective nouns as singular, he may render them in the plural, as in *The committee were in disagreement*; instead of *won't* he may say *shan't*; and at some times in history (as Lord Peter Wimsey fans well know), he may even affect the double negative. As for pronunciation, the British phonemes may sound quite different from the American ones; *terribly* may come out *teddibleh*, *schedule* may become *ssshedule*, and even the everyday diphthong in *I* may sound like *oy*. All in all, standard British, like Black English, is a mutually intelligible variant that shows certain describable and characteristic differences that combine to yield a pattern which we are quite able to identify whenever we hear it. How we may feel about it, of course, is another matter.

Researchers have tried, with varying degrees of success, to measure the specific differences between BE and SE. In one of the most comprehensive comparative studies, Walter Loban elicited samples of informal talk from a number of schoolchildren during every year from kindergarten through ninth grade. His informants included poor black children, poor white children, and upper middle class white children. In each sample, Loban counted the number of deviations from standard English per thousand words of conversation. He found that the average "High Caucasian" first-grader would deviate from SE eleven times in each thousand words, while the average "Low Caucasian" child would do so twenty times, and the average "Low Black" child fifty-five times. By ninth grade, the High Caucasion group averaged about ten deviations per 1,000 words, the Low Caucasian group about twenty-five, and the Black group about forty-one. In other words, fourteen-year-old black children used nonstandard forms about 4 percent of the time, poor whites about 2.5 percent and wealthy white students about 1 percent. The differences between the scores of poor black and poor white children were mostly attributable to the recurrence of just five dialect-based constructions which the black students employed throughout their schooling. When the these exclusively Black English features were deleted from the calculations, the difference between the two groups of poor students dropped to less than 1 percent. Obviously, these percentages are quite small for all children, regardless of which groups are being compared. More than anything else, Loban's study is a good reminder of the great overlap between the rules of various English dialects.[19]

However we try to measure the differences between BE and SE, we will inevitably find them small. But even these modest findings may overstate the case, since many differences are not invariable but optional. Most black speakers know and can elect to use the standard form in slots where distinctive BE features commonly occur. For example, a BE speaker may in some contexts say *John bite the sandwich* but in another situation might prefer *John bites the sandwich*. This choice is similar to the option which all English speakers have in choosing between *It's a tough decision* and *It is a tough decision*—both mean the same thing, though they may show differing levels of formality. (Many BE speakers also have a third option in this series: *It a tough decision*). The same sort of option applies to constructions like the "double" negative: a BE speaker may multiply negation throughout one sentence, but not in another sentence similarly constructed; or he may use this feature consistently in one social context but not in another. In summary, then, many of the distinctive features of BE (particularly grammatical and lexical ones) are not obligatory, but are options used in variation with the complementary SE forms.

To suggest how this relationship between SE and BE rules works in practice, I include the following transcript of a conversation between two black high school girls from an inner-city neighborhood. When this exchange was recorded, they were working together in class on a list of questions covering Shakespeare's *A Midsummer Night's Dream.*°

(1)   A: Oooh, I hate that imagery crap. Firs' time I been in a
(2)   classroom today.
(3)   B. Really?
(4)   A: Un-huh.
(5)   B: (Reading) Personification. A metaphor is what?
(6)   A: She mark these wrong when that on the test.
(7)   B: What?
(8)   A: Comparison of personification and metaphor. Uh, how 'bout
(9)   this one: (Reading) "Demetrius, Helena, Hermia, and Lysander
(10)   are involved in a love chain. Who loves who?" Helena . . .
(11) B: She's jealous of what's-her-name. She's in love with Demetrius
(12)   and she wants him back, and she's gonna tell on him. . . .
(13) A: Uh-huh. (Writing) Dis de firs one.
(14) B: (After working for a few moments) It's between Hermes and
(15)   Helena.
(16) A: She's telling Hermia. . . .
(17) B: I think he did her wrong, though.

                              (Later)

(18) B: So what's the theme?
(19) A: Lovers being together, and one might get killed.
(20) B: (Writing) . . . the chance of one getting killed.
(21) A: (To the teacher, who has walked over) You gon give the tess? It gon
(22)   be easy? I gon be able to pass. See, we ahead. (Reading the
(23)   next question) "Why do you think Shakespeare chose the names
(24)   he did for Bottom and his crew? Can any connections be drawn
(25)   between the names and occupation or personality?" Why did
(26)   he choose the names?
(27) B: Because they were crazy men!

°In this transcription, I have tried to be faithful to the girls' sound systems (without resorting to International Phonetic Alphabet), however imperfect the resulting spellings may be. In much of their conversation, they use what I would call standard English phonology; for example, word-final consonant clusters are fully articulated. But at other moments, as in lines 36–39, there are quite dramatic and audible shifts from standard to BE phonology which I've tried to spell accordingly. While there are many alternative ways of representing these differences, the fact that they occurred is the essential point.

(After a few minutes, they come to the character of Bottom)

(28) A: Bottom. He think he looks good in anything he be—portray.
(29) B: It doesn't make sense.
(30) A: No, it doesn't make sense. (Suddenly she discovers the
(31)   *dramatis personae* in the front of her book) Look in the
(32)   front where it says what the characters are! (With mock smugness)
(33)   See, you gotta sit down and *analyze.* Zero points for you!
(34)   (Calls to the teacher) See if you came up with the same thing
(35)   we came up with.

(Later)

(36) A: (B has started playing with A's dictionary) Don you mess wid
(37)   mah book! Ah paid a whole forty cents for dis! (Grabs book)
(38)   Yo cah gon be mess up aftah school today, girl. Teacher,
(39)   teacher! (A is pretending that she is going to report the
(40)   book theft to the teacher) We're having difficulty.
(41) T: Did you look up Snout yet?
(42) B. Yeah. It said elephant's trunk.
(43) B: What's that got to do with Snout?
(44) A: Maybe they don't like elephants.
(45) B: That's logical, if I do say so myself. (Laughter)

These two girls were regarded by their teachers as speakers of Black
English (occasionally of street talk), which indeed they are. But these lines
also suggest the wide range of variation existing within that dialect. There
is repeated shifting of styles, with an attendant shifting from BE to SE
rules and back again. Compare, for example, A's remarks in lines 6 ("She
mark these wrong when that on the test") and 38 ("Yo cah gon be mess up
aftah school today, girl") with her utterances in lines 31–32 ("Look in the
front where it says what the characters are") and the triumphant deception in line 40 ("We're having difficulty"). Not only is there variation from
one sentence to the next, but even inside single sentences both BE and SE
rules are applied: in line 28, for example, A omits one third-person
singular verb tense marker while employing the -*s* with a second verb, and
later in the sentence backs away (apparently consciously) from a BE *be*
construction to produce the more nearly standard *portray.* Generally, the
shifts between BE and SE rules in this conversation appear to be socially
governed. When the task is Shakespeare, SE rules predominate; when the
topic departs from the worksheet, BE rules take over. Contrary to some
social expectations, however, when the white teacher comes over she is
addressed not in standard, but Black English.

This transcript, like any other sample of human talk, is remarkably rich and complex. It certainly provides, in its complexity, a better sample of Black English than does some cartoon caricature of gang rapping in an imaginary ghetto alley. And besides affording a glimpse of BE in use, this conversation also serves to introduce some of the characteristic features of the dialect that we should review briefly before proceeding. The following list includes many of the specific features which linguists believe distinguish BE from other dialects of English. Though this may not be a final tally of Black English variations, it at least demonstrates the systematic and logical operation of some differences that do exist.

Lexicon

The vocabulary of Black English speakers is essentially the same one employed by speakers of standard English. A relatively few words are used exclusively in the black dialect, and many of them have been cataloged in helpful, if slender, volumes like *A Dictionary of Afro-American Slang*, by Clarence Major.[20] As this book and others demonstrate, many of the unique word items of BE tend to be appropriated for use by younger white speakers, and some eventually pass into standard or near-standard usage. Recently incorporated words include *hip, right on, rap*, and the like. Other terms, of course, do remain within the black dialect without appreciable seepage into local white speech: in Chicago BE for example, *ride* means *car* and *crib* refers to one's home or apartment.

Just because the vocabulary differences between BE and SE are small, however, does not mean that they cannot attract attention. When BE speakers invent such apparent semantic inversions as *bad* meaning *good* (in spite of the fact that context makes the meaning clear even to an outsider), there is a tendency for some SE speakers to insist that such vocabulary differences require the reclassification of BE as "another language" or "a nonlanguage." Such lexical debates reached a comical climax in Chicago recently when a black basketball player was quoted in a newspaper as congratulating one of his teammates by saying: "Moses, you is a bad damn shootin' individual!" This nonstandard exclamation engendered several columns by local reporters condemning such language as a bad (in the standard sense) example to young black sports fans; there also appeared a rebuttal from one black sports star who was proud to demonstrate his own facility with standard English, and who reproached his brother for sliding into the vernacular.[21] This whole *bad* debate seems quite inconsequential when we realize that the most needed and perishable of slang terms in *all* dialects are synonyms for *good: great, far out, cool, hot, outasight, groovy, mellow, together, bitchin'*, *super*, and so forth.

Of course, I am not saying that every black (or white) person regularly uses the entire half-million-item lexicon of the English language. Many speakers employ a relatively small vocabularly because their range of experience or education is limited. However, the fact that a given speaker may not have learned, or does not typically use, certain English words, does not place them outside of his mother tongue. It is in this sense that arguments, like Richard Mitchell's, that BE lacks the sophisticated vocabulary necessary to build a B-52 or to discuss philosophy, are specious. All people who speak a dialect of English (or any other language) are capable of adding to their personal word stock whatever items are necessary to deal with these subjects.

Phonology

The sound patterns of a dialect are often its most noticeable but least understood differences. We identify speakers of different languages primarily by their "accent," by the systematic differences between their phonological rules and our own. We recognize Henry Kissinger's German roots not by his syntax or his lexicon but by his phonology, which "sounds German." He often says *vill* for *will*, and *ziss* for *this*, and so on. In fact, the durability of Kissinger's accent (and of John Simon's, to use a more familiar example) serves as a reminder that the sound patterns of our childhood language are deeply ingrained and, for most people, not subject to complete change after adolescence. As adults, we can learn the lexicon and syntax of another language quite well, but we can never fully eliminate the subconscious interference of our native phonology.

The situation is similar for Black English. The dialect has certain sound patterns that differ from those of other varieties of English, and these patterns are often recognizable even when a speaker's lexicon and syntax reveal no BE features. Here are some of the most distinctive examples:

Vowels

The SE dipthong vowel *ay*, as in *ride* or *tied*, is often realized as *rod* or *Todd* in the black dialect. This contrast, however, is lost only before the consonants *b, d, g, n, m, r,* and *l,* and not before *p, t, k, f,* or *s.* Similarly, the dialect's lack of a vowel contrast between *pin* and *pen* (the target of many teachers' wrath) does indeed constitute a difference— but one that occurs only before *n, m,* or *ng.* In other words, a BE speaker who pronounced *pin* and *pen* alike would still distinguish between *pit* and *pet, sit* and *set,* and so forth. Another vowel contrast lost in BE is the one between *sing* and *sang,* with both words tending to sound like the latter. But again, this variation occurs only when a nasal consonant follows the vowel—the contrast between such pairs as *chip* and *chap* is maintained. There are several other vowel patterns which the interested reader could review in Robbins Burling's helpful *English in Black and White,*[22] but the above examples should suffice to make the general point. Though some vowel sounds in BE differ from those of standard English, they differ in an orderly, rule-governed manner, according to the phonological environment in which they occur.

Word-Final Consonant Cluster Reductions

In BE, words ending in consonant clusters may be pronounced with the final member of the cluster absent. Thus, *nest* or *band* in SE may sound more like *ness* or *ban* in BE. This rule results in homonyms like *build* = *bill* and *find* = *fine.* The dropping of final consonants by black speakers is particularly stigmatized when it occurs in the past *(-ed)* marker. Since the past marker is often realized in SE as /d/ or /t/, words like *looked* or *messed* end in consonant clusters: *lookt* and *mest.* Therefore, when a black speaker reduces the standard *lookt* to *look* or *mest* to *mess,* a white listener may believe that the past marker is absent, even in utterances like *Tom got mess up.*

r-lessness and l-lessness

These two consonants, whose phonetic properties are quite similar, are not pronounced by BE speakers in certain environments. Thus, such pronunciations as *It's fo clock* or *I need some hep* are possible. While *r*-lessness is also characteristic of the prestigious white Boston dialect, the dropping of /r/ is more widespread in BE than in any regional form of white English.

The th Sounds

In SE the letters *th* represent two different sounds—a voiced interdental fricative, as in *they* and *these*, and a voiceless interdental fricative, as in *three* and *think*. In BE, the rules for the pronunciation of these sounds are a bit different. In word-initial positions, the voiced *th* is often realized as *d*, as in *dese* and *dose* and the voiceless *th* somewhat less often becomes *t*, as in *tink* or *tin*. Within words, *th* sounds may also diverge from standard pronunciation. The voiceless version may yield *nuffin* or *auffor*, while the voiced *th* can produce *bruvah* or *bavin*. When the *th* sound appears at the end of a word, it will sometimes be pronounced like an *f*, as in *Shut your mouf*. Complex as the rules governing *th* are, it is important to note that most BE speakers alternate between these distinctive dialect forms and their standard equivalents.

Syntax

The grammar of BE differs from that of SE in a relatively few ways. Below are several examples.

Possessives

BE speakers often indicate possession by word order rather then by using the *'s* marker. Thus, *the girl dress* corresponds to the SE form, *the girl's dress*. The SE form employs redundancy, requiring both word order and the marker to indicate possession, while the BE version needs only one such indicator. Again, most BE speakers employ both the dialect and the SE form, although past schooling may have left some of them with other divergent possessive forms, such as *Tom's Johnson's car* or *mine's food*. These latter possessives, however, are not a systematic feature of BE, but rather are hypercorrections that belong to no dialect at all.

Plurals

The suffixes used to mark plurals in SE may sometimes be absent from some words in BE. In Chicago, for example, *fifty cent* or *twelve year old* would be common realizations of the plural. As with the BE possessive form described above, this variation simply drops a redundant marker (both *fifty* and the SE *s*, for example, show plurality), and the meaning of the sentence remains clear. This rule operates in variation with the SE plurality rules and tends to be quite idiomatic: as the above examples suggest, the plural marker is most likely to be dropped, at least among Chicago BE speakers, from the words *dollar, cent,* and *year* and is generally retained with other nouns.

Copula Deletion

The deletion of the verb *to be* in certain circumstances is one of the most striking features of BE. Teachers who hear their students say *My mother gone* or *He so bad,* sometimes believe that their students are incapable of forming even the simplest verb constructions. The copula deletion shown in these sentences, though, systematically parallels the SE rules governing contractions. While SE allows its speakers to shift from *My mother is gone* to *My mother's gone,* BE allows its speakers to delete the copula altogether: *My mother gone.* In other words, BE speakers have one additional option for forming such semantically equivalent sentences.

Habitual Be

Part of the confusion about *be* in Black English concerns the copula deletion described above, but this common verb is also used in another nonstandard way. BE has one verb tense, which many linguists have called the habitual, that simply does not exist in SE. If a black speaker says *He be standin' on the corner,* this statement is not the equivalent of the SE *He is standing on the corner.* The *be* means that he is always standing on that particular corner, or that at this time of day he can always be found standing on the corner. This verb tense denotes recurring or continuing action—something that SE speakers can only express by adding a word like *always, usually* or *regularly.* There is some evidence that this unique feature traces back to West African languages that were spoken by slaves brought to America.[23]

Third-Person Singular Present Tense Marker

Another BE feature which is very common and highly frustrating to schoolteachers is the omission of the third-person singular present tense marker, as in *John walk to town.* This form, of course, has the effect of regularizing the whole verb conjugation: *I walk, you walk, he/she/ it walk, we walk, you walk, they walk.* Several linguists have speculated convincingly that this feature, like the habitual tense, may trace back to some of the African languages upon which the black slaves' first English pidgin was partially based.[24]

Negation

One of the more commonly cited "errors" of the black dialect is the use of "double negatives." In SE, there are rules which prohibit the manifestation of more than one negative within a sentence; in BE, however, an alternate set of rules provides for the "copying," or reinsertion, of negative elements throughout a sentence. Thus the sentence *I don't got no money* is correct in BE, as is one like *I don't never get no money from nobody.* Like all of the features outlined above, however, this multiplication of negation is not a fixed feature of all BE utterances, but an option which the dialect's speakers may use when the subject or the social setting make it appropriate.

This brief catalog of features is worth presenting because it underscores the logic and the order—in that sense, the normality—of Black English as a communication system. Like other languages and dialects, it operates by its own set of consistent and explicable rules. Its speakers may, if they wish, use their language to build bombers, study Kierkegaard, or search for God. In no sense can Black English be called cognitively or intellectually inferior to standard English, Swedish, Ukranian, or Tagalog.

But, needless to say, hardly anyone outside of the friendly local linguistics department believes any of this. Encouraged by Mitchell *et al,* the managers of the real-world-out-there continue to view BE as a sign of mental weakness, a predictor of poor job performance, and evidence of indifference, if not contempt, for mainstream society. And because such beliefs are so widespread, and receive so much endorsement, they themselves become the major language problem facing blacks in this society. It is the tastes, the prejudices, of the majority which render the language of the minority "inferior." If those who are doling out degrees or jobs believe that nonstandard speech bars upward mobility, then it will. If co-workers believe that a fellow employee's dialect marks him as stupid, he may be treated as stupid. If landlords believe that people who sound black on the telephone don't make good tenants, they won't rent to them.

As we consider these examples, we see linguistic issues fading into the background. Here, language is merely being used as a marker, a classificatory tool that activates the listener's social prejudices and not his rational powers. When an employer decides, "I'm not going to hire this guy. He doesn't sound too bright," he may be using the applicant's language (along with his skin color and other clues) in a stereotyped, dismissive way—or, of course, the employer may be correct. But in this elemental confrontation (which is always presented when white people discuss what to do about Black English) the applicant, if he wants the job, has *not* been talking some impenetrable street talk. He has not been shucking and jiving and rapping and sounding, but rather has been trying to shift toward a more formal, more accessible style of speech. If he is like most black people in America, he is perfectly able to make himself understood, though he cannot disguise his "accent." It is up to the employer, then, whether to respond to whatever stereotype this accent conjures up, or to the person sitting in front of him.

We may recognize that social attitudes, and not the language itself, constitute the essential "problem" with Black English. It is quite another matter to change those attitudes, which have been enshrined through centuries of white ridicule and rationalization. The only practical alternative which seems to remain is to teach black people, and especially black schoolchildren, some kind of standard English that they can then use to circumvent the prejudices of the various white people who will, from time to time, have power over them.

This sensible and humane-sounding policy—which is usually called bidialectalism—is now the generally accepted theory, if not always the practice, in most American schools. Teachers try to convince their students of the need to master SE, to explain the differences between the prestige dialect and the one the students speak, and to devise exercises and experiences that will teach and reinforce the desired new forms. All of this is supposed to be done without seeming to reject or denigrate the children's first dialect. Even John Simon, who believes that black children should be marched from their homes to standard English preschools, outlines this approach with some delicacy: "Care must be exercised to avoid insulting the language spoken in the youngsters' homes. There must be ways to convey that both home and school languages have their validity and uses and that knowing both enables one to accomplish more in life." Teachers, Simon suggests, can turn this kind of instruction into a game: "At home you speak one way; here we have another language." The teacher can then "make up names and explanations for standard English that would appeal to pupils of that particular place, time, and background."[25] Reasonable and respectful as it sounds (except, perhaps, for Simon's conjugation camps) there are a number of problems with the bidialectal approach: it doesn't work, it alienates children from their schooling, and it supports, reinforces, justifies, and perpetuates exactly those prejudices which it is designed to help black people escape. All things considered, it is still probably the right thing to do—but we should at least consider all of those things before we do it.

Until the middle 1960s, most educators agreed that the proper treatment for the black dialect was eradication. In the few places where white teachers taught black children, they tried as best they could to replace their students' language with another one—namely, the teacher's own version of standard English. Needless to say, for black children who came from and remained in BE-speaking communities, this approach failed utterly. However, with the slow but steady integration of schools, the problem of nonstandard dialects began to receive some special attention from educational leaders.

The work that finally spurred some serious study of Black English in the early 1960s, oddly enough, involved not American Negroes but lower-class speakers of British English. Basil Bernstein, in a series of articles beginning in 1958, offered a theory of lower-class dialects based on his model of "restricted" and "elaborated" codes. This theory views the development of particular dialects as tied to the social environment in which they originate. Thus "the particular form of a social relation acts selectively on what is said, and how it is said; the form of the social relation regulates the options that speakers take up at both syntactic and lexical levels." Based on his study of the social relationships in middle-class and lower-class homes, Bernstein concluded that "certain groups of children, through the forms of their socialization, are oriented toward receiving and offering universalistic meanings in certain contexts, whereas other groups of children are oriented toward particularistic meanings."[26]

The "restricted" code, Bernstein claimed, facilitates "closely shared identifications" and "creates social solidarity at the cost of the verbal elaboration of individual experience." This sort of language seems almost tribal; it is a common, virtually ritualistic affirmation of group beliefs, attitudes, and expectations rather than a tool for the investigation and understanding of reality. While Bernstein was careful not to explicitly derogate the restricted code, it was clear that he saw the middle-class elaborated code, with its ability to create "a complex hierarchy for the organization and expression of inner experience," as a higher form of language.[27]

Bernstein's theories were promptly and enthusiastically applied to the study of Black English in America. Here, at a time when the problems of racial minorities had suddenly appeared in the limelight, was a conceptual framework that could accommodate the divergences of black dialect. The theory did seem to account for some observed facts: the apparent simplification of English rules which characterized the black dialect; the strong sense of community among its speakers; the academic failures of many lower-class black children. Unfortunately, Bernstein's terminology of *restricted* and *elaborated* was immediately translated into *inferior* and *superior*, and little attention was paid to the subtleties and qualifications of his dichotomy.

Bernstein's influence first surfaced in a U.S. Office of Education Conference on "Improving English Skills for Culturally Different Youth," held in 1962. In the volume of collected papers that issued from this meeting, Bernstein's studies are used to support the arguments of several participants. Marjorie Smiley, in a review of the current research, offered the following: "Bernstein's analysis of lower class speech in England leads him to conclude that such speech is not merely 'different' but deficient. To describe it merely as a dialect, though it may be this as well, is to miss the fact that the simplifications in language structure characteristic of lower class speech make it almost impossible to formulate intellectual generalizations."[28] Though Bernstein had been careful to note that restricted codes were inadequate only for certain kinds of activity, the notion of black cognitive inferiority had long since taken root among American educators, and no such complexities were going to hinder their efforts to catalog the evidence of language deprivation in ghetto family life.

One prominent psychologist studied the language of black urban families and concluded:

The behavior which leads to social, educational, and economic poverty is learned; it is socialized in early childhood. This socialization takes place in large measure by way of language. Since the mother is the primary socializing agent in most instances, this learning takes place in the context of the mother-child communication system. The deprivation that leads to poverty is the lack of cognitive meaning and cognitive and linguistic elaboration in this communication system.

Ellis Olim had discovered that, in the presence of a visiting researcher, black mothers often tended to communicate with their youngsters through a few clipped utterances. Ignoring the possible influence of the psychologist's presence in the home, Olim was satisfied that he had discovered the essential difference between black and middle-class language styles: "The consequences for the child of the use of personal-subjective and cognitive-rational [i.e., middle-class] approaches is to orient the child away from external standards as reference points and away from uncritical acceptance of authority and existing institutions.... Where the status-orientation [i.e., lower-class] approach is dominant, the child is led to attend to authority figures for direction, to develop a compliant, passive approach to learning." Neither Olim nor his colleagues seemed to notice that this interpretation of black intellectual deficiency completely contradicted one of the most widely accepted facts of school life: that the middle-class child uncritically accepts the authority of the teacher and the school. while the lower-class child is more often skeptical and defiant. [29]

Similar interpretations of language and life in ghetto homes became the foundation of a remedial program in the Philadelphia public schools. The program's publicity asked rhetorically:

What is it like to never hear standard English spoken in your home?
What is it like to never have had a newspaper, book, or magazine in your home?
What is it like never to have had anyone speak to you except in terms of abuse?
What is it like to have no one to see that you get to school everyday?
What is it like *never* to have known a kind adult?

Not only did Philadelphia black children have the problem of not knowing standard English, apparently, but they lived in a community where every single adult was either cruel or indifferent to kids. [30]

Even the National Council of Teachers of English, today reviled as a citadel of permissiveness and relativistic demagoguery, enthusiastically supported these crypto-Bernsteinian researches into the degradation of black family life. In 1965, the Council issued a task force report on "Teaching English to the Disadvantaged." Among its conclusions:

The inability of the disadvantaged child to express himself is one of the first noticeable things about him.

By the time they are five years old, disadvantaged children of almost every kind are typically one to two years retarded in language development. This is supported by virtually any index of language development one cares to look at.

Furthermore, they (black students) are not in the habit of expressing subjective emotions and feelings, a very important possibility of language.

... the disadvantaged child typically does not have the words to express emotions such as displeasure or love, and he hits, spits, or kicks when he is angry and similarly, hugs or kindly touches when he is pleased or gratified.

A major function of language is its role in the process of thought, in the assimilation of specific pieces of information into meaningful concepts. The disadvantaged child has an even less adequate grasp of this use of language than he does of language as a means of expression.

This description of black children's linguistic and cognitive abilities, which placed them about at the level of a cocker spaniel, stemmed from the panelist's comparisons of middle-class and lower-class language:

> People who live in the lower socio-economic disadvantaged groups use language primarily for immediate concrete situations. For that reason, they are able to use many partial sentences. The tired father says to the older boy, "My slippers." He means, "Go get my soft shoes." The mother says to the daughter, "The table." She means, "It is time now for you to set the table." Children are making a lot of noise outside. The middle-class mother would say, "Now you children know that Mrs. Jones has rheumatic spells once in a while. She has pains in her shoulders, and at such times she is very unhappy and easily upset. When children are running around making a lot of noise, it makes her even worse. Now children, how would you feel if you were Mrs. Jones? So, then, what must we do, children?' The lower-class mother says, "Quiet!"

Looking back just fifteen years later, it is hard to believe that the NCTE could have offered this transparently false little scenario as a description of *anyone's* language. But bidialectalism requires sharp contrasts, polarized choices, black and white (if you will) distinctions, and if none of these exist, they can always be invented.[31]

All people use language "primarily for immediate concrete situations." *All* people use many partial sentences and elliptical responses. These are simple facts of linguistic life. But the report's purported exchanges between parents and children are so misleading that they could not have been mere mistakes. Has there even been a middle-class (or lower-class or upper-class) father who said *soft shoes* when he meant slippers? This awkward expression is a clumsy and obvious attempt to complicate the "sample" of middle-class speech. In real life, probably both the middle-class and the lower-class father in this situation would say, *Get me my slippers.* Similarly, it is doubtful that the typical middle-class mother issues commands in the stilted and unnecessarily elaborate style of *It is time now for you to set the table,* just as it is unlikely that the black mother ordinarily pares her orders down to *The table.* Both mothers would probably say, *Will you set the table,* possibly with a *please* inserted somewhere.

The final example, about poor old Mrs. Jones and the noisy kids, is designed to contrast the intricate, cognitively sophisticated messages of the middle-class mother with the brutally reduced commands of the ghetto parent. But it is a pretty thin piece of deception. Somehow, this model mother who says, *So, then, what must we do, children,* doesn't quite ring true. Real mothers would probably say, *Be quiet. Mrs. Jones is sick.* While in a moment of extraordinary patience a white mother might attempt the "reasoning" rather than the prescriptive approach to behavior, the same is true for the black mother (*How would you feel if you was sick?*).

Using the kinds of research and speculation outlined above, the NCTE task force strongly encouraged the adoption of bidialectal language arts programs. Among its specific recommendations: "The NCTE Task Force recommends that first grade disadvantaged children not ready to enter a formal reading program should be enrolled in an intensive, language-oriented program.... The NCTE Task Force recommends that secondary English programs include oral work in standard informal English for students with non-standard dialects. Instead of downgrading or attempting to eliminate the students' dialects, teachers should teach standard informal English as a second dialect."[32] This latter suggestion marked a crucial point in the development of language arts programs for the disadvantaged. Though similar proposals had been made by individual educators for several years preceding the task force, this was the first time that functional bidialectalism had been introduced and recommended to the body of English teachers as a whole. From 1965 forward it rapidly began to replace eradication as the treatment of choice for speakers of Black English. Bidialectalism continues to be the official policy of most all-black and integrated schools to this day, although it has not always been successfully or consistently implemented in actual classrooms.

As the comments of the task force clearly indicate, the switch to bidialectalism certainly did not arise from a new respect for or understanding of the black dialect. It was, in fact, the result of a new academic reevaluation of the dialect that had found it cognitively wanting. The tradition of suspicion, acknowledged distaste, and confusion about Black English had set the stage for an elaborate and persuasive taxonomy of its intellectual and cultural degradation. Educators now had specific grounds upon which to base their efforts to alter their students' speech, and had been given some new weapons to bring to the battle—not the least of which was "proof" of black people's stupidity, docility, and cruelty to children.

Just as this consensus was being forged, however, the linguists appeared on the scene with some new and startling information. Spurred to new research by the furor among language educators, a number of investigators had begun to discover elements of a system in the "degraded" black dialect. Studies by Raven McDavid, William Stewart, Roger Shuy, and others[33] showed that BE constructions previously attributed to "lazy tongues" or improper mothering were actually aspects of a fully developed, logical, but different dialect of English. Work begun by several linguists during this period later led to the assertion that contemporary black dialect was the ultimate product of a creole tongue based on the early pidgin English of slaves brought to America from Africa.

The single most important line of linguistic research on BE was that pursued by William Labov. More than any other investigator, he was able to systematically demonstrate that the dialect had structure, order, and logic—and he also showed how previous researchers had been misled by their own cockeyed methodologies and intrusive prejudices. Labov realized that in order to find out what black children could and could not do linguistically, it was necessary to remove white-coated psychologists from the environment where speech samples were being collected. Working through a number of alternate approaches, Labov finally obtained his best samples of black children's language simply by leaving them alone in a room with a running tape recorder and a live rabbit. The resulting conversations revealed that these children had the full range of language skills available to their white age-mates, and that they used all of these skills freely when there was no threatening observer around. Labov reported these results in "The Logic of Nonstandard English," an article that served not only as a review of black children's linguistic competence, but also as a rebuke to researchers who had so tirelessly promoted the notion of linguistic deprivation among these youngsters.[34]

By 1974 the NCTE leadership, won over by the arguments of the linguists, had recanted. Instead of endorsing the deficit theories it had promoted just a few years before, the Council now issued *The Students' Right to Their Own Language,* a tract which horrified many NCTE members, not to mention outside critics. The thrust of this pamphlet was simple: it applauded the linguistic research which had upheld the legitimacy of nonstandard dialects, and warned teachers that they should respect the language which their students bring with them to school. Nowhere did the statement argue against the teaching of standard English, nor did it call for students to be taught nonstandard dialects instead. But it did note that standard English derives its importance primarily from the fact that rich and powerful people use it, rather than from any inherent superiority it might have.[35] This point, predictably enough, raised the hackles of many teachers and writers. John Simon's hackles were as high as anyone's. "I begin to despair," he wrote. "Could anything be sadder than the fact that those quotations marks around educated English come from the pen of an eduator—someone who ought to be proud of the fact that generations of educators have labored to evolve and codify that English?" Unable to fit all of his responses to the NCTE document into a single column, Simon moaned: "One difficulty with address-

ing oneself to the absurdity of this pamphlet is that where every sentence
... pullulates with logical and moral errors, one doesn't know where to
begin with a rebuttal."[36]

Despite the NCTE's flip-flop, and the attendant bad publicity, little had
changed. What was being debated in 1974 was the foundation of bidialectalism, not its practice. Everyone agreed that black students should
be taught standard English, and that they should not have their own
dialect removed in the process. One could argue about why such teaching
was necessary, about what its assumptions and goals might be, but the
classroom experiences of black students were not much affected. Bidialectal programs were being designed and implemented all around the
country from the mid-sixties on, and many such programs are still in operation today.

One of the earliest bidialectal programs was instituted in Detroit, and its
director outlined the basic approach in a U.S. Office of Education report:

We say to them, "This brand of English you are using is a language in itself, which
may have its uses for you. It is like an old suit of clothes which we do not throw
away because we still may want to wear it on some occasions. But we would not
think of wearing the old suit for a job interview or a dance, if we have something
better to wear. Here in this class you can acquire the language used by most
Americans in the business world. This language will then be yours to use when you
want it and need it."

The procedure through which students in this program were supposed to
shed their "old suit" of dialect and slip into something more appropriate
(if not comfortable) consisted chiefly of drills patterned on techniques of
foreign language instruction:

The set of fourteen taped lessons we developed are of the listening-repeating type,
but they incorporate some writing. They serve as a type of teaching machine to
explain the structure of the language as well as to change particular usages by giving the student opportunities to handle and to practice using the better forms.
Skinner's theories are involved in that the tapes give immediate reward and reinforcement. The taped lessons are also built on linguistic concepts, but retain some
traditional terminology. To hold interest, because each tape runs under thirty
minutes, we use a variety of rich voices, both male and female, and a variety of
teaching techniques and student activities.

Between trips to the "phonojack boards" around the room, students were
also required to "spend a few minutes on general oral drill": "If someone

says 'fave cent,' we may take a minute to count in unison from 'one cent, two cents' up to 'ten cents,' stressing the "s" sound. When trouble occurs in agreement of third person singular noun and its matching verb, or if we hear 'seen' instead of 'saw,' we may take time out to drill on the conjugation of the verbs, jazzing up the rhythm to make the activity fun as well as to reinforce it in the memory."

In spite of this program's considerable technological sophistication, its director was quite cautious about claiming success: "One never knows how truly successful some speech efforts are because so much of the learning may be a delayed process. If we hold to high standards, yet make speech activities pleasant and memorable, there will be positive results. We cannot change the student's speech habits for him, but we can help him to become aware of the need for change by becoming a more critical and discerning listener, we can give him good examples to imitate; we can encourage his efforts at self-improvement." It must have been discouraging, after setting up such an elaborate experiment, to have only the distant hope that the desired "learning may be a delayed process." When the director admits that "we cannot change a student's speech habits," she has probably discovered that the black child's "speech habits" are a fully functional dialect of English, and therefore extremely resistant to change.[37]

Another noteworthy bidialectal program was designed by Carl Bereiter and Sigfried Engelmann, cognitive psychologists who had earlier reached the conclusion that black children did not really have any language at all, and that their vocal output consisted of primitive animal cries emitted as an accompaniment to action. Viewing this condition as a kind of teaching opportunity, the psychologists devised a program of behavioristic language drills which purported to teach black children the structures of language for the first time. One of the program's instructors described her activities as follows: "For correct responses the children are firmly praised, and in terms directly related to what they are doing, 'that's good talking' or 'you said that just right.' . . . corrections are made in a clear and forthright manner, 'John, you haven't said it right. I want to hear every word,' or 'No, you're wrong,' followed by the correction." For this teacher, the ultimate goal is a conversation like this:

Teacher: Andy, find a figure that is triangular.
Andy: This figure is triangular.
Teacher: What size is it?
Andy: This figure is triangular and big.
Teacher: Good, what color is it?
Andy: Green.

Teacher: Can you tell me all that you know about the figure?

Andy: This figure is triangular and big and green.

Teacher: That is good talking.

One cannot help wondering what compliant Andy made of all this.[38]

If Andy felt somewhat demoralized, so too did many of the teachers who, in various school districts around the country, were (and still are) expected to make their students bidialectal. In the Pittsburgh schools, for example, teacher morale seemed to sag under the weight of an experimental "Standard Speech Development Program." Designed to "give high school students control of standard English speech through patterned drills," this program outlined its strategy as follows: "Using the prepared drills according to the prescribed directions, in a typical lesson the teacher begins by motivating the drill while the students listen and the pattern is established. Then the teacher gives a cue and the students respond. The process is repeated, with appropriate variations as to individual and group responses, for the duration of the drill." In the trial program, it was discovered that seventeen of the twenty-two carefully selected teachers had failed to hold the required number of sessions per week. In fact, among those who had held some sessions, all but four had cut the time scheduled for them by one-third or more. A crash "in-service" meeting was called in an attempt to save the program, during which the bidialectal principles involved were reexplained to the experimental teachers. Following this meeting, the teachers held even fewer and shorter drill sessions.[39]

Clearly, the drill method used in this program was a significant source of its difficulties. But the lack of teacher support was equally important. In a later survey the instructors reported that their unwillingness to teach the drills stemmed from their belief that other elements of the curriculum were more important. The teachers believed that they each presided over a small, functioning speech community, and that basic reading, writing, and talking activities were more central to their duties than the dialect program. Beyond this essentially professional objection to the program, there must have been personal misgivings as well. How difficult it must be for a teacher to spend class time drawing attention to the differences between her language and that of the students—differences which they, as a functioning group, have long since accommodated.

One other typically unsuccessful bidialectal program was reported by Richard Rystrom. Working with a group of black first graders, Rystrom hypothesized that:

1. In eight weeks, Negro children can be taught to use elements of Standard English dialect which do not occur in their native dialect.

2. The knowledge of this additional dimension of dialect will have a positive and significant influence on word reading scores.
3. Dialect training will have a positive and significant influence on word reading tests in which the relationship between letters and sounds is controlled.

Rystrom constructed a set of intensive response, translation, and substitution drills of the type recommended by Berieter, Engelmann, and other experts. Though he confined his efforts to a handful of contrasting BE and SE features, Rystrom found at the end of his program that none of the three hypotheses had been supported. Only some slight changes were detected in the post-tests of the children; none was statistically significant, and few even came close. Rystrom concluded:

It is difficult to change language behavior, and perhaps more complicated to teach a dialect than to teach a different language. With a new language, students know they are unfamiliar with the features that they are learning. In the case of dialect lessons, there is the possibility that many of the experimental group students were never convinced of a real or important difference between their native dialect and the dialect being taught. Failure to note this difference could have resulted in a lack of motivation.

Rystrom's last fond hope was that a program like his might succeed if it lasted for "two or three years."[40]

One program which is neither experimental nor explicitly aimed at black children is the *Chicago Curriculum Guide for Language Arts, 4-6.* This volume is simply the official description of the things which fourth through sixth graders are supposed to learn about English in the Chicago public schools. Obviously, however, the *Guide's* writers were aware that black students constitute the district's single largest ethnic group—and indeed, the text confirms that its authors were trying to help teachers "do something" about Black English among their students. The *Guide* reminds teachers that "Standard American English has been defined as the language in which the main business of the community is carried on," and urges them to encourage its use "by means of personal example." Apparently this standard, at least in the Chicago public schools, consists mainly of the avoidance of common Black English pronunciations: the *Guide* instructs teachers to root out *foun* for *found, kep* for *kept, nex* for *next, agin* for *again, goin* for *going, dat* for *that, dis* for *this,* and dozens of others. (Some of the "correct" target pronunciations given by the *Guide* appear to belong to no real dialect at all, standard or other: *offten, re-a-lly,* and *fam-i-ly* are among the puzzling "proper" forms given.)

One recommendation of the *Guide* is strongly reminiscent of the language pledge recited by American immigrant children in the 1920s, and, when it is combined with some of the book's other suggestions, reproduces the spirit, and nearly the letter, of that oath:

Participate in an Acceptable Speech Campaign conducted by: a committee on a classroom basis; the student council on a school-wide basis.

Remind pupils that unacceptable speech patterns may have an adverse effect on their success in school and in their chosen vocations.

Encourage pupils to eliminate unacceptable expressions. Call attention to expressions which are inherent in: their national origin; their local or regional environment.

Compile a class list of the words in which the group departs from standard pronunciation. Design a bulletin board to arouse interest in eliminating the differences. ... Help pupils to eradicate unacceptable pronunciations.

Identify the speech patterns which are accepted and understood by society. Imitate these patterns. Resolve to "retire" indistinct, inaccurate speech patterns.

Make a list of social situations in which indistinct and unacceptable pronunciations might have serious, humorous, or embarrassing consequences.

If such a program were indeed devised for a group of black ten-year-olds, it is hard to imagine what they might find "humorous" about any of its applications.[41]

The quite consistent failure of bidialectal programs to graduate skilled dialect switchers—students fluent in both standard and Black English—is hardly surprising. Leaving aside for a moment the fact that most of these efforts are shot through with ill-concealed contempt for the students' language, homes, and culture, they do not even take into account the most elementary principles of learning. For the inner-city black children involved in such programs, there is little motivation and even less reinforcement for the changes they are asked to make.

Though teachers may carefully outline the consequences of not becoming competent in standard English ("You will need it to get a good job"), it is doubtful that a six-year-old or even a twelve-year-old child will find this argument very meaningful. What the black child *does* know is that she already speaks a language which serves her needs very well. She is able to navigate through personal, family, and community matters efficiently, and engages in satisfying verbal play with her friends. She has no difficulty communicating with the significant people in her life. The way she speaks works as well for the black inner-city child as it does for children in other circumstances. Whether she, or any other preadolescent child understands the abstract social dimensions of language well enough to appreciate the teacher's pragmatic arguments about standard English is questionable. While quite young children do have some sociolinguistic awareness, and soon become masters of several speech styles, the ability of first graders to realistically project themselves into adult job interviews has never been shown.

If this offers a bleak picture of the motivational prospects for bidialectal teaching, the complementary process of reinforcement does not appear any more promising. What encouragement is a black child likely to receive for using standard English outside—or even inside—the classroom? In most cases, all of the other people in his peer group, family, and neighborhood are BE speakers. If he tries to speak standard English to them, he may find it dysfunctional. While they will understand him, his family and friends may find this behavior odd, or even "stuck up." By speaking standard English, the child separates himself from his speech community—and particularly from the language customs of his peer group, in which the pressures to conform are likely to be quite intense. If the child is offered no significant reinforcement for the standard forms he may have learned (or gets some negative reinforcement), it is not very likely that he will continue to practice them—at least not in public.

All of the foregoing programs were aimed at remediating only one particular deficiency of black children—their oral language. But many of the bidialectalists saw a broader and even more troubling problem. Since the predominant language of most teachers and schools was standard English, they reasoned, the interference between BE and SE might be an underlying cause of black students' general failure to do as well as white children in school. The fundamental linguistic mismatch, in other words, might explain black children's characteristic reticence to work, their misunderstanding of subject matter, their inability to follow directions, and especially, their failure to learn to read.

This may be an appealing explanation of black children's academic difficulties, but it oversimplifies the problem considerably. In the first place, bidialectalists typically describe dialect interference as a two-way street: the kids can't understand the teachers and the teachers can't understand the kids. In point of fact, black students *understand* both their own and the standard dialect quite well by the time they enter school, while white students and teachers do not usually have such effective cross-cultural comprehension. In one useful investigation of this phenomenon, Paul Weener played taped messages in various dialects to groups of black and white children, and then asked the listeners to repeat the taped messages verbatim. The result: "The performance of the [white] group ... was sharply reduced by having a message presented by a speaker of a different dialect, but the performance of the [black] group of children was not significantly reduced when presented with messages by a speaker with a dialect unlike their own dialect." Weener concluded on the basis of his experiment that black children develop a receptive facility for the standard dialect at a very early age, while no reciprocal skill seems to develop among young white speakers. It seems likely, then, that black children have a pretty good understanding of what the school and its teachers are telling them, and that if they ignore certain messages it is not because they cannot understand them.[42]

The problem of dialect interference nearly always comes down to the matter of reading. Bidialectalists are unanimous in their belief that the differences between black and standard English are the source of black children's perennial reading difficulties:

"*The more divergence there is between the dialect of the learner and the dialect of learning, the more difficult will be the task of learning to read.* This is a general hypothesis. It applies to all learners. If the language of the reading materials or the language of the teacher differs to any degree from the native speech of the learners some reading difficulty will result."

While differences in the dialect of the teacher are not necessarily crippling in themselves, the other part of this hypothesis—that reading materials in an alien dialect can cause reading difficulties—is perfectly reasonable. We therefore need to determine the degree of divergence between school reading books and Black English.[43]

There are three aspects of language in which divergence would seem likely: lexicon, syntax, and phonology. Since the vocabularies of BE and SE overlap almost entirely, no one has seriously argued that lexical differences impede black children who are learning to read. Syntactic differences are a more complex matter. Our previous list of the features of BE included such grammatical contrasts as possessive marker deletion, plural marker deletion, third-person singular tense marker deletion, habitual *be*, copula deletion, and multiple negation. While this list may sound fairly substantial, we must remember that most black children use distinctive BE forms in variation with the standard versions, and that they have already developed a good receptive facility for the standard dialect generally.

Many linguists who have studied the grammatical features of BE as they relate to learning to read believe that the dialect itself should pose no particular hurdle—provided that the classroom teacher is knowledgeable about the dialect. If a black child reads the sentence, *Tom has two ducks* as *Tom have two duck*, the teacher must realize that the student may not only have understood the sentence but may have translated it into her own dialect. If anything, such an operation would demonstrate an even fuller understanding than simply reading the standard form, since the child has to understand the meanings of the words before they can be altered to fit the rules of a different dialect. Such translations are not uncommon: in one Chicago reading test, many of the black children who were asked to read the sentence, *A nest is in a big green tree*, instead produced *A ness in a big green tree*. According to the scoring protocol, this version was to be marked as an error, though the consistency with which these children deleted the form of "to be" (and not any other word in the sentence) strongly suggests that they were understanding the standard form and translating it into a "correct" BE sentence when they read it aloud.[44]

I do not suggest that black children will invariably comprehend and transform different grammatical features into their own dialect forms. In many cases, their passive command of the standard dialect and the variation of many of its features within their own speech will allow them to simply read the construction in standard. Of course there will also be genuine instances of interference, when none of these aids will help a black child decode a standard grammatical construction. But in general, the grammatical conflicts are few in number, and the black child's resources for overcoming them are considerable—and we have no reason to believe that syntactical differences between BE-speaking students and SE textbooks should be a significant source of reading problems.

Phonetic interference may be a more serious problem for black children who are learning to read from books written in standard English. Because most beginning reading programs are based upon teaching some set of letter-sound or phoneme-grapheme correspondences, the BE-speaking student's divergent phonological rules may present difficulties. If the child, for example, says *ness* for *nest*, she may have some difficulty in grasping the teacher's insistence that there is a sound missing when she reads the word aloud. Similarly, if the black child reads *Ah* for *I*, the teacher may tell her that the sound of the word is wrong. In both of these cases, though, the approach of the teacher is as important as the individual phonetic differences. If the teacher believes that the student is unaware of the final *t* in *ness*, she can test the student's pronunciation of related forms: *nesting*, *nested*, and so on. If the *t* sound is pronounced in these forms, then the teacher knows that the student controls the full form of the word and that the loss of *t* in *nest* is simply a BE consonant cluster reduction. If, on the other hand, the child says *nessing* and *nessed,* the teacher will know that she does not have the *t* in her underlying conception of the word, and will have to be taught it. With *Ah,* the problem is simpler: the teacher need only understand that this is the normal and consistent BE rendering of the vowel and that there is nothing to be gained by correcting it. Probably the most important phonological complications which black students encounter in reading have to do with homonyms: pairs of words that they pronounce alike, but the teacher contrasts. These children will have to learn the ambiguities of *ride* = *rod* and *build* = *bill* just as SE-speaking students must master *threw* = *through, no* = *know,* and the like. Without question, black-dialect-speaking children will have to learn to distinguish more such pairs than their white peers typically do.

Some educators have argued that the differences between BE and SE are significant enough to require that black children first learn to read from books written in their own dialect, using these nonstandard readers as a bridge to deciphering SE textbooks. Perhaps the best-known example of this approach was developed in Chicago and is still in use in some public school classrooms. The primers written for this project, the *Psycholinguistic Reading Series,* have one central theme: that there are two kinds of language, "School Talk" and "Everyday Talk." These alternate codes are repeatedly contrasted through the reading books:

I got a mama—I have a mama
I got a daddy—I have a daddy
I got a grandmama—I have a grandmama

Teachers are instructed to present the students first with the "Everyday Talk" version and later to have them read the same story in "School Talk." The authors' theory is that students who first encounter the friendly, familiar dialect form will not only be able to read the story more easily but will then be better prepared to tackle the more challenging standard version.[45]

But this series of books also illustrates some of the difficulties which arise when school authorities half-heartedly try to accommodate their nonstandard-speaking students. In the pamphlet dealing with past constructions, for example, black dialect is represented as follows:

Yesterday my daddy work hard.
He wash the walls.
He wash the floors.
My brother help him.

"School Talk," predictably, expresses these same concepts as:

Yesterday my daddy worked hard.
He washed the walls.
He washed the floors.
My brother helped him.

The assumption of the textbook writers is that black children do not have command of the past (*-ed*) marker. But this makes a grammatical problem out of one which is phonological. Indeed, these children may reduce word-final consonant clusters which sometimes include past markers. They do not do so invariably, however: the marker is often retained when it precedes a vowel (*He washt a car*) and may be lost only before consonants (*He wash the car*). The booklet, in other words, overgeneralizes the absence of a feature that all black children understand and often use. The result of this inadequate attempt to mimic the black dialect, then, is mainly to confuse students about something they already know. It makes no more sense to omit the *-ed* markers from the past forms in books for black students than to delete the *b* from *comb* in a suburban dialect primer.[46]

In a similarly inept attempt to deal with another black dialect feature, the "School Talk - Everyday Talk" series offers one whole pamphlet aimed at the habitual tense. *We be jumping when it be thundering* and *We be yelling when it be lightning* are given as examples of this BE construction. But such sentences are rare, perhaps impossible in the children's actual dialects. *We be jumping when it thunder* or *When it thunder, we be jumping* would be more idiomatic patterns. Equally mistaken is the "School Talk" translation: *We jump when it thunders* and *We yell when it is lightning*. *We always jump when it thunders* would be more equivalent, but still not exactly parallel. The habitual tense, after all, does not exist in standard English, and these artificial translations are bound to be confusing. Again, the lack of accurate information about the dialect, combined with the program's evident intent to move the students from an inferior ("Everyday") to a better ("School") kind of language, works against the usefulness of these materials.[47]

Still, black dialect readers, carefully done, may be a small step in the right direction. As long as they do not stereotype Black English or black culture (*I don't got no Daddy*), they may reduce a bit of the interference which black children face in learning to read. It is still true, however, that from a strictly linguistic viewpoint such interference is relatively minor—and dialect readers which concentrate upon the few syntactic contrasts do little to solve the phonological problems which are the main source of interference between BE-speaking students and SE textbooks. All things considered, the archetypal Dick-and-Jane reading book should not present insurmountable difficulties for black students whose teachers understand the nature of their language.

Why then do black students generally have more trouble learning to read than their white counterparts in middle-class schools? The breakdown is primarily attitudinal, not linguistic. Imagine the black child's experience in first grade. She comes to school with a full, functioning command of the language spoken by most of the people who are significant in her life. She has learned to use her language as the primary tool for investigating things, forming relationships with people, and gathering information about life. If she is unlucky, she will be placed in the classroom of a teacher who feels obligated to reform the dialect her students bring to school. When the student asks a question (*When we goin' to lunch?*), the teacher may correct her (*Amanda, you mean "When ARE we going to lunch?"*), or may use the Silent Treatment, refusing to answer the question until it is rendered in the correct form. Probably Amanda will repeat her mistake: *When we goin' to lunch?* Silence. Confusion and discomfort will build until the teacher either explains what she wants (*I will not answer any questions unless they are put properly*) or the student tries to guess: (*When is we goin' to lunch?*). Anyone who thinks that some teachers do not use such tactics has not visited very many urban schools.

What Amanda is being taught in those early days of school is a lesson that white children rarely hear: "Your language is wrong and not accepted here. We will be reminding you of that fact from here on in." This sort of message is similar to telling a mountaineer that his ropes are frayed, his pitons cracked, his hardware weak, his boots worn out, his axe broken, his gloves slippery—and then telling him to start climbing, confidently. The major cause of academic failure among black children, in other words, is not that their dialect interferes with learning but that, all too often, their teachers do. To start a child's career in school by ridiculing, rejecting, criticizing, or attempting to immediately change her fundamental learning tool—her language—is stupidly counterproductive. Nevertheless, exactly this is done in many inner-city schools, often by teachers who sincerely but misguidedly have the children's best interests at heart.

Black children who enter the schools with an effective command of their dialect may, by the end of their instruction in English, become confused about, if not hostile toward, the whole enterprise. What should be an opportunity to refine and broaden their language skills turns into an endless, stupefying series of socially graded usage drills. Instead of learning to read involving books, they may be presented with dialect readers that misrepresent their language, attitudes, and culture. Perhaps as the children grow older, and begin to understand the social realities of their community as it interacts with "mainstream" society, they will begin to sense the prejudice implicit in the school's bidialectal teaching. "School Talk" may become "Honky Talk"; school books may become symbols of a culture to which they owe little allegiance. In the end, they may come to see the study of standard English as just another arbitrary imposition by white people.

But such drastic outcomes are not very common. Black children, like white children, are tremendously resilient and learn early in their school careers how to deal with the minor idiocies of education. Since bidialectalism is only one of many messages of rejection which the schools offer black students, it is unlikely that many of them will recognize it as a particular tool of white oppression. Chances are, in fact, that the students' parents, who see education as their children's only way up and out, wholeheartedly support the school's efforts to teach the "good language" they themselves somehow never mastered. The child is left stuck in the middle, speaking a language which seems to work for most of his purposes, but hearing from time to time that it isn't good enough, and being occasionally drilled in a white dialect which he understands but can't quite speak, or feel quite right about speaking. What bidialectalism offers the black child, in summary, is a tedious, difficult, and somewhat mysterious task which must contribute to his sense of school as an alien, inhospitable place.

So, by a roundabout route, we have worked our way back to the problems of those young black children whom John Simon would dispatch to standard English camps while their parents work. In spite of all we know about language, dialects, and education, most people still believe that if you can just get them young and teach them standard English, they will get better jobs and be forever grateful. The history and the assumptions of bidialectal programs do not offer much hope that this is true.

Instead we should accept the kids as they are, welcome them to school, and encourage them to talk, read, write, and think in the language they already have. Once they are off to a good start, and once their sociolinguistic awareness has developed sufficiently (when they are eleven or twelve at the earliest), we can tell them the story about standard English being the key to a better life. If they believe it, we can help them to learn the contrasts. But we should make no grand promises. As long as the general public retains those prejudices against black *people* which have infected the study of Black *English*, no semistandard we can teach them will offer our students much protection against the bigotry they may encounter later in life. Nor will such teaching diminish the differences between black and white dialects of English. For as long as the black and white communities in this country are largely separate—geographically, socially, politically, and economically—their languages will continue to be different. Black English will not disappear, no matter what the schools or other social institutions may do to eradicate it, to modify it, or to punish its users.

8

Politics and the Orwellian Language

It seems clear by now (at least to me) that much of the work of the language critics is trivial in the extreme. They devote page after page, speech after speech, talk show appearance after talk show appearance to morose breast beating over minor, inevitable changes in the language as a whole and to excoriating certain groups of people whose speech habits are somehow different from their own. The pettiness, the self-aggrandizement, and the sheer waste of time that such activities bespeak are quite staggering. Unfortunately, the effects of such efforts are not always as insignificant as their substance.

The critics have helped to create a climate in which it is once again chic to ridicule the language of foreigners and minorities; to abolish bilingual education programs in favor of the sink-or-swim method of acculturation; to subject six-year-old black children to stupid and demoralizing usage drills; to use more unreliable or meaningless standardized tests of language skill to screen individual citizens and employees; to believe, if you are older, that people who are younger—employees, students, children—are stupider than you ever were. It is not incidental that the 1980 election swept in, along with a conservative federal administration, a new ordinance in the city of Miami prohibiting the local government from doing or saying anything official in Spanish—the language of 45 percent of Dade County residents. The letter of this law, if followed, would prohibit any city official from issuing, for example, hurricane warnings in Spanish.[1] Presumably there will be no Spanish courses for firemen in Miami like those in Chicago. If you sit and think of all the situations in which a government's inability to use the native language of half its constituents might cause problems, you will probably come to the conclusion I have. This law will probably cost a few people their lives. The language critics, I repeat, have helped create a national frenzy of worry about language which makes the passage of such laws possible, if not inevitable.

But there is one area in which the protests of the critics appear, on the surface at least, to have potentially salutary effects, and this concerns the language of politics. Though few critics spend much time on the subject, each has at least briefly asserted that the English language is being wounded by politicians who employ its resources to mislead, bamboozle, and swindle the public. As Edwin Newman gently puts it: "our politics would be improved if our English were, and so would other parts of our national life. If we were more careful about what we say, and how, we might be more critical and less gullible. Those for whom words have lost their value are likely to find that ideas have also lost their value."[2] Richard Mitchell formulates the same view in considerably more striking terms:

I have read—and I believe it—that the Nazi bureaucracy generated thousands and thousands of pages of routine paperwork related to the business of killing Jews, but in all that paperwork the word "killing" appears nowhere. Those who think that a concern for precision in language is finicky and pedantic should ponder that for a while. . . . If our values happen to be abhorrent, as they often are, we can know that only through stating them plainly. It's not impossible that thousands of Germans could have done what they did only because they spoke carefully of "transportation" and "resettlement" and "solution" rather than of "killings."[3]

The issue, in other words, is propaganda—the willful use of language to mislead others or to camouflage abhorrent behavior. Propaganda, according to the *American Heritage Dictionary*, is "1. The systematic propagation of a given doctrine or of allegations reflecting its views and interests. 2. Material disseminated by proselytizers of a doctrine." In everyday usage, most of us (including the language critics) attach some distinctly negative connotations to this rather mild definition. We tend to think of propaganda as language designed to persuade an audience by means of certain disreputable techniques: name calling, exaggeration, oversimplification, omission of relevant information, distortion of the facts, base appeals to passion and prejudice. This human problem, unlike the splitting of infinitives or the failure to enunciate *whom* in the correct slots, appears to have real importance, and any contribution to its understanding would be useful.

Many of the language critics got interested in this problem around the time of Vietnam and Watergate, when the propaganda was coming thick and fast from the American government. They noticed that our leaders were always trying to put the best face on things. Burglaries showed not criminality, but "an excess of zeal"; napalm resulted not in incinerated human beings, but in "interdiction." Any number of subsequent newspaper columns and books observed that the officials of our government, in the effort to preserve their own power, had lied, evaded, exaggerated, euphemized, and generally "misused" the English language. While the critics who took the time to dissect and expose each instance of untruth and manipulation certainly provided something of a public service, they often showed an excess of zeal themselves by insisting that the English language itself was being damaged or even destroyed by all this prevarication.

Many of the critics picked up this idea from one or both of two works by George Orwell: his novel *1984*,[4] which depicted the attempt of a totalitarian government to systematically impoverish language, and his 1948 essay "Politics and the English Language," in which Orwell offered some terrifying predictions about the drift of political language in the real world.[5] In his essay Orwell gave to modern discussions of language a theory that had been offered many times in the past (dating back at least to Confucius, and probably further): "If thought can corrupt language, then language can corrupt thought." The great influence of this handy formula is evidenced by the fact that *Orwellian* has become a word itself: an adjective denoting a dystopic world where language is cut adrift from meaning. Orwell's essay about language and politics is now probably the single most widely reprinted piece in freshman English and composition textbooks. So revered are Orwell's ideas on this subject, in fact, that when the eminent historian Arthur Schlesinger took it upon himself to update the master's essay with his own "Politics and the American Language," he felt it necessary to apologize for such presumption: "It takes a certain fortitude to pretend to amend Orwell," he genuflected at the opening of his article.[6]

Since Orwell's ideas are so central to our interpretation of modern political language, the seminal essay itself seems worth a look. In my own modest library, I find "Politics and the English Language" reprinted in seven different books. The one that I have chosen to use here introduces the piece with an admiring editorial note: "Occasionally an essay becomes a classic, usually because it makes an important statement about some subject with unusual effectiveness. Such is the case with this essay, written in the 1940s. Here Orwell discusses the condition of the English language and the ways in which it has seriously deteriorated. It concludes by suggesting a number of remedies to help restore the language to a more healthy state."[7] I quote this introduction not only because it summarizes the essay, but because it summarizes it exactly as it is usually construed—as a masterpiece of insight into the problems of human language.

The first sentence of Orwell's classic says: "Most people who bother with the matter at all would admit that the English language is in a bad way, but it is generally assumed that we cannot by conscious action do anything about it." It is clear from the outset that Orwell is not going to waste much time *proving* that there has been a general decline in the English language—since by implication anyone with an ounce of sense already knows as much. Only someone who thought the earth was flat would contest such a statement. For the rest of the first paragraph, he summarizes the idea introduced in the second part of his opening sentence, that many people mistakenly believe language to be a "natural growth" not much subject to conscious remediation.[8]

The second paragraph of the essay begins: "Now, it is clear that the decline of language must ultimately have political and economic causes; it is not due simply to the bad influence of this or that individual writer. But an effect can become a cause and producing the same effect in an intensified form, and so on indefinitely. A man may take to drink because he feels himself to be a failure, and then fail all the more completely because he drinks. It is rather the same thing that is happening to the English language. It becomes ugly and inaccurate because our thoughts are foolish, but the slovenliness of our language makes it easier to have foolish thoughts." Notice that the decline of English which was announced in the first paragraph is reiterated here as a simple fact about which there can be no dispute among reasonable people. But nowhere in the essay does Orwell mention exactly when or where the English language is deteriorating *from*. This is a problem. If you decline, you must decline from somewhere up there to somewhere down here—but Orwell never tells us which way is (or was) up. He simply places us in the middle (or toward the end) of a disastrous but unplotted decline.

This omission is clearly not accidental. At what point in the history of English-speaking people might you find a "Golden Age" when politicians (or kings) routinely told the truth, and told it with style, precision, and grammatical propriety to boot? But at least Orwell is shrewd. Instead of falling into the trap that caught such luminaries as Swift, Beattie, and Landor (who each argued that the language had been in fine shape until just lately), Orwell sidesteps the issue and advances his case with the age-old persuader: "As all thoughtful people know ... " The second idea in this paragraph—that a person's use of bad language can be a self-perpetuating, vicious cycle akin to alcoholism—makes sense as long as we believe that liquor itself, rather than certain physiological or psychological weaknesses of people, is the cause of alcoholism.[9]

Next Orwell presents five samples of contemporary language, picked, he claims disingenuously, "not ... because they are especially bad" but because they illustrate "various of the mental vices from which we now suffer." The five passages are these:[10]

(1) I am not, indeed, sure whether it is not true to say that the Milton who once seemed not unlike a seventeenth-century Shelley had not become, out of an experience ever more bitter in each year, more alien [sic] to the founder of that Jesuit sect which nothing could induce him to tolerate.

Professor Harold Laski (Essay in *Freedom of Expression*).

(2) Above all, we cannot play ducks and drakes with a native battery of idioms which prescribes such egregious collocations of vocables as the Basic *put up with* for *tolerate* or *put at a loss* for *bewilder*.

Professor Lancelot Hogben (*Interglossa*).

(3) On the one side we have the free personality: by definition it is not neurotic, for it has neither conflict nor dream. Its desires, such as they are, are transparent, for they are just what institutional approval keeps in the forefront of consciousness; another institutional pattern would alter their number and intensity; there is little in them that is natural, irreducible, or culturally dangerous. But *on the other side*, the social bond itself is nothing but the mutual reflection of these self-secure integrities. Recall the definition of love. Is not this the very picture of a small academic? Where is there a place in this hall of mirrors for either personality or fraternity?

Essay on psychology in *Politics* (New York).

(4) All the "best people" from the gentlemen's clubs, and all the frantic fascist captains, united in common hatred of Socialism and bestial horror of the rising tide of the mass revolutionary movement, have turned to acts of provocation, to foul incendiarism, to medieval legends of poisoned wells, to legalize their own destruction of proletarian organizations, and rouse the agitated petty-bourgeoisie to

chauvinistic fervor on behalf of the fight against the revolutionary way out of the crisis.

Communist pamphlet.

(5) If a new spirit *is* to be infused into this old country, there is one thorny and contentious reform which must be tackled, and that is the humanization and galvanization of the B.B.C. Timidity here will bespeak canker and atrophy of the soul. The heart of Britain may be sound and of strong beat, for instance, but the British lion's roar at present is like that of Bottom in Shakespeare's *Midsummer Night's Dream*—as gentle as any sucking dove. A virile new Britain cannot continue indefinitely to be traduced in the eyes or rather ears, of the world by the effete languors of Langham Place, brazenly masquerading as "standard English." When the voice of Britain is heard at nine o'clock, better far and infinitely less ludicrous to hear aitches honestly dropped than the present priggish, inflated, inhibited, school-ma'amish arch braying of blameless bashful mewing maidens!

Letter in *Tribune*.

Orwell notes that despite their individual faults, all five of these samples suffer from two common problems: staleness of imagery and lack of precision. "This mixture of vagueness and sheer incompetence," Orwell claims, "is the most marked characteristic of modern English prose, and especially of any kind of political writing." He promptly goes on to catalog the specific "swindles and perversions" that are the earmarks of such language: the use of dying metaphors (*toe the line, Achilles heel*), verbal false limbs (*with respect to, greatly to be desired*), pretentious diction (*veritable, deregionalize*), and meaningless words (*freedom, justice*).[11]

These five samples of "bad" language illustrate one of the problems running throughout Orwell's essay: though he claims to be talking particularly about political language, most of his chosen passages and much of the accompanying commentary have to do with language in other spheres—or with English in general. Of the five passages quoted, only one (the fourth) is clearly political writing, and it certainly does sound like the kind of language that Orwell especially wants to attack. It is vague, imprecise, full of moribund metaphors, and "meaningless" words. It clearly seeks to incite people to the kind of mob belief, or even mob action, which Orwell deplores. But the other four snatches of language do little to support Orwell's particular point about politics—or even his more general contention about the decay of language. Surely the inept sentence from Professor Laski, the jumbled sense of Professor Hogben, and the silliness of the essay from *Politics*, all leave something to be desired. Yet none of them degrades the language in any particularly serious way and no proof is offered that any of them represents some genuinely novel kind of writing. Nothing, in fact, could be easier than surveying the writing of academics from just about any era with a view to collecting examples of pompous, confusing, or jargon-filled prose.

The fifth passage presents a different kind of problem. Certainly this letter to the editor is rather overwritten and florid, but Orwell insists that its "words and meaning have almost parted company." I find its words and meaning quite clear. It is a spirited attack on the BBC's steadfast maintenance of Received Pronunciation in all of its broadcasts—a style of speech that the correspondent finds far too effete to represent what he feels is the stouthearted and unstuffy character of the English people. This letter is not really vague or imprecise—if anything, it suffers from an excess of detail. The language of the BBC broadcasters isn't just effete, it's also stuffy, priggish, inflated, inhibited, school ma'amish, and arch. Not all the images are stale—I think that the "languors of Langham Place" has a nice ring and it helps me to visualize those prissy newsreaders simpering around the newsroom with their pinkies extended, comparing school ties with each other. Still, of course, I can forgive the excesses of this letter because I tend to agree with one of the sentiments behind it—namely, that it serves no admirable purpose for a government to officially exalt upper-class speech. Orwell, I suspect, found this passage to be *bad* language on similar grounds: he was reacting not to the form, the metaphors, or the vocabulary but to the content. He apparently was so appalled by its main idea, in fact, that he failed to recognize that the passage wasn't a very good example of the vagueness and imprecision he was trying to illustrate.[12]

Orwell's essay, in general, is a more effective attack on *what* some people in his world are saying than on *how* they are saying it. For all his talk about staleness of imagery, mixed metaphors, and so forth, Orwell is mainly angry about some people's ideas, their purposes. When he directly addresses this problem, later in the essay, he presents some examples which have deservedly become classics:

Defenceless villages are bombarded from the air, the inhabitants driven out into the countryside, the cattle machinegunned, the huts set on fire with incendiary bullets: this is called *pacification*. Millions of peasants are robbed of their farms and sent trudging along the roads with no more than they can carry: this is called *transfer of population* or *rectification of frontiers*. People are imprisoned for years without trial or shot in the back of the neck or sent to die of scurvy in Arctic labor camps: this is called *elimination of unreliable elements*.

These quotations remind us, perhaps chillingly, of the American army officer in Vietnam, mentioned earlier, who insisted that bombing was "air support." It was just this kind of political language which led Orwell to assert: "All issues are political issues, and politics itself is a mass of lies, evasions, folly, hatred and schizophrenia."[13]

Here, Orwell was on the brink of a valuable truth about language and human affairs. He had discovered and amply demonstrated that many of the politicians of his time were using language to accomplish or conceal horrible acts. He had grown sufficiently angry about this discovery to assert that *all* politics is lies and corruption—an exaggeration, certainly, but perhaps not a great one. The next logical step, it seems to me, is to recognize that the root problem of propaganda concerns human purposes. Orwell might have reminded himself that politicians did not suddenly discover lying in 1948. He might have thought back over the centuries and millennia of lies told in the name of the state or the motherland; of propaganda preparing the citizenry for the king's next war; of the hysterical tracts denouncing this individual or that group; of the glittering justifications for the slaughter of innocents which litter much of human history. If he had recalled these matters, Orwell would have realized that what he was witnessing in 1948 was not a sudden deterioration of human language and conduct. It was a deplorable but nevertheless altogether routine manifestation of political language as usual.

This same lack of historical perspective led Arthur Schlesinger to write, thirty years after Orwell: "The process of semantic collapse has gathered speed, verified all of Orwell's expectations, and added new apprehensions for a new age." On the contrary, the "process of semantic collapse" hasn't changed at all, unless we are to believe that the propaganda of Watergate and Vietnam is measurably worse than the propaganda of Dachau and Hiroshima. The problem hasn't worsened or "gathered speed." It is just still there.[14]

A fundamental truth is that human beings often have bad ideas, and they talk about them. This is the only way that any idea—good or bad—can be introduced, spread around, and perhaps acted upon. Language, in other words, always serves as the medium through which human beings express the full range of ideas that they are capable of thinking up, from the most sacred and humane to the most insane and cruel. Considered in this narrow sense, our habit of calling the expression of bad ideas "abuses of language" is not especially helpful.

It remains for us to probe the relationship between language and thought, and its significance for propaganda. The main problem is this: can bad ideas somehow get built into the language itself, can they become so much a part of everyday speech that they become assumptions, guide our behavior, and obscure the truth from us? It seems evident that if this happens, the process is not, as Orwell insists, cumulative. If English, for example, had actually absorbed and been diminished by every bit of propaganda uttered by one of its speakers, the language would have been hopelessly crippled, if not reduced to gibberish, long before Orwell wrote in 1948.

Still, we realize that the language we use does to some extent condition our interpretations of the world. If we speak a language which has names for only three colors, for example, we have a different construction of the world than someone whose language names nine colors. But then we may also have modifiers or other ways of making distinctions among our three colors that are equivalent to the nine colors used by the other language. Similarly, some of our assumptions about things are apparent in the way we talk about them. As Neil Postman has pointed out, we would be surprised if our doctor told us sternly, "You've done a bad case of arthritis there," while the judge down at the local courthouse said sympathetically to a defendant, "You seem to have contracted a serious case of criminality." [15] We think of a disease as something you get without asking for it and criminal behavior as something you are responsible for. We might choose to view these matters the other way around, but we usually don't and our language reflects that fact. Yet we should also notice that in spite of our habitual way of talking about crime, there have always been people who saw its causes as essentially environmental and at least partly beyond the control of the criminal; and always some healers have suspected that people sometimes cause their own illnesses and can cure themselves when they are ready to do so. In short, we are always partially, but never entirely, controlled by the language which we happen to speak. Reality, fortunately, is always there, enabling us to test our ideas and our habitual ways of expressing them.

Although reality offers us the opportunity to validate our ideas and our language, we do not always bother. We may settle down with a few comfortable notions and slogans, often devised by someone else, and live the unexamined life. This tendency lies at the heart of Orwell's argument: "A bad usage can spread by tradition and imitation, even among people who should and do know better." The mere existence of certain tempting lies in the semantic environment, Orwell insists, precludes independent thought: the invasion of one's mind by "ready-made" phrases "anesthetizes a portion of the brain." If language can infect people's minds in this way, it is only logical to propose that "political chaos is connected with the decay of language, and ... one can probably bring about some improvement by starting at the verbal end." [16]

This rather attractive notion of linguistic hygiene would be more help-ful if propaganda existed only in language—if lies were generated or sustained only by language. But all lies exist in a context composed not just of linguistic phenomena, but social ones as well. Our most horrifying modern example of the power of propaganda comes from Nazi Germany where, as Richard Mitchell notes, language was used to create some of the most insidious distortions and euphemisms ever devised by man. Yet the Reich did not achieve its ends simply by building certain combinations of words into the everyday usage of the German people. As Haig Bosmajian points out:

The verbal and non-verbal means of persuasion—including the flags, marching, heroes, music, monuments, mass meetings, goose-stepping parades, fire, blood, eagles, and scores of other symbols, accompanied by killings and beatings—psy-chologically pounded millions of Germans into accepting Hitlerism; yet still other millions of Germans who were fascinated with and attracted to the atavistic per-suasive appeals willingly and enthusiastically succumbed to the Nazi persuasion, making it possible for Hitler to attain power.

Hitler's propaganda was not simply linguistic deception, but deception by a whole range of persuasive devices: visual imagery, mass hysteria, and the everpresent threat of violent compulsion.[17]

Equally important, all of this persuasion depended upon a particular context without which none of these techniques, however powerful and diversified, would have succeeded so spectacularly. As Bosmajian de-scribes the context:

The democratic Weimar government, established by the World War I victors, was unable to solve the problems faced by the nation; the victors would not let the peo-ple forget the humiliation of losing the war; countless Germans were unable to feed themselves. Not only had their nation been defeated in war, it was plagued with internal unrest, inflation, and then depression.

The malaise of the German people in the 1920s and 1930s has been vari-ously described: Paul Tillich referred to fear, uncertainty, loneliness, and meaninglessness; Charles Odier called the feeling a mixture of helpless-ness, insecurity, and self-devaluation. Whatever the symptoms, it is clear that the German people at this time were extraordinarily vulnerable to the sort of propaganda which Hitler offered.[18]

Under such conditions, Hitler's "incessant official demonization of the

Jew" offered the German people a satisfying target for their own rage and sense of impotence. Against the backdrop of powerful imagery, Hitler told the people, for example, that Jewish religious ceremonies required the drinking of the blood of slaughtered Aryan children, that Jewish men were "black parasites" who sought to "defile our inexperienced young girls," that Jews were not people but "bacilli" against which the Aryan people needed to be "immunized."[19]

Although Hitler was certainly insane in one sense, he knew exactly what he was doing, and wrote prodigiously and enthusiastically on the subject of propaganda. He discussed, for example, his preference for having mass meetings at night, when people's resistance was lower and their susceptibility to passionate response heightened. He spoke about the necessity of building the movement through oratory rather than through writing, since the detachment and solitude of reading worked against the frenzied emotion of the crowd. He noted how important it was to gather all the conceivable enemies of the people into one overarching, if imaginary, enemy (in this case, *das System):*

It belongs to the genius of a great leader to make even adversaries far removed from one another seem to belong to a single category, because in weak and uncertain characters the knowledge of having different enemies can only too readily lead to the beginning of doubt in their own right. Once the wavering mass sees itself in a struggle against too many enemies, objectivity will put in an appearance, throwing open the question of whether all the others are really wrong and only their own people in the movement are in the right.

As this passage suggests, Hitler was thoroughly contemptuous of "the people" whom he constantly told of their greatness. In *Mein Kampf,* he describes the masses as sentimental, respectful of force, intellectually lacking, desirous of simplicity, susceptible to emotional contagion, moved by exaggeration, impressed less by knowledge than by fanaticism, and influenced to action not through the mind but through the heart. "What luck," he exulted, "for governments that the people they rule don't think."[20]

Given the Fuehrer's own commentary, we can appreciate the idiocy of Richard Mitchell's notion that the holocaust was primarily a language problem. The organizers of the holocaust certainly did not invent their insidious euphemisms to protect *themselves* from what they were doing—they knew exactly what they were doing, and believed in it, tens of thousands of them. If anything, these "bureaucrats" might have been even a bit prouder if the columns in their ledgers had read "Jews Killed" instead of "Jews Resettled."

The euphemisms were created for the consumption of those outside the program—the general German citizenry as well as the rest of the world. The Nazi leaders were not stupid. They knew that a clear and precise description of what the "resettlement" program entailed could cause problems for them: some weak-willed German citizens might have ceased supporting the government (or as Hitler himself put it, objectivity might have put in an appearance); the Allies, who didn't understand the true nature of the Jewish problem, might redouble their war efforts upon hearing how the final solution was being achieved. The Nazis knew, in short, that even though their course of action was "right", it was not universally popular, and that revealing all the details could cause them trouble.

The history of propaganda in Germany suggests several important truths about the general nature of propaganda and also about Orwell's theory of the mutual corruption of language and thought. In the first place, any given lie is not automatically believed and integrated into the language of the people who happen to hear it. The lie must relate to some human purpose of its hearers: it must appear to explain some previously existing complexity, to solve some problem, to answer some question. We generally consider it a fine piece of irony, when thinking about the holocaust, to say: "It couldn't happen here." But, if we are talking about America in 1983, it probably couldn't. We have a few Nazis here, and they are trying their best to get the Fourth Reich under way. But most Americans lack the pervasive feelings of helplessness and frustration which might make Hitlerian propaganda attractive. Many of us (not all, but many) enjoy relative prosperity, a sense of social calm, and general faith in the future. Obviously, these conditions could change, and then it could happen here. But the conditions would have to change *first*.

Even if the prerequisite social and economic conditions did develop, the Nazis would still have much work left to do. Although there is plenty of mild and latent anti-Semitism in America, they would have to devise specific procedures for heightening and spreading this feeling. They would need not just words, but contexts and events—ceremonies, gatherings, symbolism, sound, fury, and mass action. The demagogues would have to prohibit free public discussion and debate. They would have to stifle all sources of unapproved information, both written and spoken. They would have to provide demonstrations of violence against the "bacilli" and their sympathizers. They would have to threaten any citizens who publicly resisted or doubted the movement. In short, they would have to act as well as talk.

Notice that such propaganda would depend not just on words but on the control of information—or, if you will, on the absence of language.

Though we Americans have luckily not had to deal with full-scale Hitlerian demagoguery, our own recent political crises illustrate both the linguistic and nonlinguistic dimensions of propaganda. During the Vietnam War, we were told that a sinister Communist army had invaded a helpless sovereign nation and was trying to topple its democratic government. At first it was hard for Americans to test the accuracy of this story because Vietnam was distant and all information about it was effectively monopolized by our government. Later as other sources of information began to report, we learned of a more complex reality: North and South Vietnam were essentially a single people fighting a civil war; many of the "enemy" were citizens of the South; the government in Saigon was hardly democratic and was quite corrupt; and so forth. The slogans and buzzwords worked, in other words, until contradictory information began to circulate. Since the American government was not willing to make all the statements and take all the actions necessary to reinforce its propaganda, public support diminished. As the "invasion by a foreign power" rationale broke down, American leaders increasingly resorted to a less subtle form of propaganda, announcing: "We have certain information which you do not have. We can't tell you what it is, but if you knew it, you would support us." Propaganda, as our politicians demonstrated, thrives on ignorance—and ignorance is not necessarily an attribute of people, but a condition which leaders who systematically control the access to information can *create*.

The subsequent American propaganda crisis—Watergate—was an even better illustration of information control. The Nixon administration was accused of certain crimes which it, naturally, denied. The president appeared repeatedly on television announcing in grand terms that he could not—and would not—have done the things he was accused of. He had much of the traditional apparatus of propaganda at his disposal: the symbols and trappings of his office, the ability to control where and when he spoke, the freedom to couch his explanations in whatever language suited his purposes, and the ability to prevent himself from being publicly questioned. But in this circumstance the factual information—the truth—was potentially verifiable in the White House tapes. In order to make his propaganda work, Nixon had to curtail the public's access to reality—hence, the invention of "executive privilege." As we know, he did not finally succeed; the tapes were released, their contents were compared with his statements, and ultimately the president was forced from office.

But it was clear even before the existence of the tapes was revealed that Nixon was in trouble. His propaganda was not working, he was not being believed. Much of the language he and his subordinates used to defend themselves, in fact, became the object of public ridicule, both for being inarticulate and for being so thoroughly transparent. In Watergate, we saw an example of failed propaganda; clumsy, bumbling propaganda quite effectively overthrown by the sudden appearance of the facts.

The central role played by television in the Watergate scandal received much comment at the time, and deserves some attention here. Most commentators on the language of politics refer with great apprehension to the power of television to mesmerize and brainwash the whole of a public. Whereas in the old days, the argument runs, a demagogue could only manipulate whatever number of people would fit into some public square, today's leaders have the frightening ability to place their lies and distortions simultaneously before huge segments of the public. The invention of television, therefore, is seen as making the vast majority of us extraodinarily vulnerable to manipulation. But neither Adolf Hitler not Sigmund Freud, if either were with us today, would be much impressed by television's potential for the delivery of propaganda. Hitler believed firmly that "the power which has always started the greatest religious and political avalanches in history rolling has from time immemorial been the magic power of the spoken word, and that alone." He argued that while writing could form the theoretical base for the leaders of a movement, it was necessary to assemble potential followers bodily and for them to hear and react as part of a crowd to "demagogues in the grand style." He consciously relied upon the passions of crowds to convert.[21]

Hitler had simply discovered through historical study and through firsthand practice something that Freud, as a student of group psychology, described in remarkably similar terms: "The intense emotional ties of groups are quite sufficient to explain one of their characteristics—the lack of independence and initiative in their members, the similarity in reactions of all of them, their reduction, so to speak, to the level of group individuals. But if we look at it as a whole, a group shows us more than this ... weaknesses of intellectual ability, the lack of emotional restraint, the incapacity for moderation and delay, and inclination to exceed every limit in the expression of emotion and to work it off completely in the form of action."[22] Television, though we commonly regard it as a "mass" medium, actually offers its messages not to groups, as defined by Hitler and Freud, but to individuals and families in their own homes. This is a very different semantic environment from the public square in which the listener is surrounded by other incipient comrades in arms.

Watching television is more like reading a book. The audience is fragmented, its members isolated from one another—there is no crowd, no crowd psychology. The event depicted cannot surround, engulf, and

overhelm the individual with its fire and blood and sound and fury, because it is entirely contained in a twenty-one-inch box and transmitted
through a three-inch speaker. There is no smell of smoke, no rumbling of
the ground under marching feet, no crush of arms as fists rise in salute, no
deafening roar that fills the whole head and body of the submerging
individual with the passion of the moment. More likely, the individual is
sitting in his own living room, perhaps with one or two other family
members, with a can of Bud resting on the arm of his chair—in every important sense a spectator, rather than a participant, in the event being
broadcast to him. He may agree with what is being said, to be sure. He
may even get excited and pound his fist on the arm of the chair. But the
structure and nature of his experience is vastly different from that of a
member of the mob, different in a way which drastically reduces the
potential for hysteria, for loss of identity, and for immediate action. While
the crowd in the public square may go on to smash store windows and beat
up "enemies," the television watcher will probably go to bed.

Understanding all of this about television, it is hard to argue that it now
is, or ever will be, a very effective tool of totalitarian political propaganda.
It may or may not be harmful in other ways, and the isolation and pas-
sivity it seems to promote may have other dangerous effects. But as a
direct tool of large-scale political propaganda, television seems a minor
threat.

Still, we are right to worry about propaganda. It has facilitated all of the
vilest acts of mankind. The fact that propaganda depends on much more
than language does not make it any less fearful or dangerous. Still we are
not, nor have we ever been, completely vulnerable to it. For every line of
crazy talk that has ever been invented, there has always been some group
of people who saw through the lie and resisted it. Hitler achieved power in
Germany by 43 percent of the vote in the election of 1933—and while
many of the remaining 57 percent eventually acquiesced to what they
knew of his subsequent actions, thousands fled the country, and a brave
few tried to resist.[23] If Hitler had not withheld information about the
destinations of all those cattle cars, perhaps more Germans would have
fled or fought back.

In America many people believed in the justice and moral integrity of
human slavery for 200 years, but always a vocal and persistent minority
pronounced it repugnant and criminal. Amid every recurrent human
abomination—war, persecution, slavery, organized brutality—there have
always been those on whom the lies didn't work, however common their
use or however routine their metaphors. Given that people have certain
values (for example, that dropping flaming jellied gasoline on children is

wrong) and that they have just enough information to know or suspect what is going on, some people will usually decipher the truth and share it with others. Neither wealth nor education has been a reliable hallmark of such clear-sighted people—the wealthy and educated have just as often administered abominations as they have opposed them. The only completely effective way for political leaders to suppress this truth-finding process is to institute a wholesale, wholehearted program of propaganda *and* information control *and* violent repression—and not even this potent combination always works.

In considering the nature of propaganda we are compelled to face some of the most awful acts of human history and, perhaps, some of the enduringly bestial aspects of the species itself. Perhaps this is why we are often so eager to exchange our horror about what people do for horror at the language they use to get it done or to rationalize it afterward. Still, for all of the insanity and cruelty, there is also a continuing strand of rationality and regeneration. There is a kind of balance in the history; though we repeat our horrible acts over and over, we also occasionally stop and pause and regret—and make restitution and resolutions. All in all, I cannot see that we have either progressed or regressed.

Orwell gave us a precious gift, one which we ought to treasure. He encouraged us to be suspicious of political language because it is so often full of lies and so frequently tries to enlist us in cruel or crazy behavior. He reminded us more generally that human purposes are often ignoble, and that it is usually healthy to look for the intentions behind any given words. But Orwell has also left us a problem. His realistically cynical ideas about the nature of politics became so popular and so powerful that his accompanying remarks about the decay of language and the operation of propaganda (which are misleading and wrong) have been accorded similar reverence. Therefore, when we hear some modern expert deploring the "Orwellian" problems with our language, we should take a close look. We should check to see whether "the classic essay" has been upgraded as well as updated. We should be sure that Orwell is not simply being used as an unexamined touchstone for more-of-the-same complaints about the "death of language."

Arthur Schlesinger's "Politics and the American Language," which announces itself as a straightforward and humble amendment to Orwell's essay, is a helpful test case. Schlesinger does closely follow the main lines of Orwell's argument, substituting more recent examples of bad language for the ones Orwell used. Instead of the holocaust or the Spanish Civil War, we hear about Watergate and Vietnam and "the utter debasement of language in the mouths of our civilian leaders." Schlesinger bemoans the "horrid military bureaucratic patois" that transmuted the slaughter in Vietnam into "pacification" (a term which our government freely used in spite of Orwell's having exposed it thirty years earlier). He asserts that in the final days of Watergate, "language not only fled the reality principle but became the servant of nightmare." And just as Orwell argued that remediation of mankind could begin "at the verbal end," Schlesinger argues that "as we combat the corruption of language, we work for the health of the social order." To the extent that Schlesinger's article provides a careful translation of certain lies, it is, of course, valuable. But Schlesinger is no less susceptible than Orwell to sweeping generalizations about the mutually corrupting relationship between language and thought, and no more interested in viewing propaganda as a phenomenon related to human purposes and actions, as well as words. He refers without qualification or explanation to "the massacre of language," "the persecution of meaning," "semantic collapse," "linguistic pollution," and "the dissociation of words from meaning, language from reality." In Schlesinger's text, all of these interchangeable disasters are seen as achieving a distinctly new, post-Orwellian level of seriousness and are identified as general conditions of the American language itself.[24]

Here and there, Schlesinger does try to innovate or at least expand upon Orwell's arguments, and with consistently modest results. While Orwell was clever enough to sidestep identifying some golden age when language was at its peak and from which we have since descended, Schlesinger shows no such reticence. The glory days of American English occurred, he says, when the founding fathers were putting together our country. They produced "lucid, measured, and felicitous prose, marked by augustan virtues of harmony, balance, and elegance." Confining his examination of American language to the Constitution and the Federalist Papers, Schlesinger is able to marvel that the typical American utterance of the late eighteenth century was "so closely reasoned, so thoughtul, and analytical." Understandably, he neglects to mention some of the propagandistic tracts which circulated at about this time, nor does he offer any defense for his highly selective sample of the political language of the day. But such quibbles are ultimately insignificant, since in Schlesinger's history of American English, corruption began to set in before the ink was dry on the Constitution.[25]

He excoriates Jefferson for pandering to the agricultural voters, whom this particular founding father had called "the chosen people of God . . . , whose breasts He has made His particular deposit for substantial and genuine virtue." This courting and flattering by Jefferson, according to Schlesinger, "sentimentalized and cheapened the language of politics" and initiated the deterioration of American English. From Jefferson on down, it is a quick, grim spiral. By the time of de Tocqueville's famous visit, the language was already gravely weakened, and unscrupulous orators abounded. By the time of Emerson little was left but the postmortems. Society, according to Schlesinger, had assumed forms which "warred against clarity of thought and integrity of language." Now, in the late twentieth century, Schlesinger concludes, we are saddled not only with this lengthy history of linguistic degradation but also with "dictionaries who [sic] propound the suicidal thesis that all usages are equal" and by homosexuals who have brazenly tried to "kidnap that sparkling word [*gay*] for their specialized use."[26]

Schlesingers only other noteworthy reworking of Orwell is to make a distinction between degradation and *degradation*. While Orwell had tried in his essay to hold both ends of the political spectrum to an equally stern accounting (even though he was personally committed to the Left), Schlesinger takes pains to note that however deep we Americans have sunk into linguistic corruption, our propaganda is nothing compared with that of you-know-who. "Language deteriorates a good deal more rapidly in communist and fascist states . . . nowhere is language more stereotyped, mechanical, manipulated, implacably banal and systematically false, nowhere is it more purged of personal nuance and human inflection than in Russia and China." Are Russia and China actually fascist states? One could have an intriguing debate on this point. But obviously Schlesinger is treating himself to a little propaganda of his own. Surely the official party pronouncements of the Chinese and Russian governments are banal and mechanical (as official American policy statements sometimes are). But I doubt Schlesinger has any evidence that the language of, say, the people in the Ukraine, as they go about their daily chores, fits this description. I would expect that the language spoken by ordinary people in these "communist and fascist" countries is probably about as lively, and as personal, and as inventive as that spoken in Wayzata, Minnesota.[27]

Though both Schlesinger and Orwell present themselves as hardened realists looking bravely into the face of human deception and degradation, both are also idealistic utopians, pursuing the hopeless dream of a world in which, the language having finally been tamed, everyone behaves himself. And how is this language-based salvation to occur? Schlesinger stirringly calls upon American teachers to rise to the occasion, to "expel the cant of the age" and "to rally to the defense of the word." This hardly seems a specific enough instruction to revitalize "the health of the social order."[28]

Orwell was considerably more specific. He presented a list of rules for writers that would both prevent them from producing bad language and help them to recognize it in others:

1. Never use a metaphor, simile, or other figure of speech which you are used to seeing in print.
2. Never use a long word where a short one will do.
3. If it is possible to cut a word out, always cut it out.
4. Never use the passive where you can use the active.
5. Never use a foreign phrase, a scientific word or a jargon word if you can think of an everyday English equivalent.
6. Break any of these rules sooner than say anything outright barbarous.[29]

Notice how little protection from stupidity or craziness these rules actually afford. They don't prohibit our saying "We want peace" when we don't mean it. They wouldn't have prevented a Nazi bureaucrat from saying "We haven't killed any Jews." In fact, none of the first five rules restricts any meaning whatsoever. If I should say "Let's burn down the library" and I don't muck it up with stale metaphors or excess verbiage, I have followed the rules which are supposed to prevent just this kind of crazy idea from being spread. The only real defense in Orwell's list of injunctions may be the last item, but it is not even clear what sort of barbarisms Orwell had in mind. According to the *The American Heritage Dictionary*, *barbarism* may refer either to "an instance, act, trait, or custom characterized by brutality or coarseness" or to "the use of words or forms considered incorrect or nonstandard in a language." If Orwell was referring to the latter kind of barbarism, then his list prohibits no idea at all; if he had in mind the former difinition, then he implicitly acknowledges that you can't really do much "at the verbal end" after all—and instead must police people's intentions and actions. Whatever sort of barbarism Orwell meant, his six-point plan for truth-telling is still predominantly editorial—it focuses on the forms that a piece of language uses, not on what it says. The truth, however, does not always come to us with all the conventional punctuation marks in place or even in the dress of the prestige dialect; lies, on the other hand, are often elegant and well edited.

Here is another list of rules designed to help people identify and protect themselves from bad language. It was written by Neil Postman and appeared in his book *Crazy Talk, Stupid Talk*. Postman's approach to propaganda, lies, distortions, deceptions, and euphemisms involves considering them in relation to human purposes and actions rather than solely in terms of the form of language that expresses them. While some of these questions incorporate terminology from elsewhere in Postman's book, the general approach of the list should be clear.[30]

> What is the general area of discourse I am in? Is this the language of law? science? commerce? religion? romance? education? social lubrication? politics? patriotism? entertainment?
>
> Is there ambiguity or confusion over what sort of situation this is?
>
> How has such confusion been created?
>
> What are the avowed (or hypothetical) purposes of this environment? To satisfy the need for knowledge? for spiritual uplift? for love? for economic security? for social cohesion? for freedom? for protection? for aesthetic pleasure?
>
> What are the purposes that are actually being achieved by the way this environment is organized?
>
> Is there a correspondence between the avowed and actual purposes?
>
> Are there contradictions in purpose between the environment and its subsystems?
>
> Are there conflicts between the purposes (either hypothetical or actual) of the situation and the needs of individuals within the situation? Who are the people performing within the situation? How well do they know its rules? How well do they know its language?
>
> What are the general characteristics of the atmosphere of this environment? How are these characteristics made visible? What attitudes are required, and of whom? What is the role-structure of the environment? Is it fixed or fluid? What are the possibilities of changing the atmosphere?
>
> What are the technical terms used in the environment? What are its key terms, including its basic metaphors? Who is controlling the metaphors? Who or what is in charge of maintaining the definitions?

Postman presents this list with many qualifications and sensible limitations, noting that such questions will usually be extremely difficult to answer and that reasonable people will answer them differently. But even with its imperfections, this guide to the assessment of language behavior is vastly more helpful than Schlesinger's pieties or Orwell's editorial tips. It is more useful because it acknowledges, in fact is based on, the need to understand how human language functions in a vast array of real contexts.

Throughout this discussion of propaganda, I have implicitly accepted Orwell's and Schlesinger's and all of the other "good guys'" assumptions about the moral content of the events I've discussed. I share, for example, the belief that the systematic extermination of millions of people on the basis of their religion is wrong and immoral. I also share the assumption that it is wrong for leaders to break the laws they themselves are supposed to enforce and that it is wrong to drop flaming jellied gasoline onto children. These are views which I believe many people share. When we discuss language used to justify actions like these, it is convenient to call it *bad language* in the sense that it either distorts the way we see reality or aims to create a reality we find abhorrent.

But the *we* is important, because *we* is not usually such a clear majority. While most people may agree that dropping flaming jellied gasoline onto children is wrong (and, hence, any language used to defend it is "bad"), reasonable people are more evenly divided on any number of other issues that engender propaganda. Is it the promoters or the resisters of school integration who are guilty of bad language? Who is the propagandist—the individual who promotes strip mining as being "beneficial to the landscape" or the person who decries it as the "rape and pillage" of an environment? Is it an abuse of language to call abortion "murder," or to call it "a matter of personal choice"? It obviously requires the beliefs and values of people to assess the moral content of any given issue—and to assign, if it seems necessary, the label *bad language* to the statements of people on the other side.

The language crisis itself—the central problem addressed by this book—is also a subject ripe for propaganda, and quite a lot of "Orwellian language" has in fact been written about it. I am going to spend the rest of this chapter discussing one such piece of writing: an article called "Sentimentality," which was written by A. Bartlett Giamatti shortly before he was elevated from a professorship to the presidency of Yale University. The article appeared in the *Yale Alumni Magazine* as part of a special issue on the problems of college writing and literacy and was reprinted in the *National Observer*. While this three-page essay certainly did not have the impact of, for example, *Newsweek's* cover story on illiteracy, Giamatti's piece received wide comment and circulation in academic circles.

I devote considerable space to this article for several reasons. In the first place, I find it to be full of bad language. As a mater of fact, I think it contains more bad language per sentence, per paragraph, per page than any other single piece of writing about the language crisis that I have seen. According to my values, "Sentimentality" is a rather staggering "misuse of English" and a fine example of the ways in which political, social, economic, and cultural propaganda may be disguised as salutary remarks about "the language." Naturally, I want to show how Giamatti, like so many of his colleagues, has "abused the language"—or to put it a better way, lied.

Giamatti's article also offers a convenient test of the notion, shared by Orwell, Schlesinger, and so many others, that one can discover the truth of utterances simply by examining their language: by scrutinizing their vocabulary, euphemisms, grammar, or metaphors. I notice, for example, that in "Sentimentality" Mr. Giamatti has followed all of Orwell's six rules for the prevention of propaganda: all metaphors are fresh and original; the vocabulary is rich but never prepossessing; there is no excess verbiage; passive constructions are commendably scarce; jargon never intrudes; and nothing in the article, I trust, would strike the average reader as barbarous. Nevertheless, this article is full of patent untruth.

I freely acknowledge that my designation of it as bad language comes from my own contradictory beliefs about its subject matter. John Simon or Edwin Newman would undoubtedly find it accurate, honest, insightful, and informative. But whether or not we call Giamatti's piece propaganda, even the briefest examination of it demonstrates the hopelessness of Orwell's attempt to test the truth of statements by studying their *form*.[31]

Giamatti's beginning assumption is that "today's college students . . . have lost touch with the language." They are the products, he argues, of the "anti-structures" of the late 1960s and early 1970s. These students are unable "to listen to anyone else," "to take a direction," "to multiply," "to take the pressures of grading." Many of them, in fact, cannot "cope with their work, their time, themselves." "But most of all," Giamatti asserts, "these present college students, and those now in junior and high school, cannot handle the English language, especially as it is written." As evidence of this breakdown, Giamatti cites "the real and terrifying" drop in SAT scores, and his observation that "many Yale students cannot make a sentence or a paragraph, cannot organize a paper, cannot follow through—well enough to do college work." The immediate cause of this deterioration, according to Giamatti, is an educational system which offers children open classrooms, modular buildings, new math, individualized instruction, elective systems, personal development, and creativity. But the root cause, the phenomenon which nurtured the development of such a perverse educational system in the first place, was the linguistic sentimentality of the 1960s.[32]

Here, then, is the chief subject of Giamatti's article: the effect of 1960s-era youth (whom he insists on calling "the Movement") on our language and our teaching about langauge. He declares:

I believe that of all the institutions attacked in the past dozen years—governmental, legal, and educational—the one that suffered most was the institution of language itself, that massive, living system of signs which on the one hand limits us and, on the other, allows us to decide who we are. This institution—language—was perceived as being repressive. It was thought to be the agent of all other repressive codes—legal, political, and cultural. Language was the barrier

that blocked—blocked access to pure feeling, blocked the communal experience of
the kind that flowered at Woodstock, blocked the restoration of Eden.

One begins to hear the inevitable rustling as the straw man is lifted into
place. Giamatti wants to prove that the "denial" of language was explicitly on the agenda of the Woodstock generation. "The first shot in the
revolution," he confides, was fired by the 1964 "Free Speech Movement"
at Berkeley. Those of us who remember this minor uprising as being
primarily concerned with profanity are corrected: "It was also intended to
free us from the shackles of syntax, the racism of grammar, the elitism of
style. All those corrupt and corrupting elements in American society, those
signs that we had fallen from paradise, could be located in an aspect of
language."[33]

Next, Giamatti recounts a speech given at Yale in 1970 by Abbie
Hoffman:

Don't listen to people who say we got to be serious, responsible. Everybody's
serious and responsible but us. We gotta redefine the _____[fucking, presumably]
language. Work—W-O-R-K—is a dirty four-letter word.... We need a society in
which work and play are not separate. We gotta destroy the Protestant ethic as well
as capitalism, racism, imperialism. That's gotta go too. We want a society in which
dancin' in the streets isn't separate from cuttin' sugar cane.... We have picked the
Yale lock.

This quotation represents some of Giamatti's strongest proof that Hoffman
and his ilk were out to smash the mother tongue—"the most cunning, the
most resourceful, the last enemy." But even as Exhibit A, Hoffman's own
words undermine the case. He specifically talked about redefining, not
destroying, the language and clearly indicated that his enemies (however
vaguely denoted) were "the Protestant ethic, as well as capitalism, racism,
imperialism." Giamatti is thus forced to buttress his lame interpretation
with the aside: "And although Abbie Hoffman didn't say so, he might
have said 'Shut it down to open it up.' If language is a city, let it fall."
Abbie Hoffman did not say these things, however, and Giamatti is reduced
to arguing from statements that Hoffman *might* have made. One wonders
whether Professor Giamatti rose to prominence as a literary critic by
interpreting things which the Great Authors *might* have written.[34]

Beyond presenting and embellishing his few shabby bits of "evidence,"
Giamatti can do little but sling contemptuous epithets at the 1960s
generation: "People for whom Zen, the occult, Indians, organic garden-
ing, transcendental meditation, the 'I Ching'—the whole frozen dinner of

the new primitivism—were superior to words." For language never was the enemy of the 1960s protesters (of whom I was one). Surely we did develop a jargon of our own, full of the shorthand of demonstrations, political alienation, suspicion of authority, and general hostility. We also resented much of the language of the opposition: "peace with honor," "defending the democratic process," and "supporting the legitimate aspirations of the Vietnamese people."[35]

But the central problem of that time, and the root of the turmoil among young people, was not the language but the Vietnam War itself. The expressions of anger, defiance, and disorder were originally aimed at stopping the war—and certainly at saving ourselves from having to participate in it. Probably the protests simply made the war an even greater test of will to the presidents who conducted it, and may actually may have firmed their resolve not to "cut and run." But though that question can never be settled, some related ones can. In spite of the inanities and excesses of some of "the Movement's" leaders, I believed then and believe now that the vast majority of student protesters were sincere, literate, intelligent people who had no designs, evil or otherwise, on the English language.

If anything charaterized the 1960s, it was talk. There was endless discussion of the government, the war, and the tactics of protest. There were interminable teach-ins, during which students sat for hours listening politely to lectures on Southeast Asian history and politics. There were special courses and seminars hastily offered by professors who wanted to "do something within the system." There were songs—not always screaming, unintelligible rock-and-roll gibberish, but often comprehensible and sometimes passably poetic. And of course there were angry slogans and shouted profanities delivered through battery-powered bullhorns. In short, the 1960s were full of language of all kinds, from the scholarly to the crude. I do not remember that all this talk was sophisticated or beautiful or honest, though some of it was. But I do remember this clearly: the English language was not the enemy.

Giamatti's argument is a good example of the pitfalls of ascribing to language problems which are not primarily about language. In the 1960s a large segment of American youth decided that the war was wrong, that they didn't much want to fight in it, and let their displeasure be heard in dramatic, sometimes destructive, ways. And certainly a by-product of the tension was a wider-than-usual "generation gap" as well as the creation of an extraordinarily discrete youth culture with all of its attendant preoccupations—both selfish and altruistic. Without a doubt, this was a period of serious, even critical, turmoil for our country.

But Giamatti insists on viewing it all as a linguistic phenomenon, and look at the mess it gets him into. He must concoct a flimsy story about language being the explicit enemy of the protesters. He has to twist the offhand sentiments of a self-described clown to make his case. He has to feign amazement that politics sometimes descends to the level of sloganeering. He necessarily ignores the parallel "language abuses" committed by the elders and statesmen of the era. He has to omit the fact that many college professors and administrators openly or tacitly supported the students' aims. He must convince us that students were attracted to hobbies like meditation or "Indians" because these enterprises offered an escape from language (what if the kids had taken up ballet or cello playing?). And he has to quietly back away from his own announced belief that language helps us to "find out who we are," because it apparently only allows us to become something of which Giamatti approves.

I suspect that for Professor Giamatti, the language of the 1960s is not so much the problem as it is an emblem of a period and an attitude that he did not like. He has had plenty of company in this view. As I noted in chapter 2, many other language critics have also rummaged around in the decade looking for, and often claiming to find, a cause for the present decline of the English language. All this cultural archaeology reflects an abiding anger at a generation of young people who refused a call to arms. Especially for men who served in Korea or in World War II, it must have been a bitter, disillusioning experience to listen to the self-righteous defiance of fist-shaking twenty-year-olds. I am tempted to say that Giamatti should simply have come out and expressed what was really on his mind—but his real purposes are so thinly veiled by talk about "the language" that he has probably come close enough already.

There are a few passages in "Sentimentality" where Giamatti's ideas about language appear to stand apart from his sociocultural assumptions, and these reveal little understanding of the nature of language. "The ability to use language," he asserts without qualification early in the article, "is withering rapidly." If this were the case, it would surely mark a turning point in the evolution—or the beginning of the devolution—of the human race. Giamatti probably meant to say that the ability or inclination of certain people to use particular forms or styles of speech is declining. Still, he says something quite different. Later, Giamatti notes: "Try as you can, you can neither wholly avoid words nor wholly make them mean only what you feel. Words resist ... language won't change its essential shape for anyone. If you engage it, you must honor its deep tides." No, human beings cannot avoid words altogether, nor can individuals change the essential shape of language. Yet neither of these platitudes has anything to do with the idea that language has "deep tides" that "resist" sentimentality. Here, Giamatti is trying to have it two ways: that there are people who wrongly use language as a vehicle for expressing feelings; but that these language-abusers cannot finally win, because the language somehow prevents such abuse.[36]

Neither individual words nor the institution of language offers resistance to the varying shades of meaning that different speakers may elect to employ. If I choose to use language in the sentimental expression of feelings, the words themselves will not stop me from doing so. However, other *speakers* who find my sentimentality offensive may very well oppose my ideas and the language I use to express them. Language itself has no internal policing mechanism which prevents certain kinds of expression—whether they are sentimental, literary, scientific, racist, or religious. But then this passage is really not so much a commentary on the ability of the English language to repel inappropriate talk as it is a rallying cry for the users of New Haven standard English to band together to resist the bleeding-hearted feeling-mongers whose meanings Giamatti cannot abide.

If this seems a harsh interpretation, let us consider one of Giamatti's other flatfooted statements about language: "A group of people who cannot clearly and precisely speak and write will never be a genuine society." This rules out as "genuine" all of the preliterate societies which many historians revere, not to mention the scores of modern peoples in Africa, Asia, and South America who seem to have societies even though they cannot write. Again, Giamatti probably means to say that writing is an important skill in modern industrial societies—as, of course, it is. But the constant burden of dismantling Giamatti's exaggerations and misrepresentations of the workings of language grows tiresome.[37]

There is more to Giamatti's article than self-serving fictions about the nature of language and revisionist cultural history of the 1960s. Though he finds the roots of the language crisis in the past, he also sees it branching throughout the present. He argues that degraded, "sentimental" views of language are reflected in the "corrosive" writings of Kurt Vonnegut, Herman Hesse, Rod McKuen, and Kahlil Gibran. One mistake of these authors and the people who read them, Giamatti explains, is their belief that "language [is] a medium for expressing feelings." It would have been so easy for Giamatti to protect this statement with a qualifier—language is not "mainly" or "primarily" for expressing feelings. Instead he leaves his assertion unqualified and therefore indefensible. *Of course* language is a medium for expressing feelings. It is the *main* medium for expressing feelings. It is also the main medium for expressing ideas about history, politics, art, space, time, truth, beauty and Ping-Pong. But we are people; people talk; and one of the subjects we love to talk about is our feelings.

Must we deny this utterly self-evident fact in order to criticize the books of Kurt Vonnegut?[38]

Surely the authors Giamatti flays are "sentimental" in the everyday sense of the term. Writings like theirs have always been popular with young (and older) people. Simple melodramas and mystical self-help books are enduring, if not much respected literary forms. But was it ever fair to describe Kurt Vonnegut as "the perfect writer for people who felt that words were crowding them, impeding them"? Was it true in the 1960s that "the only texts to be trusted were Eastern ones that might lead to trance or offered no resistance to it"? What about Vonnegut? Are his the texts of "Eastern" New York? And does lowbrow poetry really "satisfy the sentimental longings for absorption of those for whom real politics or drugs were either too dangerous or too distant"? Does this mean that the housewife blubbering over Rod McKuen is in fact sublimating her fundamental choice of taking to heroin or to the barricades? But now I am beginning to sound like Giamatti, full of bluster and exaggeration. And I think that it is also becoming clear that what Giamatti fears is not sentimentality but sentiment.[39]

This abhorrence of feeling is also evident in Giamatti's comments on contemporary American education, as is his characteristic disregard for factual accuracy. Here is some of Giamatti's evidence for the deterioration of English teaching:

It is this sentimental attitude, now running throughout our system, that led the editor of "English Today," the organ of the National Council of Teachers of English, to write an article last April deriding the call from colleges for more "fundamentals" at the high school level.... "The English teaching profession—for the most part—has progressed," he wrote, "well beyond thinking of writing instruction solely or principally in terms of basic skills instruction."

Giamatti further accuses the editor of encouraging his teacher-readers to abandon "discipline" and "hard work":

Judging by the titles of two suggestions for courses in his journal—"Creative Writing Without Words" and "A Visual Approach to Writing"—he would rather have students avoid meaning and grope for feeling. He would urge them not to face the reality of language, though, of course, the consequence is that they will not face or find the reality of themselves.

Giamatti's pet dichotomy between feeling and meaning is upheld here, along with the corollary insight that finding the "reality" of one's self necessarily *excludes* feelings. But there are a number of other problems with this apparently straightforward summary from a teachers' magazine.[40]

First of all, the publication is called *English Journal*, and it is not "the organ" but one of several organs of the NCTE. Next, Giamatti has sufficiently detached the editor's statement about the progress of the profession from its context to make the editor sound as though he equates progress with the diminution of effort. The editor was assessing the repeated finding of research that certain "basic skills" approaches, such as diagraming sentences, are utterly useless in improving writing skill. The editor was not "deriding" the call for more "fundamentals" (although he did deplore some of the exaggerated reports in the popular press) so much as calling for a discussion among the various parties as to ways of teaching basic skills effectively and sensibly.[41]

More important, this editor never counseled any student or teacher to "avoid meaning." Nor did he, or would he, tell them: "Hey, be sure that you don't ever face the reality of language." Giamatti is here engaging in distortions of a low order, attributing to the editor statements and sentiments that were never expressed. The buried disclaimer "judging by the titles for two suggestions for courses in the journal," does not suffice. There are nineteen other articles in this particular issue of *English Journal*, reflecting a wide range of teaching concerns—and many of them recommend plenty of "discipline" and "hard work." As a matter of fact, the "titles" Giamatti attacks actually head two of nine one-paragraph teaching ideas presented as sidebars to the issue's main articles. Some of the other such paragraphs are headed: "Instruction in Style"; "Poetry Writing: A Suggested Curriculum"; "How to Write a Novel"; and "The Rhetoric of Imagination." If these paragraphs are to be considered "articles," then the whole issue contains about twenty-nine articles. And Giamatti knows perfectly well that a journal editor's views cannot be reliably deduced from 7 percent of one issue's table of contents.

But given Giamatti's slip on the title of the *Journal*, one has to wonder whether he actually saw the offending document at all. Perhaps he just studied Xeroxed selections or looked at someone else's notes. Is it a trivial error to misidentify a source in this way? Certainly. But we can easily imagine what Giamatti himself might make of this mistake if it had occurred in a student essay: "symptomatic of the breakdown of habits of precision and thoroughness." But the error did not end there. Clifton Fadiman, in drafting his book *Empty Pages: The Search for Writing Competence in School and Society*, picked up and reprinted the essence of Giamatti's attack on "English Today" intact and unverified. Here is Fadiman's version: "In 1975, the editor of *English Today* suggested that courses be given in 'Creative Writing Without Words' and 'A Visual Approach to Writing.'"[42]

Curiously, Stephen Judy, the maligned *English Journal* editor, remained silent for many issues. Then, in the January 1980 installment of the magazine, he finally refuted Giamatti, calling him an "elitist humanist" with little understanding of students, teaching, or the English language. More useful and less predictable was Judy's presentation (spread over 15 pages) of a mock issue of *English Today!*—the journal as Giamatti's exaggerations had described it. The lead editorial in this bogus journal satirized Giamatti's contention that *English Today!* was an organ of permissivists. Commenting on the fatal attraction of television for young people, the "Editer's Page" announces:

In keeping with the editorial policy of English Today!, in which we argue that whatever feels good must be educationally sound, I say, "Let them watch it!" Responsibly, of course. That's why next month's issue will contain two seminal articles dealing with critical TV viewing: "The Commercial: Dangling Participle or Misplaced Modifier?" and "Hyperbole and Synthetico-Tragesis in *As the World Turns.*"

Another ET! article was apparently inspired by Giamatti's indignation over the entry, "Creative Writing Without Words" in the *English Journal*. Here we have "Toward a Core Curriculum: You Are What You Throw Away."

Depression engulfed me one night as I scraped the remains of dinner into the insinkerator. Sad lettuce, desultory corn cobs, whirling into oblivion. The steady crunch and grind of the disposal brought home to me my failure as a teacher of nonverbal composition. My students were learning, but something was missing from their media compositions this term.... But then as the last potato peel disappeared into the vortex, it came to me: What was missing from the students' compositions was the students themselves—their lives, their guts and souls, their garbage! I realized that I must—*we* must—help students rediscover their sensory voices. And what better way to do this than through the medium of garbage, the very mirror of the self? For too long we have stressed the product and not the by-product.

Guided by his conviction that "garbage arranged is not random," the author describes classroom activities for writing with refuse:

Scream and wave your arms like coffee grounds. Convince a classmate to put you

in a potted plant. . . . Role-play orange peels. Try them first as aggressive, then passive. Make them supplicate.

   . . . Analyze the structure of burnt toast. Explain your thesis in a five-minute
documentary slide show.

   . . . Construct a smell-o-gram for a classmate. (Remember, sequence is important!)
Exchange, and cook a response.

   . . . Using whatever is collected on the bottom of your shoes, make a collage expressing your favorite dream. Sing it for the class.

All in all, this jocose response to Giamatti's slipshod and ill-tempered attack was probably more effective than any extended refutation could have
been. The one-time issue of *English Today!* dramatized not only Giamatti's inaccuracies, but his self-righteous humorlessness as well.[43]

   The indictment of "English Today" is not the only example of Giamatti's ignorance of actual educational practices. Early in his article, for example, Giamatti asserts that during the late 1960s and early 1970s "creativity
was the highest goal." It simply was nothing of the kind, as anyone who
was working in the elementary or high schools during this period can at-
test. Creativity in some areas of the curriculum did enjoy a brief spurt of
increased respectability, but by no stretch of the imagination did it ever
become a higher official or unofficial goal than reading, mathematics, or
any of the other usual school subjects. Similarly, Giamatti tells us that today's college cripples "have come out of vertical grouping, modular buildings with 50 pupils to a room." This, presumably, is Giamatti's ill-in-
formed attempt to describe the open-classroom schools experimented with
during this period. In fact, many of these institutions had (and some still
do have) 100 or even 200 pupils in a single, huge room—supervised,
though Giamatti neglects to mention it, by the appropriate number of
teachers. The main false implication, however, is that a substantial number of today's college students were schooled in such innovative institutions, which is far from true. Though no reliable statistics have been kept
on this subject, a very generous guess would be that 5 percent of current
college students were actually victimized by open classroom schools—a
system, by the way, which is a common form of school organization in
Britain.[44]

   Giamatti also informs us that today's college students emerged from the
sentimental 1960s, when "arbitrary" and "repressive" grades were done
away with. Since he is in the midst of a point-by-point condemnation of
American elementary and secondary education, Giamatti must mean that
these schools abolished grades during this period. I am aware of no public

or private school which did such a thing. Some colleges and universities did, during the semester in which the Cambodian invasion (that is, *incursion*) occurred, institute special forgiving grades for students who either caused or were hindered by the closing of their schools. But in the lower levels of education, no record which I can find describes the abolition or suspension of grades, "repressive" or otherwise.

Perhaps the final factual inaccuracy in Giamatti's article (it occurs in the next-to-last paragraph) lies in this assertion:

High school and college students have been encouraged to believe that language does not require work—that if they wait they will suddenly blossom and flower in verbal mastery.... Clearly, to have been told all these things—and millions of school children were and are told these things—is to have been lied to.[45]

But as usual, it is Giamatti's readers, rather than the helpless schoolchildren of America, who must fend off the lies. Giamatti would have us believe that the English teachers of America are willfully sabotaging their students' literacy at every turn. To the extent that we lend credence to such a notion, we obscure our view of a real problem; to the extent that we gather up all the members of a diverse profession into one, overarching "enemy" of Good English, we obstruct our efforts to teach better.

In the end, "Sentimentality" tells us very little about language but plenty about its author. Like much of the other writing on the literacy crisis, it is social and literary opinion masquerading as commentary on the state of American English. Giamatti has simply written an article attacking the people he doesn't like—past and present students, popular authors, English teachers without a Ph. D. The article employs many of the classic techniques of propaganda: it revels in name-calling, reductionism, exaggeration, and the depersonalization of the "enemy"; it omits much relevant and most contradictory information while distorting the few facts it does contain; and it shamelessly massages the prejudices of its academic and alumni audience.

In spite of his considerable efforts, though, I doubt that President Giamatti actually added much fuel to the fires of the literacy crisis. His audience, after all, was relatively small, and his case was stated in terms so sweeping that even some potentially sympathetic readers might have been offended. Probably the odd professor here or there found his despairing assessment of those cretinous freshmen confirmed; maybe a handful of Yale alumni, now employed as captains of industry, felt vindicated in their contempt for the younger fellows around the office; perhaps a few parents of current Yale students felt encouraged to go out and vote down the next school bond issue in their own community. But beyond these modest outcomes, Giamatti probably accomplished little.

If only he could have assembled his readers in the Yale Bowl, lit a few torches, played some martial music, and thundered on about the "bacillus of illiteracy," Giamatti might have achieved more gratifying results.

9

Welcome to Bonehead English

I have repeatedly accorded credit (deservedly, I think) to *Newsweek* magazine for inaugurating the writing crisis as a semiautonomous arm of the larger literacy crisis. Its 1975 cover story "Why Johnny Can't Write" elevated what had previously consisted mainly of the staff-room grumblings of freshman English instructors to a matter of general public concern.[1] Six years after "Johnny," *U.S. News and World Report* printed a rather self-conscious update on *Newsweek*'s original exposé: "Why Johnny Can't Write—And What's Being Done." While this headline implies that some progress may have been made, the text of the article mostly argues otherwise.[2]

"Appalled by the second-rate writing ability of many students", *U.S. News* commences, "America's schools are counterattacking with remedies ranging from courses in bonehead English to cash awards for outstanding essays." The choice of the term *counterattack* perhaps tells as much as one needs to know about the editorial stance of *U.S. News*—just when, one wonders, did students mount the *attack* which is now being *countered?* Except for one glancing reference to the fact that some schools are now turning out more "acceptable" student writers, the first thirteen paragraphs of the article aim to reinforce the idea of a continuing and still-pre-cipitous decline in student writing competence. This argument is some-what harder to make now than in 1975, since the National Assessment data from 1969 to 1979 do not show any significant deterioration. So *U.S. News* simply recasts the facts: "Latest evidence of the decline came in the recent National Assessment of Educational Progress on writing, which found scant improvement since 1970 in the ability of high school students to put words on paper correctly."[3]

Later in the article, there is a list of new writing programs ("weapons") that are being tried out (for "cracking down") on students around the country, and these range from remedial writing laboratories to industry-sponsored technical writing courses. In addition, of course, there is the now-obligatory sidebar offering a sampler of unskilled student writing for the delectation of the readers:

"Chaucer was the greatest middle-aged writer"; "She called him an idiot and other epitaphs"; "She was pure as a vestigal virgin."

The overall impression created by the article profoundly contradicts its hopeful title: it describes a crisis in writing which appears to be deepening and outlines remedial efforts which sound paltry and impotent in the face of such a massive problem.[4]

U.S. News's report is typical, in several ways, of both the popular and the professional descriptions of the writing crisis which have followed *Newsweek's* clarion call to literacy. It insists on seeing imperfect student writing as something new and ominous; it lays the blame on irresponsible teachers and lame-brained theorists; it holds the weakest student writers up to public ridicule; it repeats the common and pointless exaggeration that writing is "the most basic and important of the three Rs"; it happily passes along the ludicrously inaccurate advice, "Don't say you know it but can't write it. There's just no way to separate the two"; it describes efforts to improve student writing in terms of enmity, violence, and war; and it indiscriminately applauds a whole grab bag of new "writing programs" which, taken as a group, reflect not a coherent and sensible national effort to upgrade student writing, but a fragmented, confused, and occasionally regressive collection of mixed-up schemes and tricked-up panaceas.[5]

Before I explain why *U.S. News* is wrong and why many of the writing programs it cheers are likely to fail, I should say a few words about my own frame of reference. In the first place, I tend to agree with the media and the popular critics that writing *is* important and valuable. It does trou-ble me that so many of my students cannot write well—cannot use the medium of the written word to get things done for themselves, to write successful college papers, to analyze or interpret their experience, to communicate effectively with others. Like many other teachers, when I read unskilled student writing I often find myself frustrated, stymied, confused, and angry.

On the other hand, I do not happen to share the popular belief that these inadequacies of student writing are either catastrophic or entirely new. If there is indeed a "writing crisis" today, then there was also one in 1956 when that anguished professor wrote: "Students at Yale are less competent to write an effective composition than were students of ten years ago." And there was a crisis in 1917, when that worried teacher moaned: "From every college in the country goes up the cry, 'Our freshmen can't spell, can't punctuate.'" There was a crisis at Harvard in the 1880s, where even the "picked youth" of the country consistently produced "dreary" compositions, filled with "bad spelling, incorrectness as well as inelegance of expression," poor punctuation, and "tedious mediocrity." There was trouble in England in 1711 when Addison complained about the jargon-filled prose of young British soldiers writing home. And if *Newsweek* had posted a correspondent to ancient Sumeria, we would doubtless have been handed down a stone tablet detailing the literacy crisis of 2500 B.C. ("Why Kahlil Can't Write").[6]

A crisis in writing seems to be as much a shift in perception as an objectively measurable event. What changes, perhaps, is not so much the nature of the writing which people do, but our level of awareness of its qualities and limitations. Recently, thanks to the media, the National Assessment, and a flock of individual critics, we have been reminded of the fact that much student (and adult) writing continues to be ineffective. But while the current writing crisis is essentially the resurgence of an old problem, a few contemporary conditions *are* different and deserve some attention.

It is insistently reported that the number of students being required to take "bonehead English" (as it is called even by students at many colleges) has doubled or tripled or octupled in recent years. We are usually instructed to view such developments as evidence of the deterioration of the writing skills of eighteen year-olds. Yet these trends really show change less in literacy than in American higher education. At the start of the 1960s, about one-quarter—presumably the "top" quarter—of high school graduates went on to college. The admission process was more or less selective, and going to college was, or seemed to be, a virtual guarantee of a good job and a nice salary.

Relatively suddenly, the ideal of universal educational opportunity was expanded to include higher education. Colleges and universities were slapped together at a brisk rate until every state seemed to have a Northern, Southern, Eastern, and Western State University (often Southeastern State and Midcentral State, too), a Community (née Junior) College on every corner, and a many-branched City College system in each burg. All this construction was accompanied, of course, by advertising which extolled the benefits and increasing availability of a college education. Many American parents of modest means and modest educations clutched to their breasts the dream of sending little Johnny Jr. or Janey off to State U. By 1975, about *half* the high school graduates were going on to college.

This remarkable expansion of higher education gave rise to the altogether predictable complaint that standards had declined. Though this was certainly true in one sense, there were other ways to describe the situation. The change was not so much in the nature of the colleges as in the people who were there to learn. The society had engineered an arrangement by which anyone with a high school diploma was welcome to go to some college; society then began fussing when many nontraditional students accepted the invitation. But when you think about it, who else could have enrolled?

This expansion of enrollment and broadening of the student body helped precipitate the writing crisis in a fairly direct way. While the average teacher of freshman composition in 1964 could reasonably have expected that most of her students would speak something resembling standard English, would have read many of the same books, and would have had some training in the production of college-style essays, today's teacher of English 101 cannot always make such assumptions. She probably faces twenty students from diverse ethnic and linguistic backgrounds, with high school training ranging from the vocational to the academic, with attitudes varying from the compliant to the skeptical, and with writing skills more assorted than they were among the fondly remembered and more homogeneous class of 1968.

But if this population shift is a main cause of the writing crisis in the colleges, how do we explain the fact that the crisis apparently extends beyond Midcentral State, where most of these "new" students would be expected to enroll, and into the elite institutions—Yale, Harvard, Berkeley, and others—schools which presumably are still free to choose the cream of the standard speaking and writing crop?

To a great extent, the announced arrival of the writing crisis in New Haven and Cambridge simply reflects professorial bandwagon-jumping. These schools do retain their opportunity to select the most academically skilled high school seniors in the country, and no statistics, no trends, not even the most worried critics of education deny that at least a handful (tens of thousands) of perfectly bright, fully literate students are out there for the picking. If Yale students cannot, as President Giamatti suggests, "make a sentence or a paragraph" well enough to do college-level work, then either a cog has slipped in the admissions office or else the president is simply joining in the general me-tooing without much reference to what's really happening on his own campus. I am sure that the writing of Yale students can use some work, as it probably always has. But I seriously doubt that the quality of writing at the most selective colleges has actually declined as much as their proprietors apparently like to think.

One anecdotal report on this puzzle comes from Dartmouth College, where, for some reason, no one on the faculty seems ready to acknowledge any deterioration in student writing. Dartmouth's alumni magazine, perhaps following the lead of its sister publication at Yale, set out to investigate the writing crisis in Hanover, but couldn't find one. The editor in charge was startled to encounter the faculty's apparently unanimous belief that the writing skills of undergraduates had remained stable thoughout the period when a grave slide was noticed nearly everywhere else. The chairman of the history department said: "I've been teaching for 15 years—here and at Harvard—and I don't think there's any new crisis in writing." A writing teacher reported: "There has been no decline in literacy among Dartmouth students in the 11 years I've been here." Similar testimony came from the chairman of the English department, the director of the Reading and Study Skills Center, the head of the freshman English course, the director of the Resource Center for Composition, the chairman of the sociology department, the dean of the engineering school, a spokesman for the medical school, and the staff of the admissions office.[7]

The author of the alumni magazine article confessed: "I had not expected such an answer, and I certainly had not expected it so consistently." What most of the professors *did* talk about, after dismissing the notion that writing had deteriorated, was how many problems their students have *always* had with writing, and in this their anguish was as great as that of teachers elsewhere. The Dartmouth case presents an interesting contrast to the goings-on at Yale. Either the Dartmouth admissions boys have been aggressively out-recruiting Yale's, gathering in nearly all of the few remaining American teenagers who can speak and write, or else some element in the bracing New Hampshire air has helped the Dartmouth faculty to retain the perspective which teachers in other, more frantic locales have long since lost.[8]

So then, is nothing new? Is student writing just as good (or bad) as ever? Since the clientele of the colleges has changed so greatly in the past couple of decades, one could certainly say that the writing of the average freshman today is "worse" than his counterpart in the previous generation. But when we talk about "worse," we really mean (or should mean) that more of these students are coming from homes and communities where standard English is not routinely spoken, from families without a history of college attendance, and from schools lacking a curriculum attuned to the styles of language and writing which most colleges continue to demand. The resurgence of freshman English, in this context, represents the rather explicit attempt of higher education to assimilate such students into another culture—to teach them ways of talking and thinking and behaving and writing which, unlike many freshmen of the past, they did not learn at home. To the extent that the elite institutions have recruited, admitted, and tried to educate some of these students, they have also shared in this effort.

Having said all this about changing populations and about the perpetual difficulties with student writing, I am still willing to entertain the possiblity that other changes may have left today's students less prepared to write than their predecessors. I think that some such changes have occurred, though they are relatively minor. As I noted earlier, high school enrollment figures do show a considerable decline in the amount of English studied during the 1970s. And, of course, some of the remaining English courses which students do take fall into the dreaded category of "electives." While the actual silliness and triviality of classes in film study and media ecology have been vastly exaggerated by critics, the fact remains that such courses probably require less writing than the more traditional literature/grammar/composition program offered to earlier students. All of these changes certainly do imply a modest decrease in writing practice among current high school students. Still, if there were a direct correlation between the amount of English instruction and the quality of writing, we should have seen at least a 10 percent drop-off in the National Assessment writing scores of seventeen-year-olds over the last decade, while in fact the scores have stayed the same.

There has been another, less recognized factor working against the practice of writing in the high schools over the past three decades. From the time of President Eliot at Harvard, one of the main requirements for entry into college was the writing of admissions essays. These papers were written on assigned topics by prospective students and were then scored, usually by members of the college faculty. We recall, no doubt, Adams Sherman Hill's exhaustion in 1881 after having read 5,000 of these "dreary" writing samples. However discouraging they may have been, most of the selective colleges retained the essays as a criterion for admission for almost a century. They even went so far as to establish the College Board, a body whose task it was, among other duties, to organize the collection of the samples. But in the middle 1950s, the College Board itself proposed a new approach to admissions testing which was to do away with all the "dreary" samples and usher in a new era of efficient, scientific admissions. Thomas Wheeler has described the impact of the Scholastic Aptitude Tests on the teaching of writing in high schools.

When the university dropped the essay requirement, it failed to recognize the power of the system it had launched. Once the college entrance exams were objective, secondary schools asked for less writing. Urged on by test manufacturers, high schools began to use objective tests both to prepare their students and for their own examinations. The university, by sanctioning the objective system, bears a terrible responsibility for the decline of writing in the United States.

While I am obviously less convinced of the gravity of the decline than Wheeler, I think his point is valuable. Not only did the rise of objective testing discourage teachers from working on writing with their students, it helped to create the atmosphere in which all those maligned elective courses quite naturally developed. And the irony recirculates and compounds itself as jolly ETS researchers now churn out bundles of new multiple-choice tests of *writing*.[9]

Given all of these changes in testing, schooling, and society, we may concede that the average teenager today has somewhat less experience and proficiency in writing than his precursor of ten or twenty years ago. His shortcomings are not disastrous, and he is capable of learning, but he mainly lacks practice. To be sure, my definition of the writing crisis is milder than those that commonly appear in the popular and scholarly press. Yet mine does acknowledge an authentic problem: much student writing is poor and ought to be better.

In the rest of this chapter, I want to review some of the new techniques and programs—"weapons," in the parlance of *U.S. News*—which American high schools and colleges have aimed at their students in response to the announced crisis in composition. It would be impossible, of course, to comment on every new textbook, curriculum, and teacher-training strategy invented in the wake of the crisis. But by selecting some of the more typical efforts of the secondary schools and colleges, I hope to convey the general flavor of the crusade, as well as its inevitable futility. What *U.S. News* and other authorities see as a vigorous and coherent—if long overdue—national effort to upgrade student writing is in fact nothing but turmoil. There is little consistency in these efforts to improve writing, and the few approaches which *are* used consistently are unpromising at best.

As I write, there seem to be two prevailing conditions in the writing crisis: a panicky sense of urgency and the incoherent proliferation of quick-fix "solutions."

American secondary schools have certainly been affected by the crisis, at least in the sense that high school English teachers have been blamed for it and are now trying both to shift the blame and to mend their ways. Statistics from the National Assessment suggest that English teachers now spend more classroom time on writing than they did in 1974 and that they mark their students' written work more thoroughly and scrupulously than they did before the arrival of the crisis. *English Journal* frequently bristles with articles exculpating English teachers and prescribing redoubled attention to composition. In many school districts, both city and suburban, writing has become a new focus of curriculum development and teacher retraining. At local and national conferences of English teachers, programs which a decade ago would have heavily favored literary topics now feature writing as the central theme. Sales of high school writing textbooks have increased dramatically, and most large educational publishers who don't yet have a new composition series on the market have one under hurry-up development. Writing, in short, has indeed become a pressing concern to American high schools.

What have been the results of this often frantic recommitment to writing? One way in which I have personally and involuntarily studied the results of these innovations has been by reading the essays and papers of my own beginning college students. Over the past three or four years I have indeed begun to notice some changes in their written work which I take to be the fallout from the crisis-conscious writing instruction they have received in their high schools. For example, many of my present students show a greatly heightened concern about the proper form for their papers. While in the past I have generally been able to engage the class in a sustained discussion of topics, approaches, and evidence gathering, these days I am peppered by apparently more urgent questions: "Do we need footnotes *and* a bibliography?" "Should we use commas or semicolons in the footnotes?" "Should the title be on a separate page?" "Do you want it in a folder?" "How wide should the margins be?" When the papers are actually submitted, I find that certain rules about writing are being observed more scrupulously than in the past. Almost all students avoid referring to themselves as *I* (though this maneuver jacks up the passive count), they paste topic sentences (sometimes two or three) conspicuously at the head of each paragraph, and quite a few hang their discourses on a sturdy but obtrusive five-paragraph skeleton (*tell 'em what you're gonna tell 'em, tell 'em three things, tell 'em what you told 'em*). In what I take to be a related development, many of these students now include an unasked-for formal outline with every assigned paper, Roman numerals and all. When I study these curious prependages, they seem entirely post hoc—a suspicion that is confirmed by a round of knowing laughter when I mention it in class. And when I announce that instead of concocting fictitious outlines we will work together in class on planning and constructing their term papers, and that we will set aside parts of two class periods to share notes and drafts with each other, they look at me (though this is nothing new) with expressions ranging from mild puzzlement to outright suspicion.

Whatever happened in their high schools, these students do not initially write any better (or worse) than the ones I had ten years ago. They do not make any more or less sense on paper, nor do they express themselves more or less correctly (despite their frantic concerns) than their predecessors in 1971. The main difference between my post-crisis students and my earlier ones is that the new crop seems to have been taught a few more specific (and often unhelpful) rules about writing—and taught them more emphatically—than the alumni. That they remember many of these rules does not seem to help them produce good writing.

This fetish for rule-giving has been studied by Muriel Harris of Purdue University. She asked several hundred incoming freshmen to describe what they had been taught about writing. Among other things, 53 percent reported that they had been taught never to use the pronoun *I* in school writing, while 37 percent had been told it was acceptable. An even higher percentage had received related instruction about never using *you* to address a reader. Seventy-five percent said that they had been told never to begin a sentence with *and, but,* or *because.* When asked to list any other words that were not supposed to appear at the start of a sentence, students reported forty additional items, including *a, although, also, furthermore, however, if, so, there, when,* and *yet.*[10] (If these prohibitions were applied as a group, they would disqualify perhaps a third of the sentences in this book, including this one.)

On the final question of her survey, Harris asked students to report any other specific rule for writing that they had been taught in high school. She discovered that for almost any student who had been taught a particular rule, there was another who had been taught its opposite. Some of the pairs:

Extend your vocabulary—Avoid big words
Keep sentences short—sentences shouldn't be short, but long and interesting
Don't use a lot of adjectives—Write with many adjectives
Use different styles—Have a uniform style that fits yourself

Write what you feel and don't worry about how the reader feels—Write so that the reader experiences the paper and doesn't just read from the sidelines

While the contradictions are troubling, probably more serious is the notion that *any* such rules, or combination of rules, can serve as a useful description of what successful writers do. Students who carry around such a set of rules in their heads—whatever the individual rules may be—are unlikely to have learned to view writing as a process of communication in which the requirements of form and style shift with the nature of the subject, the audience, and the purpose of the task at hand.[11]

My own freshmen's high school teachers (as well as teachers in Indiana, apparently) tried to "do something" about their students' writing. According to the National Assessment, something that these teachers did *not* do, amazingly enough, was to assign their students much actual writing. Despite the ubiquitous publicity about the writing crisis the amount of writing assigned to secondary students actually declined between 1974 and 1979. In an average six-week period, 14 percent of high school students do no writing at all, 12 percent write only once, 17 percent write twice, and only 27 percent write five or more assignments—and these figures represent a slight reduction from five years before. If, as NAEP reports, teachers are spending more classroom time on writing, then what are they doing? As I noted in the discussion of test scores in chapter 6, teachers apparently spend their increased class time not on guiding actual writing but on teaching rules, reviewing grammar points, supervising workbook exercises, and the like. These activities may reflect the teachers' awareness of the writing crisis and their sincere desire to address the problem, but such measures are extremely unlikely to cause any improvement in the students' applied writing skills.

How could English teachers fail to implement the single most important (and most obvious) remedial activity for unskilled writers—practice in writing—in the face of all the publicity about a crisis in composition? In reality, most English teachers know little about how writing skill develops. During their own preparation as teachers, they were never specifically trained to teach writing, never studied much rhetoric or linguistics, and worst of all, weren't required to write much themselves. Writing has always been the stepchild of the "Three Rs," and it has been as thoroughly neglected in teacher education as it has been in public schools themselves.

I am not condemning English teachers; I am simply describing a lack in their training. Teachers who do have a chance to study the process of writing (as I will outline at the end of this chapter) do discover the importance of frequent writing practice, and their students' writing does measurably improve as they continue to write. But the vast majority of high school teachers remain unprepared and have no opportunity for such study and reflection. Instead, they must fend for themselves under intense pressure to "do something." Understandably, they fall back on those activities which they *have* been trained to conduct—perhaps diagraming sentences daily or vigorously red-penciling occasional writing assignments.

Occasionally, these lonely and frustrated teachers may be better off left alone, since some of the "innovative programs" designed to train them and help their students only make things worse. The Cincinnati public schools, for example, have developed a new, federally-funded project called "Minimum Competency in Writing," which introduces itself as being: "not a cure-all . . . but a good start toward improving functional literacy." The program's flyer announces with unparalleled certainty that "anyone reading, listening, or watching the news is aware of the problem areas facing our schools." The decline of basic skills, according to this document, is "one evident concern from parents, educators, and citizens." In response to this concern from "community people," the MCW staff has developed a set of "prescriptive," "self-directed," and/or "teacher directed" "tutorial units," as well as an "inservice package," some "slide tape presentations," and a packet of tests for each grade level. These tests, incidentally, have been "screened for culture, racial, and gender bias." [12]

Exactly what writing skills do the "prescriptive units" prescribe and the "culture screened" tests measure? Under the heading: "Competencies essential to the Consumer/Citizen," the program displays the horizon of its ambitions:

Skill Statements—Grade 3
  1. Identify sequence of events.
  2. Alphabetize words in a series.
  3. Write five words in cursive.
  4. Write spelling words.
  5. Write five sentences on a topic.
  6. Recognize sentences and fragments.
  7. Use subject-verb agreement.
  8. Recognize singular and plural nouns.
  9. Punctuate statements/questions.
 10. Use commas/periods within sentences.
 11. Use capital letters in sentences/names.
 12. Form contractions.

While there surely are some valuable goals on this list, the overall aim is both confused and low. Cursive writing is normally introduced in second, not third grade, and most teachers would consider themselves to have failed if their eight-year-old students could produce only five words in cursive. While this list clearly is not aimed at helping students to say something in writing, it is reassuring to know that they will at least learn how to use periods "within sentences."[13]

Moving up to the sixth-grade "Skill Statements," we find, among other goals: "Use personal pronouns,"; "Understand the dictionary"; and "Combine sentences and fragments." This is quite a developmental mishmash, ranging from skills which any second grader has ("*My* mother is pretty"), to the vaguely ominous entry about understanding (using? copying? memorizing?) the dictionary, to the sophisticated business of "combining" sentences and fragments (which I take to mean eliminating sentence fragments). At the ninth-grade level, some even more serious business is introduced: the first two entries on the list are "Write a business letter/envelope" and "Fill in printed forms." These are followed by a group of proofreading "competencies," including: "Use abbreviations appropriately," "Construct sentences from run-ons" (*deconstruct* would be more to the point), and "Choose verbs for meaning/agreement." This last item was a real revelation to me: I have always tended to choose my verbs for meaning, but now I realize that I should pick them for agreement as well. Perhaps I can enhance my ability to do this if I "listen the news" more often.[14]

In grade 11 we have the climax of the program—the list of skills which the Consumer/Citizen approaching graduation should have/possess:

1. Write paragraphs in prescribed form.
2. Fill in printed forms.
3. Edit for subject-verb agreement.
4. Edit for clauses used as sentences.
5. Edit for run-on sentences.
6. Edit for improper pronoun forms.
7. Edit for improper modifier forms.
8. Edit sentences with mixed structures.
9. Edit overloaded or empty sentences.
10. Edit all paragraphs for theme and unity.
11. Correct all mechanical errors.

Looking over this list of objectives, and those for the lower grades, it seems clear that the project's title is no misnomer. This is indeed a "minimum" program for the teaching of writing. It is minimal in its understanding of what writing is—a way of communicating information to a reader. Its obsessive focus on penmanship, punctuation, capitalization, spelling, grammar, and editing must surely limit the opportunity of students in its grasp to express ideas on paper and instead encourages them to view writing as a way of testing their knowledge of certain mysterious rules that even the authors of the program itself have not mastered. Indeed, the "Minimum Competency in Writing Program" is "no cure-all." For all of its sound and fury and trivial specificity, it signifies little and promises less.[15]

Whether a high school student is subjected to an "innovative" writing program like the one in Cincinnati or simply proceeds through a more routine four years' worth of high school teachers' sporadic attempts to mend her writing through grammar drills and composing rules, she will finally arrive (if she wishes to, more or less) at some college. And here she enters a system which has become quite obsessed with her writing problem and which has by now deployed a diversified and overlapping set of "weapons" against her insufficiencies.

Imagine that you are such a student. Though exactly what happens to you will depend on the college or university you decide to attend, the first step will undoubtedly be screening. You will be given a placement test, consisting either of a multiple-choice usage quiz or a writing sample, the score on which will cause you to be assigned to the appropriate writing course. Your first writing teacher, who may be a graduate assistant, may require you to write many short papers or a few long ones; may ask you to write in class or may assign compositions as homework; may prescribe topics or let you find your own; may encourage you to write from personal experience or may forbid it; may have you share your work with classmates or may be your only audience; may teach you any number of specific essay forms and models or may instruct you to imitate professional writers; may grade your work largely on the basis of its grammar and mechanics or may emphasize content and originality; and may or may not enjoy working with you and your peers. The one thing you can almost certainly count on is that you will never read any of this instructor's own writing, nor will you ever see him doing any writing himself.

You will undoubtedly be issued a writing textbook, and it may take any of several approaches: it may mostly provide you with models to emulate; it may encourage you to use writing as a means of self-expression; it may teach you grammatical terminology and some form of sentence diagraming; or it may describe various classical and modern systems of rhetoric and argumentation. Your textbook also may be accompanied by a workbook offering hundreds of blanks to fill in and multiple choices to choose.

In your other, nonwriting courses, your teachers will also care about and attend to your writing. But each of these instructors will probably respond to your work in slightly different ways, none of which will necessarily parallel what your freshman composition teacher has told you to expect. If you become worried and confused about these contradictions, your college will probably have a drop-in tutoring center that you can visit for help with particular assignments. The staff you find there (which may consist of either faculty members or student peer tutors) may offer to advise you on the conception, planning, and organization of your paper, or may confine its comments to your spelling, grammar, punctuation, and usage. The center will also have a long shelf of style manuals, writer's guides, usage handbooks, and dictionaries. In each of these you will find clear-cut answers to certain questions, although no two books will necessarily agree with each other or with any of your professors.

Learning to write in college, in other words, is far from a standardized and consistent process. The writing crisis has indeed spurred the colleges to make composition an issue and to assemble people and tools for addressing it. But the results of all this maneuvering are not very consistent. What is done to any given student in the name of making him literate will depend almost entirely on where he happens to enroll, and when. And the student himself, wherever he is, will still have to slog through a deluge of well-meant advice, much of it both contradictory and dogmatic, trying to assemble a set of ideas, skills, attitudes, and work habits that works for him most of the time.

Still, however diversified writing instruction may have become on many campuses, the freshman writing teacher certainly does play a central role. What kind of person is he or she likely to be? What does she know and think and believe about writing? How does he feel about teaching this subject and these students? Obviously, a great variety of persons serve in this job. Some of them are wonderful and effective teachers. Others hate their work and take a kind of painful pleasure in telling anyone who will listen about the horror of their classes. A surprisingly large number of these unhappy teachers have even taken their grievances about students to the popular or professional press.

Sometimes they give gleefully morose interviews in which they describe the shortcomings of their weakest writers. "Many students have vocabularies of about 20 slang words," said one Chicago teacher to the *Tribune.* "That's a copout, even if 'copout' is a slang expression. Half the time something is 'neat,' 'groovy,' 'bad' (good), 'super,' or 'wow!' because a person can't think of anything else to say."[16] An instructor from a state university offered the inquiring reporter a whole list of complaints: "They confuse 'to' and 'two.' They don't know the difference between 'its' and 'it's.' 'There,' 'their,' and 'they're' are confused. For some reason, many students write 'a lot' as one word. They just don't know these things."[17] Another teacher published a presumably fictional memo to her department chairman in which she diagnosed her own battle fatigue: "Thousands of them invade the campuses each fall, and the abolute worst end up in my classes. . . . I'm beginning to believe that no one under the age of 19 can write a simple declarative sentence. . . . Mr. Chairman, I am at the absolute end of my rope. . . . I really wish I didn't have to teach freshman comp." In her hand-to-hand combat with the illiterate hordes, this instructor reveals, she has to struggle against such disastrously infelicitous phrases as: "I invite your participation." "I mean, thank you very much," she replies disgustedly, "but my participation and I are busy that night."[18]

Richard Mitchell, not surprisingly, has also made a few remarks about his students:

I was certain that the Admissions Office had salted my classes with carefully selected students, students who had no native tongue. They aren't utterly mute, of course. They can say something about the weather and give instructions about how to get to the post office. They are able to recite numerous slogans, especially from television commercials and the lyrics of popular songs and recent—very recent political campaigns. They are able to read traffic signs and many billboards and even some newspapers, and they can claim certain emotions with regard to various teams and even individual athletes whose names they often know. They can spin more or less predictable reveries about the past or the future either in very simple concrete terms or in sentimental banalities, or both. But they cannot pursue a process; they cannot find examples for analogies. They've never heard of analogies. They speak and write English as though they were recent immigrants from Bulgaria, whose Bulgarian itself had been totally obliterated on Ellis Island.[19]

Charlene and Arn Tibbets, although less subject to such Mitchellian fear and loathing, are pleased at one point in their book to refer to contemporary students as "unwashed, unpleasant, and unteachable."[20]

As these examples suggest, the concerns of writing teachers are quite diverse, ranging from slang to spelling to cultural impoverishment to bathing habits. But one thing which many of these dispirited writing teachers have in common is their eagerness to provide the press with actual samples of the student writing they abhor. That instructor who was trying to get out of teaching freshman composition, for example, offered these samples of her students' mistakes:

In this story, lonliness takes place with this man.
Walking through the woods, the trees were very pretty.
The sun was slowly covered by a few clods.
In the story, a girl visits two old laddies in an Old Laddies Home.[21]

The practice of publishing snatches of poor student writing may have been invented by *Newsweek* magazine, which decorated its famous "Why Johnny Can't Write" article with sidebar samples of various Johnnies' illiteracies.

Shortly after *Newsweek* had struck, a Chicago City College teacher wrote his own long article in the *Tribune*, bracketing testimony about his own nobility with dozens of student errors:

Televusion to me is a very educational value, beneficial in a grand spectrum of helpful material in every day life.

The values I see in television isn't much because it can occupy your mine and how stable you are nowadays television mostly describing racial sex or something on that level and young children dont need to be educated in something like that.

I were born in the state of Mississippi, where I started school in the south the teacher didn't teach much about writing the little I know I learn in high school where I attented here in Chicago which isn't very much, you see.

Me and English never got along. I had problems in senecte and forming good one. I can do the work just to pass but after a month time I will for get half of what I learned.

These last two entries imply that the teacher, Professor de Zutter, might actually have been trying to learn about his students' previous writing experience—a quite sensible idea. But like too many other teachers, he has gravely misused the results of his inquiry.[22]

One wonders what Mr. de Zutter's students thought when they saw their own writing held up as examples of stupidity (and hilarity, according to the Professor's accompanying commentary) for the amusement of the million or so readers of the *Tribune*. What did these students say to Professor de Zutter the next time they came to class? What did he say to them? How, exactly, was the work of the class advanced by the public ridicule of the students' efforts? What about the student who had already confessed that what he knew about writing "isn't much, you see"? What was the purpose of humiliating someone already so humble?

Professor de Zutter, and all of his colleagues around the country who have written or abetted articles in this vein—exposés that depend upon reproducing the worst sentences from the clumsiest essays of the weakest students—have demonstrated something worse than student illiteracy: they have confirmed their own incompetence. Teaching anyone anything requires a modicum of trust—teaching writing requires perhaps more trust than teaching any other subject. The writing instructor who is filled with a perpetual sense of outrage over his students' inadequacies, who is obsessed with the shortcomings of their past training, who loathes their attitudes and tastes, who actively expects to despise both the form and content of everything they say or write, who feels that such work is beneath his dignity, who wants to get out of teaching writing, who is so contemptuous of his students' morale that he would sell their mistakes to a newspaper—such a person will never teach anyone to write. His students may learn to hate their teacher, which might be appropriate. But they will probably also learn to detest writing, which is a sad and unnecessary waste.

These negative attitudes toward students are surprisingly common among teachers of freshman composition (particularly at the larger universities) and, to a lesser degree, among high school English teachers. They are, so far as I can tell, almost unheard-of among elementary teachers. There are some understandable reasons for this curious distribution. In most universities, the people who teach freshman composition stand on the lowest rung of the English department ladder, and, as often as not, can expect to have their perch sawed off after a three-year terminal appointment. Success in an English department is normally measured by the speed with which a young faculty member can escape writing courses and begin to participate in the *real* work of the department—the teaching of literature. With the announcement of a crisis in writing, some universities have tried to involve senior members of the English faculty in teaching lower-level composition courses. Such proposals are generally met with bellows of protest or outright refusal. Full professors complain that their research will be side-tracked or the department's recruiting efforts injured if senior faculty are assigned to this inglorious job. What outstanding scholar would want to work here, the argument goes, if writing classes were part of the customary course load?

So the teaching of writing to freshmen continues to be done by junior faculty members, and most of all by graduate students who are pursuing degrees in literary studies. Few of these instructors have ever had a writing course themselves and almost none have ever had a course—or any structured experience—designed to prepare them to teach writing. In the lives of these graduate students, teaching freshman comp is simply something that pays your tuition while you finish your thesis and look for a job in your "period." As we have seen, some individuals view these assistantships as a form of torture, or at least peonage, and broadcast their misery on campus and off. Others, probably a majority of these teachers, try to make the best of things, accept their students as they are with a minimum of scolding, and to teach them as much about writing as their own experience and training will allow. What, then, will they teach?

While most instructors in freshman composition lack formal training in the teaching of writing, they have plenty of beliefs and opinions about what ought to be taught. Some of their views, naturally, stem from the treatment accorded their own written work by the senior professors they write for and from the oral traditions of the department in which they are working. This oral tradition, on many campuses, transmits an excessive concern for the surface features, the mechanics of writing, and encourages the measurement of such elements against standards of correctness that are comically archaic and reliably self-defeating.

Mary V. Taylor, who teaches at the University of Utah, studied the beliefs of freshman instructors by asking whether they would accept certain phrases and constructions in the written work of their students. Taylor took her list of potential errors from the 1938 study *Facts about Current English Usage,* in which all nineteen of the constructions she chose were rated "Literary English" by a panel of 229 arbiters. The English teachers Taylor surveyed were remarkably prescriptive, 60 percent said they would mark *My contention has been proven* as an error; 42 percent would red-pencil both *We only had one left* and *This is a man I used to know;* 67 percent would reject *This is the chapter whose contents caused most discussion;* 20 percent could even find a mistake in *I don't know if I can.* Summarizing the responses, Taylor notes: "In fifteen out of nineteen instances, more than twenty-five percent of these graduate students find unacceptable in written work for introductory composition and literature classes usages which occur in the works of major figures of every kind of literature, sometimes from the beginnings of written English records."[23]

Taylor's study also asked the instructors to note whether each questionable construction would be marked wrong in one of their own papers submitted in a graduate-level class. For every item, they reported that the senior faculty were even more likely than they were to mark these as errors. In fact, the teachers of freshman English also said that their own instructors would correct such words and phrases if they were spoken out loud, in class—although with less consistency than they would root out such mistakes in essays. Given this environment of steadfast archaism, it was not terribly surprising that Taylor found prescriptive attitudes among freshman English teachers to be quite stable; no matter how much actual experience a particular teacher might have had with students, he or she was likely to hold the same beliefs as a near-beginner.[24]

Taylor's survey suggests that when our hypothetical entering freshman is assigned to his first writing class, he is fairly likely to encounter a teacher who is both deeply concerned and profoundly out of date about standards of correctness in usage. Another study of the attitudes of college writing teachers, this one conducted by Joseph Williams at the University of Chicago, demonstrates that this teacher probably also favors verbosity along with antique diction. Williams took several good student essays and recast them into two alternate forms: the "verbal style," favoring the kind of plain, crisp language that writing teachers usually claim to appreciate, and the "nominal style," characterized by cluttered, sometimes bloated verbiage. Williams was careful to preserve identical facts, evidence, and arguments in each of the two versions so that nothing would differ but the style. A sample sentence in one of the "nominal" papers read: "In these differences concerning social and moral expectations is an accounting for the varied patterns of decision making and evaluation of answers that is the main occupation of my daily life. "The contrasting "verbal" version ran: "The way in which the generations differ in their social and moral expectations accounts for the different ways I decide questions and evaluate answers."[25]

Williams included samples of these two types in stacks of student papers being graded by groups of writing instructors. College composition teachers preferred the "nominal" version by a two-to-one margin (high school teachers preferred it *three* to one). Some of the teachers' written comments on the papers were revealing. "The language is somewhat mediocre [in the verbal version]" one reader noted, but in the "nominal" equivalent, "the vocabulary is unusually good and fits the unusual approach of the thesis." Another instructor believed that the "nominal" paper "followed a logical organization," while the "verbal" one was "not well-organized." Williams' reluctant conclusion was that the teachers he had studied "associated verbose, pompous writing with greater intelligence."[26]

Helpful as Williams's experiment was, we certainly cannot credit him with discovering the nominal style. Most college graduates can recount with some glee their success at faking their way through writing assignments by cloaking their ignorance with nominal verbiage and fluffy padding. The popular comedian Robert Klein has even built an entire comedy routine around his writing experience at Alfred University. Reminding his audience about the dangers of objective testing (you must know some-thing), Klein recalls his preference for other kinds of examinations:

How about a nice *essay* question? If you're creative—ah, nothing like a nice essay question. You can generalize, you can dispute facts, you can bullshit your way through. You can stay up two nights, walk in, look on the blackboard: "Compare the civilization of Mesopotamia with Ancient Rome." Shovel, please! Alright: Dig it up! Plop it on! Mold it nice! That's it. Ah, looks like a C+ already, just with the first load. That looks beautiful. Mold it nicely here. Some nice phrasing, good words: Renaissance, agriculture ... domestication of animals began ... the religion of the Mesopotamians was ... compared with ... in terms of the com-munity's development ... in terms of, in terms of, in terms of ... You're asking me whether that's black or white? Well, in terms of the hue or what other comparison?

Klein confesses that his sure-fire method of piling up an essay did fail him once, when a professor of International Relations returned his paper with a C– and the instruction: "Get a bigger shovel next time."[27]

The tolerance (or encouragement) of the nominal style is hardly restricted to teachers at Alfred University or at the Chicago schools studied by Joseph Williams. In fact, the mastery of bloated prose can even help students score well on some standardized composition placement tests. The Educational Testing Service, despite its general reliance on multiple-choice examinations, even for measuring writing skills, does also sponsor a number of testing programs that solicit actual essays from stu-dents and rank them according to various scales. In one testing program aimed at upper-ability high school seniors, students were asked to write an essay responding to this quotation: "Wastefulness is part of the American way of life. We use three packages of wrappings when one would do, build machines to be obsolete in five years, and generally waste time, energy, and natural resources. Yet we consider thrift a virtue and we consider ourselves efficient."

In sample responses published by ETS, the nominal style is heavily rewarded. One student, whose paper earned the highest rating, wrote: "In the late 1800's (with the existence of men such as Rockefeller, Ford, etc.) a theory of work-succeed was greatly substantiated ... [and] was examplified by the Andrew Carnegie's of that ... time period." Another student with a top score opened his essay with the nominalist's safest introductory sentence: "I feel the statements can be justified to a degree." This second student relied not only on big words but also on flashy, empty turns of phrase. "Computerization has caused a vast waste of manpower," he mourned; "Frivolity left a great void where beauty once flourished. . . . Great heaps of rubble, dirt and ugly cities appear everywhere. Gone are the beautiful vistas everyone once enjoyed." What is needed is a "progressive program" to get us out of "this menagerie of free time and wasted environment." Nowhere does the author explain the relationships of frivolity, free time, or computerization to the central assigned topic of wastefulness—but he or she avoids them with flair.

Most of the essays given the lowest grades by ETS are indeed unskilled; they often recast the assignment altogether, filling up space with some sort of personal material chaotically and incorrectly presented. Some students attempt the nominal style ("we are the largest economical nation in the world") but fail. Yet even among these low scorers there are modest flashes of the "verbal style" and general lucidity. "When a newer product replaces an older one without producing any marked improvement," wrote one bottom scorer, "then there is a waste of materials for no apparent gain but vanity."[28]

My own favorite among the sample responses to the wastefulness assignment received a middle ranking. This student makes the initial mistake of taking a clear-cut position—"I believe this statement is justified"—and goes on to argue that American manufacturers produce shoddy, faddish goods on purpose, so that customers will soon "rush to the store" to buy more self-destructing junk. The main distinction between this particular essay and the other samples is that its writer seems, for some reason, to actually care about the subject. How he or she managed to develop any enthusiasm under the conditions of the testing itself is a mystery, but nevertheless this paper has vitality and even occasional mild outrage. Commenting on the planned obsolescence of clothing designs, the author notes: "These forgotten styles hang in closets collecting dust. They'll never be worn, such a waste!" And car models are just as ephemeral: "Every year, new and different car styles appear. The men fall in love with these new cars. They scrimp and save for these cars. After five years, the car is worn out and out of style. Instead of buying a car that will run well and maybe save money on gas, men rush out and buy the new, shiny, lemon-yellow fastback. These cars are good for looks only. When it comes to a good piece of machinery, they aren't worth the room they take up." With fully conscious irony, the author remarks: "I can see why manufacturers don't use good quality material to make their products." Such simple "verbal" sentences, with their rather ordinary vocabulary, obviously cannot compete with "nominal" sagas of the days when men such as Rockefeller, Ford, etc., existed and helped to greatly substantiate things during their time period.[29]

What do these essay test scores say about the attitudes of college writing teachers? The Educational Testing Service does not operate in a vacuum—at least not any more than it can manage. Tests like the one just quoted are designed to predict success in college level writing courses. The ETS staff consults closely with advisers from college writing programs who tell them what is valued in freshman composition. The research staff in Princeton conducts countless statistical studies to ensure that the scoring system will indeed reward those students whose writing style is congruent with such expectations. In this interaction between ETS and the campuses, the nominal style is institutionalized and, for all I know, substantiated.

Perhaps the second most important element in the freshman's introduction to college writing—after the teacher's practices and attitudes—is the textbook which students are obliged to use. I have already asserted that you usually cannot help someone learn to write by teaching a set of precepts. Most of the rules traditionally thought to describe good writing are either too vague to be useful to working writers (*be precise*) or are so rigid that they misrepresent and narrow the writer's range of useful options (*avoid passives*). Yet many of the composition textbooks currently being used (often with increasing fervor) in college writing courses perpetuate just such ossified maxims. Mike Rose of the University of California at Los Angeles found these instructions, among others, in his review of twenty newly published writing texts:

If you can't list at least six points then select another topic.
Every word in your essay must lead the reader back to your thesis.
The clearest and most emphatic place for your thesis sentence is at the end, not the
    beginning—of the introductory paragraph.
Save the best for last. It's as simple as that.
Nearly all good papers begin with what the writers think is least important (though
    perhaps catchy) and work up to what they consider most important.
You will need to make at least two drafts before submitting any paper.
In the first place, outlines freeze most writers.
Begin your essay with a simple sentence.
A thesis should not be written in figurative language.

As Rose rightly observes, a student who follows any given one of these rules will not necessarily please any given teacher.[30] Making six points about a subject, some instructors will insist, is too many—better to make two points carefully and in detail. Other teachers might become quite infuriated with a student author who religiously saves his best points for the end of an assignment: "Get to the point!" the marginal comment might say. Another teacher might criticize the student for starting an essay with trivialities, while yet another might be perfectly friendly to metaphorical thesis statements. The usefulness of each of these suggestions depends, in sum, upon the teacher, the course, the assignment, the subject matter, and the attitudes and purposes of the student. Each rule may be good advice in certain circumstances and terrible advice in others. Textbooks which prescribe such rules without reference to the context in which the writing is being done are about as likely to hamper as to aid the student writer.

Beyond a fondness for rule-giving, many college writing textbooks share the belief that students must learn to write from the "bottom up": that you cannot try to say something until you know what conventions it must follow; that you must study grammatical terminology before you write; that the writer-in-training should first study words, then learn about sentences, then work on paragraphs, and finally consider the process of composing whole pieces of writing. This sequence of endeavors is exactly the reverse of the process which most professional writers describe. The *Paris Review* interviews with notable authors, for example, furnish no testimony from writers who claim to have developed their talent through grammar drills or practice with diamond-shaped paragraphs. On the contrary, most successful writers report some version of the idea that they "learned to write by writing."[31] Nor is there any reason to believe that this procedure will not work for students. It is vital for most student writers to try their hand at whole discourses—descriptions, explanations, essays, arguments, narratives, stories—and, using the reactions of their teachers and other audiences, to work gradually toward refinement. There is no purpose in having one's editorial skills, in other words, until one can produce something worth editing. Still, the most-used college writing texts preserve this hallowed misarrangement of steps and often completely ignore aspects of writing that are considerably more important.

Robert A. Gundlach has studied the *Harbrace College Handbook,* which is the single largest-selling textbook for college writers. He reports:

To get the discussion of composing in the *Harbrace College Handbook, Eighth Edition* (Hodges and Whitten, 1977) one has to work through a section on "Grammar," with chapters on "Sentence Sense," "Sentence Fragment," "Comma Splice and Fused Sentence," "Adjectives and Adverbs," "Case," "Agreement," and "Verb Forms"; a section on "Mechanics" with chapters on "Manuscript Form," "Capitals," "Italics," and "Abbreviations and Numbers"; a section on "Punctuation," with chapters on "The Comma," "Superfluous Commas," "The Semi-colon," "The Apostrophe," "Quotation Marks," and "The Period and Other Marks"; a section on "Spelling and Diction," with chapters on "Spelling and Hyphenation," "Good Use—Glossary," "Exactness," "Wordiness," and "Omission of Necessary Words"; and a section on "Effective Sentences," with chapters on "Unity and Logical Thinking," "Subordination," "Coherence: Misplaced Parts, Dangling Modifiers," "Parallelism," "Shifts," "Reference of Pronouns," "Emphasis," and "Variety." Only after all this does a reader come to a section on "Larger Elements" . . . nineteen pages on "Planning and Writing the Whole Composition."[32]

Here, between pages 331 and 350, the authors provide a few rules for composing whole essays (narrow your topic, have a good title) but they say surprisingly little about preparing to write and essentially nothing about revision. The fact that what students can write will depend on whatever material they either have or can get is irrelevant in the *Harbrace* model of composition, as is the notion that students may discover ideas (and the need to make changes) *by* writing. The text offers four passages of skilled professional prose as examples of composing, but the accompanying commentaries consistently fail to point out that each author has, above all, gathered abundant and detailed information about the subject at hand —and that each writer has undoubtedly taken the piece through a series of careful revisions.[33]

The writing process, according to *Harbrace*, begins when students spin subject matter out of their own heads, subjecting it to a series of quasi-logical operations involving appropriateness, acceptability, and narrowing. Though the text tells students nothing about prewriting activities which might help them gather some information to write about (reading, brainstorming, note-taking, talking), it does devote the better part of ten pages to the proper use of the formal outline. There is even an escape clause for the student who is trying to attach Roman numerals to nonexistent material: if you can simply state your "central idea" clearly enough, "you will already have the main plan and perhaps eliminate the need for a formal outline." Concerning the other end of the writing process, *Harbrace* is mute. Revision is not mentioned in this chapter on "Planning and Writing the Whole Composition." You simply "write the paper according to your plan or formal outline," provide an "effective" ending, and be done with it. As Gundlach notes, *Harbace* has reversed Forster's axiom: "the writer knows what he thinks before he says it."[34]

While *Harbrace* at least represents itself as a "guide" to "all the basic principles of effective writing," other popular texts set themselves humbler, if less promising objectives. Plain old-fashioned grammar texts and workbooks are enjoying a comeback, and educational publishers are appealingly advertising their new or reissued grammar guides in the professional journals serving writing teachers. D. C. Heath recently announced in the *Publications of the Modern Language Association* the imminent third edition of *An Auto-Instructional Text in Correct Writing, Form B*, a useful "alternate to the highly successful *Form A* with identical format." From Holt, Rinehart and Winston comes *The Least You Should Know about English, Form C*, covering "the indisputable essentials of spelling, grammar, sentence structure, and punctuation" and providing "one hundred practice sentences and some practice paragraphs ... for every rule." An apparently similar text from Charles Scribner's Sons, *Writing Good Sentences, Third Edition* ("long popular for its clear-cut visual aids and plentiful tear-out exercises"), promises "a practical treatment of the fundamentals of grammar and sentence structure widely used in freshman composition and remedial English classes."[35]

While these grammar books may be good for the publishing business, and may comfort anxious teachers, they are unlikely to help students much. We may recall that NCTE leader whom the Tibbetses vilified for abandoning teaching techniques that "DID NOT WORK." What this villain probably had in mind was the consistent finding of hundreds of well-controlled experimental research studies that the teaching of grammatical terminology does not improve student writing.[36] This nonexistent correlation between grammar study and improved writing is not a recent discovery. One 1920 article in the *Elementary School Journal* begins: "We were shown a number of years ago [a 1906 study is one example given] that children who have studied formal grammar do not write any better or interpret literature any better than children who have not studied formal technical grammar. We have also been taught that formal English grammar is ineffectual as a discipline."[37] In spite of the matter-of-fact tone of this sixty-year-old article, scholars and researchers have continued to try to demonstrate the usefulness of grammar study in teaching writing. Scores of subsequent studies have followed the usual procedures of social science research. Equivalent students are divided into treatment and control groups. One group receives some specific kind of grammatical training (diagraming sentences, performing syntactic drills, learning how to make transformational trees). At the beginning and end of the experiment, the actual writing of both groups is sampled and scored. Virtually all of these experiments have shown that grammar study doesn't improve writing. The evidence is copious, consistent, and undeniable.

However, teacherly faith in grammar study dies hard. It lives on at all levels of education: among elementary, secondary, and college instructors.

Charlene and Arn Tibbets, who pride themselves on having taught at all of these levels, have offered a vociferous and nostalgic case for a rededication to grammar. Although "radicals" have tried to lead teachers away from grammar, the Tibbetses argue, the few remaining good teachers and schools realize the importance of this "older, proven" method of teaching writing. They wistfully review (and recommend a return to) the days when writing courses were grounded in a grammar book: "At the beginning of the year, students would review the basics of grammar in the text, do exercises in workbooks, and practice sentence patterns in short papers." Although students will hate the grammar text "as a symbol of organized learning," the Tibbetses instruct teachers to use one nevertheless in every writing course at every level.[38]

The Tibbetses intersperse their arguments for more grammar study with certain other pedagogical opinions, perhaps the most curious of which is the idea that students will actually learn more English from female teachers than from males (though, oddly enough, the Tibbetses consistently refer to educators as "schoolmen"). Although some men make "splendid teachers of the subject," the Tibbetses insist that "on the average women are better." Their explanation of this odd opinion is a bit opaque. They note that English teaching is not considered a "manly occupation" and conclude that "the presence of many men in a high school English department usually can be accounted for by reasons other than their interest in the profession." I believe that this statement is what the mayor of Chicago likes to call an "insinuendo" about the sexual orientation of some, apparently most, male English teachers. If this seems irrelevant to you, try to remember that the Tibbetses are attempting to show that 85 percent of English teachers are incompetent, and realize that condemning such a large proportion of any profession necessarily requires a rather long and not always salient list of disqualifications.[39]

So central is grammar to the Tibbetses' ideas about teaching writing that they devote a whole chapter of their book to explaining how it ought to be taught—and this is the *only* part of their book which prescribes in detail what should occur in the classroom. Some current grammar books, the authors argue, are too theoretical, presenting students with a cripplingly vast array of abstract terms. Examples of such overspecificity are quoted from two popular school grammar texts, one traditional and one transformational. In place of these confusing systems, the Tibbetses propose one of their own, which they insist should be taught from the earliest grades so that students will have essentially mastered it by junior high school. In order to learn the Tibbetses simplified grammar, one need only acquire the following terms: subject, object, sentence base, base unit, free unit, openers, closers, interrupters, noun, verbal noun, pronoun, verb, transitive verb, intransitive verb, verbal adjective, adjective, adverb, preposition, conjunction, joiners, phrasal units, phrases, modifiers, complements, main clause, subordinate clause, subordinate and main clause, subordinate clause inside main clause, subordinating signs, subordinating clause as opener, subordinating clause as closer, subordinating clause as interrupter, subordinating clause as subject, subordinating clause as object, action statements, *is* statements, passive statements, *it/there* statements, and subjunctive. "This system makes no pretense to completeness," its authors apologize, and teachers should be careful not to get "lost in detail." Yet however "short and basic" this list may appear to the Tibbetses, it is more than long enough to take weeks, if not months, of actual writing time away from students who are obliged to learn it—and then relearn it every year.[40]

Let us pause again and consider the situation of the student beginning her first college writing course. With luck, she may have been assigned to an instructor who enjoys students, likes teaching writing, who has been trained for his work, who has studied some of the recent research on composition, and who even thinks of himself as a writer. Without such luck, she will be assigned to a teacher who is less than delighted with the project at hand, who expects his students to disappoint him in certain ways, who neither enjoys nor does much unassigned writing himself, who shares (probably to a less rabid degree) the Tibbetses' belief in grammar study as the key to successful writing, and who has adopted a textbook which reflects most of these assumptions. This teacher probably will not focus on the process of writing, but on the evaluation of its products. Much attention will be given to the identification of errors in usage and mechanics and much less to the gathering, organizing, and revising of content. Personal, or "creative," writing will not be assigned, either as an end in itself or as a step toward the mastery of more difficult expository forms. The official audience for most writing assignments will be the teacher and the teacher only. Neither the teacher nor the students are likely to enjoy any of this, nor will any of them learn much about writing.

Naturally, this writing teacher and the textbook he assigns will provide the freshman's most direct and powerful introduction to the problems and procedures of college-level composition. But now that concern about writing is campuswide, any given campus is likely to offer the student writer a host of secondary support services, guidance, resources, and advice.

One of the most common local responses to the crisis has been for the dean to coerce the English department into producing a style manual for use by students. At Yale University, where President Giamatti has declared war on student illiteracy, three members of the English department (identified only as S. A. Barney, J. E. Hunter, and B. L. Packer) have written just such a booklet, called *Writing Prose*, and it represents the genre well enough. This eighteen-page pamphlet says almost nothing about finding topics, thinking, planning, gathering material, organizing, outlining, or drafting and instead divides writing into four categories: problems in diction; problems with sentences; problems with punctuation; and problems in general. Most of these problems are illustrated by sentences taken from the essays of Yale students. And while it is traditional and necessary for writer's guides to give samples of common errors, the Yale stylists go well beyond the call of duty in their abuse of student writers. The authors typically offer a student-written sentence, describe it as "monstrous," "dreadful," "pretentious," "lifeless," "hackneyed," "awkward," "silly," "prissy," "uproarious," "slovenly," "fraudulent," or "stiff," and then correct it. Their enthusiasm for the official terminology of author abuse is shown perhaps most clearly on the final page of the text:

Here is a list of words which are used to describe prose styles. Learn their meanings, and pray that none of them appears among the reader's comments at the end of your paper: turgid, turbid, muddled, precious, elliptical, patronizing, glib, crabbed, fancy, breezy, hyperbolic, low-powered, pompous, condescending, flamboyant, vague, pedantic, tired, flaccid, padded, redundant, stilted, derivative, repetitious, wheedling, snide, arrogant, florid, tumid, tedious, dense, loose, laconic, talky, reticent, slangy, voguish, sloppy, pretentious, hackneyed, trite, purple, vulgar, facile, inane.

Obviously, some good professorial humor lurks behind all these adjectives: Barney, Hunter, and Packer don't want students shot, but simply "fed piecemeal to carnivorous computers" when they make mistakes in writing. But such grandiose, half-humorous punitiveness must perplex students who are trying to learn something from the booklet. And all this nastiness stands in contradiction to the authors' careful note in section 28 that students should not be "aggressively direct in their arguments" and in section 61 that they should avoid "arrogance," "exaggeration," and "contempt for the subject or the reader."[41]

Sprinkled throughout the Yale text are dozens of aphorisms for writers:

Be skeptical, practical, humble.
Be logical.
Be tactful.

Be brief.
A little repetition is better than a lot of confusion.
A good topic is half the battle.
A good title indicates that an essay has a topic.
An unstructured list of observations is not an essay.
Write about your subject, not your state of mind.
Firmly state, but do not over-state.
It is your business as a writer to make understanding prompt, not eventual.
Do not overwork the semi-colon.
Errors are not your typewriter's fault, but yours.

Although these maxims tend toward the vague and trivial, all contain some truth. Other pieces of advice from Barney, Hunter, and Packer are more suspect. "Your sentences," they claim, "should be clear before they attempt to be anything else." But clarity is often the end result, not the precursor, of some thinking. Sentences, one could argue, ought first of all to have some content, ought to develop some meaning. The authors elsewhere assert that "most poor writing results not from ignorance, but from carelessness." This formulation is neatly contrary to the actual problems faced by many students who, because they are ignorant of the topic or of certain conventions, write poorly. Plenty of student writers are extremely careful, even laborious, in the creation of their papers, dutifully consulting library sources, dictionaries, textbooks, and thesauruses—and still reliably produce both empty and incorrect writing. Ignorance—a word that I use not as an epithet but to describe a student's failure to write effectively because some information or skill is lacking—is the central fault of much student writing; carelessness is a minor and much more easily remedied problem.[42]

Barney, Hunter, and Packer participate vigorously in the general professorial assault on certain horrible words. Dangling *hopefully*, as one might expect, is identified as "nonsense," as are *basic* and *massive* unless the "image of a base or mass is present." *Insightful* and *enthuse*, they rule, "are not English words." More original is the authors' assertion that certain seemingly useful, common verbs are actually the last resort of mediocre writers. Such crutches include: *is, seems, appears, exists, reproduces, impresses.* Many other words fail to win the Barney-Hunter-Packer seal of approval. Either entirely outlawed or restricted by the Yale handbook are: *almost, quite, rather, dichotomy, delineate, satiate, ambience, relevant, involve, paradigm, putative, committed, aspects, manifest, depict, evoke, blatant, obvious, elicit, real, ostensible, sympathize, empathy, emblematic, overall, evince, factor, function, positive,* (or *negative) feelings for, reactions, impact, utilize, relative to, interpersonal, feedback, parameter, extrapolate, options, input, interface,* and *life-style.* These words don't even merit a decent burial; they are simply lumped together in lists which imply that almost any conceivable use of them will be wrong.[43]

The Yale pamphleteers' condescending tone and vacuous maximizing are minor shortcomings when compared with the abundant contradictions of the handbook itself. Within a mere eighteen pages of prescriptions, the authors cannot keep their own rules straight. Sometimes they contradict themselves within a line or two. "Avoid extensive quotation or para-phrase," they insist on page 15. On page 16 they counsel without any ex-planation or clarification: "Quote or paraphrase essential material." The authors' advice on beginning an essay is thoroughly self-canceling: "A statement about your method or approach to a topic is often welcome. You need not be over-explicit. Usually begin by making statements about your subject, not about your method." In describing the correct tone of the academic essay, they tell students to "write as if you were speaking to a class," while in the following sentence they note that "the style should be formal." Back on page 5, they were warning against a writer's "trying to impress his readers with his formal elegance of style." Later, the authori-ties advise: "Avoid self-consciousness." It is hard to imagine how any stu-dent is supposed to construct, out of these conflicting pieces of advice, a sense of the correct academic style (unselfconsciously speech-related non-elegant formality?) while simultaneously skirting the dreaded pitfalls of prissiness, turgidity, breeziness, et cetera.[44]

Two errors that receive particularly scathing commentaries in the pamphlet are the overuse of the passive and the word *this* ("the worst culprit among vague pronouns"). The authors illustrate the *this* problem with this (uh, the following) pair of student sentences: "Homer says that Odysseus is weeping when he is on the island of the sun-god and loses all the crewmen. This shows his humanity." On the following page, the au-thors present a famous sentence from Orwell's "Politics and the English Language": "Defenceless villages are bombarded from the air, the inhabi-tants driven out into the countryside, the cattle machine-gunned, the huts set on fire with incendiary bullets: this is called *pacification.*" Except for its colon, this sentence is structurally quite similar to the ones about Odys-seus, with the substitution of passive for active verbs. Yet the authors pre-sent Orwell not to reinforce their point about passives and about *this*, but as a shining example of "clarity" and "strength."[45]

Barney, Hunter, and Packer are deeply concerned with etymologies and particularly with the distinction between Latinate and Germanic vocabulary. They encourage students to "substitute concrete [Germanic] words for Latinate abstractions." Their rule is this: "don't use Latinate diction if you can translate into Germanic equivalents with no loss of meaning." They admit that this switch to Germanic words may be hard for students but advise: "Force yourself to use them anyway; your style will become livelier and more vigorous, less pretentious and less dull." A few lines down, they offer as an example of superb diction a paragraph from Joseph Conrad, in which half the words are Latinate and half Germanic. The previous rule is inoperative; you don't substitute Germanic for Latinate after all, but "keep a balance." [46]

I do not mean to suggest that Barney, Hunter, and Packer are wrong about everything. Clearly, they know how to write and they know what they like. Although the contradictions suggest some editorial sloppiness, all can be explained. There may be good reasons why Orwell's passives are better than someone else's passives, why one may want to write formally but not too formally, and why words like *dichotomy* and *interface* may offend certain readers or mismatch with certain topics. Unfortunately, the handbook doesn't begin to help students make the necessary distinctions. It simply presents them with huge, sweeping rules delivered in a tone of smug irritation at its readers' ignorance.

If students at Yale have been discouraged or insulted by the indigenous style manual, they might instead consult a much friendlier and chattier publication called *Off to College*. This glossy magazine is distributed free each fall to incoming freshmen at hundreds of colleges and universities around the country—though I cannot say for sure whether it has actually circulated in New Haven. *Off to College* is published by the nonprofit Guidance Research Group and is overseen by an advisory board of professors from such places as the University of California, Ohio State University, and Indiana University. The 1980 edition presented new students with sixty-two pages of advice about adjusting to and succeeding in the world of higher education. Amid such other tips as "Coexisting With Your Roommate" and "Managing Time for Study and Play," students are instructed in "How to Prepare Research Papers" by Norman L. Trusty, associate professor of history at Purdue University. [47]

Professor Trusty admits at the outset that paper writing is "a chore," but reassures his readers that it is really nothing more than a problem in "materials management." He offers a "foolproof" system for the preparation of research papers which will raise the student's grades and make the process fun. After a few words (and fewer explanations) about selecting a "narrow," appropriate topic, Trusty launches into the seven crucial steps of the "foolproof" procedure:

1. Establish your thesis or viewpoint early. You'll always find more after you decide what you're looking for. . . .
2. Use 3 x 5 cards for bibliography with only one complete citation on each. . . . For larger papers use alphabetical index tabs. You may prefer to use two sets of A-Z tabs, one for works finished, the others for works to be investigated.
3. "Stationery's for the hicks, scholars use 4 x 6." Every particle of information extracted from your reading should be put on lined or plain 4 x 6 cards. Each card should hold ONE unit of information, never more. . . . Build a portable research center by gluing two manila accordian files back to back, one 3 x 5, one 4 x 6, for your cards. That's all you'll need to carry to the library. . . .
4. Write directly from your cards . . . at a large table reread (a useful final review) and sort your cards by topic. You should now have five to fifteen stacks of cards. Spread out the first topic and shift the cards until they tell their story. No story? Back to the library!
5. Write your rough draft quickly. . . . Finish the first draft well before the due date and let your ideas "soak" awhile. . . .
6. Now, with your mind refreshed on the subject, go over the first draft several times, checking all aspects and elements of the paper in great detail. . . .
7. Make your paper look sharp. Use a good typewriter. . . . Keep a good black ribbon in the machine. . . . Use quality white bond paper. Make erasures with great care. A plastic or manila folder gives a professional appearance. . . . [48]

It is sobering to forecast the fate of a student writer inexperienced or naive enough to follow such trivially hypermethodical advice. I can just see poor Joe Frosh now, sitting in the library, his dutifully constructed double accordian file emptied of its contents, and the would-be author dealing and redealing his cards into assorted stacks, waiting with mounting anxiety for them to "tell their story."

But if no national or local guide to composition solves the student's problems, a telephone call can reach one of the writing "crisis lines" that several enterprising colleges around the country have established. At Illinois State University, for example, the English department maintains a "Grammar Hotline"—a phone number which troubled student writers are supposed to call for help with problems in syntax, usage, punctuation, and the like. The staff of the campus writing lab simply take turns answering the calls as they come in, providing each caller with an answer and some advice on how to use reference books to solve future dilemmas.[49] The staff of the "Hotline" confesses, however, that their service does not just reach its intended audience. "We thought a lot of students would call," says the director, "and some do. But most of the calls are from non-students." Some of the callers, it turns out, are people "who are plagued by what they think is a terrible abuse of the English language" and "want somebody to commiserate with." Other inquiries come from "businessmen, secretaries, and free-lance writers" asking questions like whether to use *a* or *an* before "Europe" (beats me). The director admits to feeling a certain anxiety in this role: "At first we were nervous. We were afraid somebody would trip us up and then say we were stupid. It's fun to see if we can answer all the questions. It's really interesting." At last report, the "Hotline" operators were pursuing the "correct" abbreviation for *bucket* and trying to find the third word in the English language that ends with *-gry* (other than *angry* and *hungry*).[50]

The student who gets her information about writing from a "Grammar Hotline," from the tutors in the campus writing lab, from her scores on writing placement tests, from the cut-and-paste instructions of a trusty history professor, from the official local style manual, from the *Harbrace College Handbook*, from her teacher of freshman composition, and from eighteen other sources is going to receive much conflicting advice. Perhaps the only consistent message she will get, both from what all these sources say and from the fact that they all exist, is that writing is an extraordinarily complicated and difficult "chore."

This, it seems to me, is the most insidious advice of all, and it comes from all corners. The writing crisis has spawned not only a whole raft of programs and materials but a continuous flow of academic flapdoodle about what dreadfully challenging, intellectually manful work writing is supposed to be. Many of the very people who are paid to teach students to write spend their off hours (when they're not ridiculing their students) declaiming with apparently unconscious irony that learning to write is learning to think—or that if you can't write about something you don't really know it, or some other self-serving piety. If the teachers who propagate these homilies ever stopped to apply them to the difficulties which students have in learning to write, they might be able to feel some sympathy instead of their customary contempt. But all these complainers want is to make themselves seem important and their tasks sound Herculean; making the connection with students' failures would take half the fun out of bemoaning them.

Clifton Fadiman has provided a good example of this unhelpful attitude in his book *Empty Pages: The Search for Writing Competence in School and Society:* "Writing is not a game. Nor is it a pleasure, though pleasure may follow the completion of a satisfactory sentence or paragraph. Writers do not 'enjoy' writing; it is simply something that their natures and talents require them to do." Fadiman goes on to assert that students who use writing to express their feelings are sadly deluded. Such a use of writing, he explains: "does not reinforce the urge to learn. There is a great difference between students who write to *express* themselves and those who write to express their *selves*." The fact that Fadiman would not (perhaps could not) go on to explain the nature of this "great difference" signals the confusion of his underlying idea.[51]

In the first place, everyone who ever learned to write, Fadiman included, began by using writing (as a child, no doubt a very young one in Fadiman's case) as a way of expressing themselves. This early use of personal writing certainly *does* reinforce the urge to learn. Some young writers become sufficiently excited about the usefulness of writing that they continue to practice their skills, gradually branching out into less obviously personal modes of discourse. But even if they become professional writers and literary critics, self-expression (even of feelings) remains an essential element of why they write and what they write. Fadiman, for example, did not compose *Empty Pages* simply because something in his nature compelled it. He wrote the book because, as he himself says, he feels "a passion for our magnificent language" and "a deep concern for . . . literacy." He senses that "we are all in some sort of trouble" and he fears the impending "impoverishment of the human spirit." In other words, Fadiman has written his book to (among other purposes he seems to find nobler) express his feelings on a subject.[52]

His advice about the funless toil of writing also has a curiously anti-intellectual twist. Fadiman seems to believe that anything requiring effort and care is necessarily unpleasant. Not only is this pedagogically self-defeating advice ("Now, class, you are really going to hate this next lesson"), it is also wrong. If you go into a class of second or third or fourth graders who are writing and ask them how they feel about what they are doing, they will tell you that they love it. Many older children, of course, learn to despise writing (as most adults do), not so much because of the nature of the work itself but because of what and how they have been taught, and because people tell them what a hard, miserable struggle it is supposed to be. But it makes no more sense to say that writing is unpleasant than to say that playing the piano or reading a book or shingling a roof is unpleasant. Certainly, when human beings do any kind of complex and absorbing work, they tend to derive much of their satisfaction from those moments when they pause to enjoy the passage played, the chapter read, or the straight line of shingles laid. But there is pleasure in the doing itself, there is pleasure and satisfaction in productive activity. To deny this is to deny that *anything* is pleasant, at least until afterwards.

Fadiman's statement that writers are people whose nature requires them to write, while it was doubtless intended to reflect the modesty of its author, actually bespeaks the opposite. He is simply passing along here the standard mythology of writing according to the professional author: writing as devilishly, indescribably difficult work that can only be done well by magically gifted creatures locked alone in barren garrets, manfully engaged in mortal combat with those deadly, empty pages. It is hard to imagine that the average student at Midcentral State could feel much in common with such "real" writers, whose "natures" make them write so well, if so painfully.

Now I want to shift from college back to elementary and secondary education, and talk about how some students are learning to write, and write well. For the writing crisis, in spite of its persistent exaggerations and misbegotten innovations, has actually had some worthwhile results.

Over the past five years I have been working with the Illinois Writing Project (IWP), a federally-funded program aimed at the improvement of writing in several dozen elementary, junior high, and senior high schools. While we have had much in common with the widely acclaimed Bay Area Writing Project in San Francisco, we have had no affiliation with it and have done many things differently. Our basic approach has been to conduct relatively long (thirty to ninety hour) in-service programs with teachers, testing their students' writing before and after the program. Our research, which has used the instruments and methodology of the National Assessment, has shown that the writing of students taught by IWP teachers typically improves about twice as much as that of matched control students. This highly significant growth in writing skill($p < .01$, for the statisticians in the audience) has allowed the program to be, in the terminology of educational research, "validated" by the appropriate officials and approved for "dissemination." In other words, we have proved to the satisfaction of various investigators that what we do works.

I want to briefly outline the IWP program here, to show how writing *can* be taught to students and to their teachers. While I make no exclusive claim for the effectiveness of our program as compared with other similar efforts, I do want to assert the importance of its underlying principles. This way of training teachers and teaching children succeeds because it respects the nature and difficulties of writing itself. Some of its assumptions and procedures intentionally run counter to many of the traditional assumptions and procedures of writing instruction—in fact, if the program did not differ in these ways, it wouldn't work.

What, as a result of all those workshop sessions, do IWP-trained teachers do differently?

1. *They write.* For the first eight hours of the program the teachers themselves write on a series of assignments and share the results with each other in certain structured ways. This experience is usually quite threatening at first, since most working teachers have had no formal training in writing and are required to do little writing in connection with their daily work. When the first assignment is given, groans and protests arise, just as they do from rooms full of students. With some encouragement, the teachers (and the workshop leaders) begin to write, and they soon discover the fear and pleasure of reading their work to small groups of colleagues. All of the initial assignments are on personal topics that move from the comic to the serious. As an atmosphere of enthusiasm, confidence, and mutual trust is built, the teachers begin to explore increasingly personal issues. By the end of the sixth or seventh hour, without prodding or finagling by the leaders, the teachers are typically writing about powerful and intimate experiences often centering on love and loss. As some of the stories are read aloud to the group, there are always cries of admiration, and almost always a few tears.

This powerful emotional experience is essential to everything that follows. It is not achieved by "sensitivity training," a "T-Group" exercise, or any other form of calculated emotional manipulation. It is a natural demonstration of the power of writing itself—of using the written word to communicate significant ideas to others in a climate of trust. Through this experience of personal writing, teachers make empathic connections with the predicament of their student writers. They are reminded that writing is risk-taking behavior; that it is often hard to anticipate the reactions of an audience; that attempts to simultaneously write and proofread often stifle the ability to say something; and, perhaps most important, that one learns to write (and grows and improves) primarily by *practicing.* Teachers who have had this experience, whatever else they may do, usually change their classroom behavior in one important way: when they ask their students to write, they write along with them.

2. *They assign more writing.* IWP teachers understand that writing, like most other skills, requires practice. One cannot learn to play chess, ride a bicycle, or play the piano without frequent attempts—and, naturally, not without being checkmated, falling off, or hitting many sour notes along the way. Accordingly, these instructors place a high priority on fluency: they encourage students to write often and at length. They realize that, like a piano teacher, they need to instruct the student directly at times,

and also to send the student off to practice alone. Reading teachers are delighted when they hear that their students are reading newspapers, magazines, or letters on their own time, at home; IWP teachers take a similar view of writing practice—learning to write does not require that the student have a teacher as overseer at all, or even most, times.

This principle is not as simple as it may first appear. Most teachers believe that their fundamental duty as writing instructors is to correct every word ever written by every student, so that mistakes and bad habits do not "take root." Nor do these teachers particularly want parents or administrators to ask: "Why didn't you circle all the misspellings on Johnny's paper?" Yet the teacher who holds to this narrow and mistaken sense of duty also becomes a bottleneck in the writing process. If the amount of writing done by students is regulated by the amount of grading time available to the teacher, then the students cannot possibly practice enough to develop fluency. If a high school teacher with a typical student load (125 pupils) assigns an essay to each student and then spends ten minutes correcting each paper, she will work for more than twenty hours. How many times per week can a teacher reasonably be expected to add twenty hours of after-school work to her schedule? Clearly, the teacher who wants her students to write a great deal must cease to be the only audience for their writing.

3. *They assign more kinds of writing.* From the experience of their own writing, as well as from the theory and research discussed in the workshops, IWP teachers learn that "expressive" writing—autobiographical and fictional narratives using language comfortable to the writer—is the base out of which other modes of writing can be developed. Although "creative writing" has by now become something of a dirty word in the era of back-to-basics, it remains the most natural and accessible form of writing for most students. Practice in expressive writing builds the fluency and confidence which students need for other, more challenging kinds of discourse.

Since schools, of course, do attach more importance to these other kinds of writing—descriptive, persuasive, explanatory—IWP teachers work carefully to help their students make the transition to these "transactional" forms. Such growth requires that students learn to anticipate the needs of a particular audience, study the purpose of any given writing task, collect and organize information, and rewrite as well as proofread. These capacities develop best when students try out whole compositions in various modes, rather than fill out workbook exercises or listen to lectures on rhetoric.

4. *Their students write for a variety of audiences.* Given the need both

to facilitate much practice and to help students discover rhetorical strategies, IWP teachers ask students to write for a wide range of audiences—both real and imaginary. While in ordinary classrooms students write only for the teacher (and more specifically, for the teacher's correction), IWP students also write for each other, for older or younger students in their building, for students in other communities, for their own families, and for displays, publications, and competitions of many kinds. The experience of sending a piece of writing out into the real world is enormously instructive: it confirms for students that writing is not merely a set of drills, but a useful way of communicating with other people; it provides them with feedback on the effectiveness of their written messages; and it exerts a natural kind of pressure to edit and revise the writing beforehand so that the intended audience will understand and appreciate it.

5. *They teach writing as a process.* IWP teachers know that writing is accomplished in a series of recursive steps or stages and not, as many students initially believe, as a single, spontaneous act. Without trying to make their students follow a lockstep model of the composing process, these teachers organize activities that implicitly break writing assignments down into the component stages. Students thus spend much time preparing for writing (discussing, note-taking, outlining, brainstorming, list-making) and come to view first drafts as "progress reports" more than as finished products. They also learn that much of the work of writing occurs in revision, and they regularly confer with the teacher, or with a peer editing group, to get help in reseeing and rewriting their work. And they copy edit with care, mostly after all these other tasks have been accomplished.

6. *They evaluate writing productively.* Based upon their own recent experience as writers, IWP teachers recognize that the evaluation of writing is a complicated and sensitive business. Since almost any piece of writing is a bit of self-revelation, sensible readers treat its contents with respect. And if we wish to show students that writing is a way of communicating with an audience, then we must treat their writing accordingly—by responding to the content, as well as to the other features, mechanical, rhetorical, or stylistic, that we may want to alter. Since IWP teachers also seek to acquaint students with the various modes of writing, they realize that different kinds of papers require different kinds of responses: it is no more appropriate to red-pencil an intimate personal reminiscence extensively than to ignore the mechanical errors in a report about to be published in the school paper.

In general, IWP teachers share several approaches to evaluation. Although they do not correct every piece of writing by each student, they do try to read it all. They prefer to grade students on a body of work, often kept in a cumulative folder, rather than on individual efforts. They try to schedule frequent individual conferences with each student: They organize students into small peer editing groups which read and comment on each other's writing. They tell students how they intend to evaluate any given assignment or cumulative folder. They correct mechanical errors in related sets or patterns, rather than trying to remediate all student mistakes at once. Perhaps most important and least definable, their evaluation is supportive: these teachers are ready to appreciate and praise whatever their students *can* do with writing, and do not nurture a constant, festering sense of outrage over the shortcoming they do discover.

7. *They care about teaching writing.* IWP teachers believe that writing is important, not just to their students' success in school, but also for its power to help individuals think and share their thoughts with others.

Though these changes in teachers' attitudes and behavior may seem modest, they do not come about comfortably. Many of these new ideas contradict the training, beliefs, and experience of the best of teachers, and older, more familiar notions are not relinquished without a struggle. The struggle is not between the teachers and the workshop leaders, however, but between the teachers and their own acts of writing. The principles—the importance of fluency and practice, the need to work in steps, the centrality of audience and purpose, the need for supportive response, the relative insignificance of rules and drills—all these things teachers discover when they write. The remainder of the training merely reinforces these ideas by providing the research and theoretical evidence that supports them and by presenting specific, practical classroom applications.

Many of our participants have reported undergoing a mild form of "conversion experience" during the training. Sometimes they half-jokingly refer to their new methods of teaching writing as "the gospel" and are frustrated when they cannot easily transmit the good news to their colleagues. What these teachers have adopted, it seems, is not just a new set of lesson plans but a whole new way of looking at writing and its teaching. For the first time, they really know *that* writing is important and *why*. For them, helping students to acquire this skill is no longer just a teacherly duty. It is the opportunity to give them a precious gift.

If the program I have just described sounds quite different from the "weapons" being lauded in the popular press, then the problem should be clear. The greatest public acclaim and encouragement is reserved for writing programs which adhere to some kind of conspicuously back-to-basics, drill-oriented, hard-nosed, rap-on-the-knuckles methodology, whether or not it works. A few valuable non-traditional programs, like the Bay Area Writing Project and ours in Illinois, have been able to evade scrutiny (or to cultivate misunderstanding) long enough to produce indisputable results. But we are exceptions. In most college English departments and public school districts, the frenzied concern over student illiteracy is still mostly generating either retrograde "innovations" or meaningless turmoil. And, I am tempted to say, until teachers become writers themselves, either independently or through participation in some program that compels them to write, turmoil and regression will continue to dominate the world of English teaching.

10

Not So Strictly Speaking

As I read over this book, as Forster advises, to find out what I think, I am again struck by the centrality of social attitudes in all debates about language. From the tiniest skirmishes—like John Simon's accusation that the *Los Angeles Times's* punctuation errors demonstrate "moral cowardice"—to the wider battle being fought out on the covers of the newsmagazines, disagreements about language are almost always matters of personal opinion, not matters of fact. As a necessary result, language itself has often faded into the background of my text as I have needed to discuss traditions, tastes, beliefs, attitudes, prejudices, and even hatreds. In a sense, this has really been a book about the apparently limitless capacity of human beings to cling to stupid ideas and to find the most trivial imaginable reasons to despise each other. Why should a fireman risk his life to save someone who doesn't even speak English? Why should black children be allowed to use the language they have grown up with? Why not use unreliable and arbitrary multiple-choice tests of usage to assign people to certain levels of schooling and income? Why should students write for pleasure when we have proven methods of teaching writing that are both painful and ineffective? Why shouldn't those who believe they speak proper English be encouraged to congratulate themselves on this feat and to excoriate others not sounding like them? As corrosive old Kurt Vonnegut might say, so it goes.

Since this book has largely addressed questions like these, and since it has acknowledged the power and persistence of certain language attitudes, it is impossible to now end it with a series of snappy, sure-fire recommendations for change. I find myself without what that high-scoring student writer called "a progressive program to get us out of this menagerie." Such a program would have to be aimed at changing the deeply held beliefs of those people—language critics, journalists, editors, college professors, usage panelists—who have been dispensing misinformation and encouraging bad attitudes about the language and its users.

But changing language attitudes is slow, hard work (not that it isn't fun, mind you). A mere application of knowledge will not do the job. John Simon could probably learn the nine principles about language outlined in chapter 4 and still recommend sending black children off to standard English day camps for their own good. Come to think about it, John Simon probably already knows, and in some sense accepts, many of the ideas in that chapter.

No, changing attitudes about language requires more than information: it requires experience. People who have inappropriately prescriptive ideas about the English language will probably never change until they have the experience of coming to value another person whose language differs greatly from theirs, or until their own language is ridiculed and penalized for a change. Such experiences might plant the seed of simple empathy—which, it seems to me, is the only tool which can effectively break down hostilities between individuals and groups. By such linguistic empathy, I do not mean the sloppily sentimental embrace of any sort of language used by anyone at any time. I simply mean that we could develop some new habits of mind: we could become as quick to seek understanding as to attack; as ready to understand *why* language is used in a certain way as to declare why it *must not* or *should not* be so used; and, perhaps most important, we could be cheerfully aware of the fact that in matters of language, someone does not *always* have to be right and someone else wrong. All things considered, however, I cannot think of a way to expose the currently practicing language critics to a combination of information and experience that might encourage the development of such empathic behavior.

Elementary and secondary school teachers, luckily, are another matter. While I have occasionally been hard on teachers in this book, I hope it has also been apparent that I believe that many of them do their work intelligently, effectively, and humanely. But when it comes to teaching about language, teachers are caught in a trap. On the one hand, their training and their professional tradition require them to describe, defend, and act as a living model of standard English for their students. This has long been a fundamental duty of American teachers and has even been confirmed by court cases upholding the dismissal of schoolteachers for grammatical errors in their speech or writing. In a real sense, teachers are expected to promote essentially the same ideas about language that are held by Edwin Newman, Richard Mitchell, and John Simon. Of course, most teachers actually accomplish this task only imperfectly, for reasons ranging from their unwillingness, to their inability, to do it.

On the other hand, teachers also have a kind of experience which the language critics lack: they must work every day with rooms full of people whose command of language is not fully mature, perhaps not even standard. In order to teach their students anything, teachers must be ready to accept them as they are and find value in them as persons. They must certainly go on to teach about English, but they cannot allow the differences between their own and students' languages to become an obsession, to obstruct the other work of the class. Back in the office of the language critic, language *can* become an obsession; the critic is free to lambast the office boys, terrorize the secretaries, or even (perhaps more delicately) correct the boss. Adults are surprisingly tolerant, sometimes even sadly thankful for, attacks on their language. Children are not, and good teachers know it. As I said in the last chapter, people who cultivate a festering outrage about the language of young people do not make good teachers. And as I also mentioned, such people are distributed in the teaching profession in a kind of ascending ratio: the older the students are, the more likely are their teachers to feel such outrage as well as to ridicule the soft-hearted practices of their colleagues at the lower levels of education.

Down in the primary grades, where the basic skills of reading and writing are taught (and where, I cannot resist pointing out, test scores are rising), there are many teachers who know a lot about language. They know, intuitively at least, what kids of any given age can and cannot do with language. They realize that the language of the individual develops in its own sequence and according to a timetable that instruction can accelerate but not rearrange. They know that their students are eager to learn about all the various uses of language and, given the chance, usually will. They accept the fact that social dialects exist and cannot be eradicated by a teacher or anyone else. They know that a teacher who relentlessly criticizes the language and other cultural traits of her students indulges her own prejudices at the cost of the students' motivation.

I say that they know these things intuitively because many teachers are not consciously aware of their knowledge or of the implications of their actions in the classroom. A white teacher working with young, black, inner-city students, for example, may claim (if asked) that she is constantly working to teach her pupils standard English. Yet a visitor to her classroom may find that Black English is being used frequently—often most of the time—as the children go about their work. The teacher and the students understand each other, and dialect differences rarely become an issue. The teacher intuitively knows that to correct every nonstandard utterance which might occur ("When we goin' to lunch?" "Get off mah case, Charles!" "This book be to hard, Teach") would be both time-consuming and counterproductive. The inevitable result of such a policy, consistently applied, would be silence among the students. This teacher has implicitly decided that her students must begin by using the language they already have, that the first priority is accomplishment and the development of a positive attitude toward learning in school, not the learning of standard English grammar.

Yet this teacher probably feels some conflict between what she does and what she thinks. She undoubtedly believes in the importance and value of standard language, and sporadically tries to teach some of its features. She tries to use good English herself, believing that if she can't teach the standard she should at least model it. But she is concerned, when she thinks about it, because the dialect of the students seems not to change. She asks herself when, if ever, they will learn standard English. She wonders, from time to time, whether ten years from now her students will be able to get good jobs. Sometimes, when she sees articles about the literacy crisis or the low SAT scores of black students, she probably feels guilty about what she does and doesn't do in her classroom. But she tells herself during these low moments that learning to read is the most important task before her students, and she devotes the most class time and the best of her energies to this job.

This is the kind of teacher whom the Tibbetses would probably call incompetent. To them, she would be incompetent because she does not consistently and thoroughly teach standard English to her six-, seven- or eight-year-old pupils. To me, it is a measure of her competence that she doesn't. But this teacher still needs help. She needs the opportunity to examine her intuitions.

There *are* parts of the English curriculum, its professional traditions, and the customary teaching methods which are wrongly based, counterproductive, which DO NOT WORK. And teachers need the chance to find out which these are. They need the chance to meet with each other, to read research, to consult with outside sources, to discuss, sift, and compare ideas. Ideally, they need time to study not only their experience with children, but also language itself: to learn about language acquisition, language history, sociolinguistics, the nature of writing, and even (so that they will understand, but not necessarily teach it) grammar. They also need a chance to learn about the history and traditions of their own profession, and about the role that teachers of English have played in the maintenance of common attitudes about language. Giving teachers such opportunities for study will obviously require that employers provide the time and money these activities require. But even more important, teachers need the professional autonomy to adopt classroom practices and materials which will meet the legitimate objectives of schooling, and not just those which will please the proponents of the latest crisis or the adherents of the back-to-something-or-other movement. Some of the things teachers will learn from their studies will be altogether familiar, and will confirm current practices. Other discoveries will probably require changes in subject matter and teaching methodology that will not immediately be popular with school boards or language critics.

Nor is it a very propitious time for teachers to stand up for unpopular, if sensible, ideas about language and its teaching. The vast and angry publicity about the literacy crisis has encouraged taxpayers and parents to demand "basic" curricula in the schools—and *basic* usually just means *old.* It is also a hard time to be a teacher in more general ways: enrollments are declining, tax bases eroding, buildings being closed, teachers reassigned, certification requirements stiffened, and multiple-choice tests increasingly required for finding and keeping teaching positions. In one school district where I recently gave a workshop on writing, 251 of the 401 teachers had just been dismissed. Some of those 251 would regain their jobs during the summer, depending on student registration patterns and each teacher's own political connections with certain administrators. Scores of others would have no jobs. It is not entirely reasonable to expect teachers in such circumstances to adopt or defend practices which, rightly or wrongly, may be unpopular with people who are free to fire them.

Yet even in this discouraging climate, the teachers in the Illinois Writing Project have been willing to take the risk. They have cared enough to spend afternoons, weekends, and parts of their summers working to improve their teaching. They have become serious and prolific writers. They have read much research, talked with each other, and written new curricula. More than this, they have had the confidence and courage to teach writing as their own study dictated, rather than as their principals or the local taxpayers initially might have preferred. They have tried to explain their procedures to others, to build support, or at least to prevent serious attacks on their own classroom innovations until the results were in. Now that all of them can show results, can show that their students indeed learn more about writing than kids taught by other methods, these teachers are admired by their colleagues, their schools, and the parents of their students. They also quite rightly respect themselves and their profession more than they did when they started.

In other words, my "progressive program to get us out of this menagerie" of language crises and grammar drills is to give schoolteachers the support and autonomy they need to teach about language truthfully and effectively. I feel no need to predict or prescribe exactly what, as a result of their own study, they will decide to teach. It will vary from teacher to teacher and from place to place, and that will be fine. But my own experience assures me that teachers provided with the time and space and encouragement to reflect upon what they do will make far more sense than any curriculum that will ever come off Richard Mitchell's basement printing press.

My final recommendation is simply this: we should learn to live with the language critics, for they will always be with us. A hundred years from now, in the stacks of a college library, some enterprising graduate student will dig up the writings of Edwin Newman (as I have dug up Richard Grant White, and Lounsbury dug up James Beattie) and have a good laugh at Newman's complaints about *hopefully* and *massive*. Chances are, too, that this same graduate student will be able to go down to the periodical room, pick up a copy of *Newsweek*, and read about the "massive deterioration" of American English just discovered by the language critics of 2082.

Some things really never change. There will always be a few people who have a strong enough conviction of their own rectitude, a sufficient ignorance of language, and enough leisure time to police the utterances of their social and intellectual inferiors. To the extent that such people are generally believed, they will always do some harm. Their efforts will reinforce and exacerbate whatever hostile attitudes already attend existing language differences at that time and in that place. But when you think of all the trouble such crusaders could cause by getting into less quixotic lines of work, you begin to realize how lucky we are that they confine their efforts to language reform. Perhaps we should simply exercise our option of ignoring them, and allow them their little hobby.

Notes
Bibliography
Index

Notes

1 Famous Last Words

1. I have more fully discussed this controversy in "Literacy and the Popular Press: Fear and Loathing at the *Chicago Tribune*," *ETC: A Review of General Semantics*, September 1978, pp. 285–87.
2. Richard Mitchell, *Less Than Words Can Say* (Boston: Little, Brown, 1979), p. 189.

2 Outlines of the Crisis

1. Ann Landers, "Dear Walter: How Do You Say 'Library'?" *Chicago Sun-Times*. April 24, 1978.
2. Shelly Ross, "TV Ruining Children's Language," *National Enquirer*, undated clipping, 1976.
3. Edith Efron, "The 'New' Illiteracy: Blaming it on TV Skirts Real Issues," *TV Guide*, October 11–17, 1975, p. A–6.
4. Arn Tibbets and Charlene Tibbets, *What's Happening to American English?* (New York: Charles Scribner's Sons, 1978), p. 4.
5. Elaine Markoutsas, "Good English? It's Foreign to Many," *Chicago Tribune*, January 4, 1976.

6. "College Essays: Freshmen Ain't So Good, Mostly," *Los Angeles Times*, November 3, 1974.
7. *Chronicle of Higher Education*, March 1, 1976.
8. For more details on the *AHD* panel and the credentials of its members, see Thomas Creswell, *Usage in Dictionaries and Dictionaries of Usage* (University, Ala.: American Dialect Society, 1975), pp. 11–37.
9. Cited in Israel Schenker, "Words," New York Times News Service, February 24, 1977.
10. Randall's plan for vocabulary building appeared, among other places, in *People Magazine*, September 24, 1979, pp. 4–5.
11. Katherine Anne Porter, cited in Richard Locke, "Jewish American Fiction," *New York Times Book Review*, July 10, 1977, p. 3.
12. Donald Janson, "The Grammarian Stalks Rapists of English Language," *Chicago Tribune*, September 6, 1978. For a similar interview, see Melvin Maddocks, "Glassboro, N.J.: A Voice Crying in the Wilderness," *Time*, January 29, 1979, pp. 5–6.
13. Janson.
14. Nicholas Walshe, "The ... Uh ... Hangout Thing," *National Review*, December 20, 1974, p. 1459.
15. Edwin Newman, *Strictly Speaking* (New York: Warner Books, 1974), p. 22.
16. John Simon, *Paradigms Lost* (New York: Clarkson N. Potter, 1980), p. 7ff.
17. Mitchell, pp. 14, 71.
18. Jean Stafford, "Plight of the American Language," *Saturday Review World*, December 4, 1973, p. 14.
19. "Watch Your Language," *New York Times*, editorial, July 10, 1972.
20. Newman, *Strictly Speaking*, p. 22.
21. Mitchell, p. 131.
22. A leading example (and one to which I will return in chapter 8) is Arthur Schlesinger, "Politics and the American Language," *American Scholar*, autumn 1974, pp. 553–62.
23. See, for example, Richard Gambino, "Watergate Lingo: A Language of Non-Responsibility," in William Sparke and Beatrice Taines, eds., *Doublespeak: Language for Sale* (New York: Harper's College Press, 1975), pp. 49–57.
24. Arthur Schlesinger, "Watergate and the Corruption of Language," *Today's Education*, September-October 1974, pp. 26, 27.
25. "Can't Anyone Here Speak English?" *Time*, August 25, 1975, p. 36.
26. Walter Simmons, "Danger—Functional Illiteracy Increasing," *Tuesday Magazine*, a supplement to the *Chicago Tribune*, October 1976, p. 8.
27. The most noted of the illiteracy studies was the Adult Performance Level survey conducted by the U.S. Office of Education in 1975. It found 23 million American adults "lacked important functional competencies" and an

additional 34 million "were functional but not proficient." For an article that adds later data from a Ford Foundation study, see Gene I. Maerhoff, "Fight on Illiteracy Found to Lag Badly," *New York Times*, September 9, 1979, p. 1.

28. Douglas Bush, "Polluting Our Language," *American Scholar*, spring 1972, p. 239.
29. A. Bartlett Giamatti, "Sentimentality," *Yale Alumni Magazine*, January 1976, pp. 17–18.
30. Simon, p. 169.
31. Clifton Fadiman and James Howard, *Empty Pages: A Search for Writing Competence in School and Society* (Belmont, Calif.: Fearon Pitman, 1979), p. 51.
32. George Orwell, "Politics and the English Language," in Paul A. Eschholz, Alfred F. Rosa, and Virginia P. Clark, eds., *Language Awareness* (New York: St. Martin's, 1974), pp. 30–31.
33. Mitchell, p. 220.
34. Berman, cited in "Why Johnny Can't Write," *Newsweek*, December 8, 1975, p. 58.
35. For a sample of such presumed causes, see *On Further Examination: Report of the Advisory Panel on the Scholastic Aptitude Test Score Decline* (New York: The College Board, 1977).
36. Mitchell, p. 111.
37. Newman, *Strictly Speaking*, p. 24.
38. Fadiman and Howard, pp. 31, 36, 35.
39. Tibbets and Tibbets, pp. 10–11.
40. Ibid., pp. 16–17.
41. Mitchell, p. 60.
42. Tibbets and Tibbets, p. 179.
43. Schlesinger, "Watergate and the Corruption of Language," p. 26.
44. Tibbets and Tibbets, pp. 170–71.

3 Something New and Ominous

1. Dwight MacDonald, "The String Untuned," cited in James Sledd and Wilma R. Ebbit, eds., *Dictionaries and THAT Dictionary* (Chicago: Scott, Foresman, 1962), p. 166.
2. *New York Times*, October 9, 1960; October 21, 1960; January 12, 1961.
3. Cited by Joseph Mersand in *Attitudes toward English Teaching* (Philadelphia: Chilton, 1961), pp. 79–80.
4. Ibid. p. 71.

5. Ibid. p. 49.

6. Ibid.

7. Philip Marsh, cited in Stephen N. Judy, *The ABC's of Literacy* (New York: Oxford University Press, 1980), p. 34.

8. Cited in Richard Lloyd-Jones, "Is Writing Worse Nowadays?" *University of Iowa Spectator*, April 1976, p. 2.

9. Thomas R. Lounsbury, "The Correct Use of Words," *Harper's*, June 1908, p. 108.

10. Quintillian, *Institutio Oratoria* (A.D. 90) cited in William Smail, ed., *Quintillian on Education* (Oxford: Clarendon Press, 1938), book I, pp. 11–14.

11. Lounsbury, "Correct Use," p. 107.

12. Roger Ascham, cited in Richard Foster Jones, *The Triumph of the English Language* (Stanford: Stanford University Press, 1966), pp. 14–15.

13. Silvester Jourdan (1613), cited in Jones, p. 32.

14. William Caxton, *Eneydos* (1490), cited in William A. Craigie, ed., *The Critique of Pure English* (Oxford: Clarendon Press, 1946), pp. 120–21.

15. Roger Ascham, cited in Craigie, p. 126.

16. Thomas Elyot, *The Boke Named the Governour* (1531), cited in Joseph M. Williams, *Origins of the English Language* (New York: Free Press, 1975), p. 93.

17. Angel Day, *The English Secretarie* (1595), cited in Jones, pp. 105–6.

18. George Puttenham, *The Art of English Poesie* (1589), cited in Jones, pp. 129–39.

19. John Locke, *Some Thoughts Concerning Education*, in James L. Axtell, ed., *The Educational Writings of John Locke* (Cambridge, 1968), pp. 276–80.

20. Cited in Williams, pp. 94–95.

21. Joseph Addison, cited in Craigie, pp. 160–63.

22. Swift, cited in Thomas Lounsbury, "Is English Becoming Corrupt?" *Harper's*, December 1903, pp. 108–10.

23. Ibid.

24. Samuel Johnson, *Preface to the Dictionary*, cited in Leonard F. Dean and Kenneth G. Wilson, eds., *Essays on Language and Usage* (New York: Oxford University Press, 1963), pp. 54–69.

25. Orrery, cited in Lounsbury, "English," p. 110.

26. Beattie, cited in Lounsbury, "English," pp. 110–11.

27. William Eddis (1770), cited in J. L. Dillard, *All-American English* (New York: Vintage, 1976), p. 55.

28. Cited in Dillard, p. 57.

29. John Witherspoon (1781), cited in H. L. Mencken, *The American Language* (New York: Alfred A. Knopf, 1937), p. 5.

30. Dillard, pp. 45–76.
31. Thomas Jefferson, cited in Mencken, p. 17.
32. John Adams, cited in Mencken, pp. 7–8.
33. Noah Webster, cited in Mencken, p. 10.
34. Benjamin Franklin, cited in Mencken, p. 7.
35. John Witherspoon, cited in Mencken, p. 5.
36. Walt Whitman, cited in Mencken, pp. 73–74.
37. *American Journal of Education* (1827), cited in Glendon Drake, "The Source of American Linguistic Prescriptivism," paper read to Linguistic Society of America national conference, San Francisco, 1974.
38. *American Journal of Education* (1830), cited in Drake, p. 3.
39. James Brown, *An Appeal From the Old Theory of English Grammar* (1845), cited in Drake, p. 10.
40. Fowle (1829), cited in Shirley Brice Heath, "Standard English: Biography of a Symbol," in Timothy Shopen and Joseph Williams, eds., *Standards and Dialects in English* (Cambridge, Mass.: Winthrop, 1981).
41. Beattie, cited in Lounsbury, "English," p. 111.
42. Landor, cited in Lounsbury, "English," p. 113.
43. *European Magazine and London Review* (1787), cited in Mencken, p. 14.
44. Thomas Hamilton (1833), cited in Dillard, p. 270.
45. Frederick Marryat, *A Diary in America* (1839), cited in Mencken, p. 25.
46. Charles Dickens (1842), cited in Mencken, p. 26.
47. Samuel Taylor Coleridge (1822), cited in Mencken, p. 28.
48. Edward Everett, cited in Mencken, pp. 67–68, 80–81.
49. Drake, p. 14.
50. *North American Review* (1860), cited in Drake, p. 16.
51. *Southern Review* (1871), cited in Drake, pp. 16–17.
52. George Perkins Marsh, *Lectures on the English Language* (New York: Charles Scribner's Sons, 1884), pp. 7–8.
53. Ibid., pp. 381–82, 9.
54. Most of White's columns were reprinted in *Words and Their Uses* (New York: Sheldon, 1870) and in *Every-Day English* (Boston: Houghton Mifflin, 1880).
55. White, *Words and Their Uses*, pp. 18–19, 26, 31, 39–43.
56. Ibid., pp. 26–27, 24, 199ff.
57. Ibid., pp. 80–182.
58. Charles William Eliot (1873), cited in Stephen Judy, "Composition and Rhetoric in American Secondary Schools: 1840–1900," *English Journal*, April 1979, p. 36.
59. Adams Sherman Hill, "English in the Schools," *Harper's*, June 1885, pp. 123–24.

60. E. S. Cox, "English in American Schools," *Addresses and Proceedings of the NEA Session of the Year 1885* (New York: National Education Association, 1886), p. 182.
61. M. W. Smith, "Methods of Study in English," *Journal of Proceedings and Addresses, NEA Session of the Year 1889* (Topeka: National Education Association, 1889), pp. 521–22.
62. Alan Chase, *The Legacy of Malthus* (New York: Alfred A. Knopf, 1977).
63. Theodore Roosevelt (1919) cited in Peter Farb, *Word Play* (New York: Bantam, 1975), p. 186.
64. Van Dyke and Scott (1923), cited in Mencken, pp. 64–65.
65. Mencken, p. 34.
66. Mencken, p. 38.
67. Mencken, p. 39.
68. George Bernard Shaw (1927), cited in Mencken, p. 40.
69. Rupert Hughes (1920), cited in Mencken, p. 77.
70. Murray Godwin (1926), cited in Mencken, p. 78.
71. C. H. Ward (1917), cited in Judy, *The ABCs of Literacy*, p. 34.
72. H. L. Mencken, cited in Gene Lyons, "The Higher Illiteracy," *Harper's*, November 1976, p. 33.
73. Mencken, p. 60.
74. "Good English," *Nation*, June 27, 1934, p. 720.
75. Raven I. McDavid, ed., *An Examination of the Attitudes of the NCTE toward Language* (Champaign: National Council of Teachers of English, 1965), chapter 1.
76. Mencken, p. 51.
77. McDavid, p. 9–10.

4 Nine Ideas about Language

1. Victoria Fromkin and Robert Rodman, *An Introduction to Language* (New York: Holt, Rinehart and Winston, 1978), pp. 329–42.
2. Martin Joos, *The Five Clocks* (New York: Harcourt, Brace and World, 1962).
3. Ibid., p. 40.
4. Ibid., pp. 39–67.
5. M. A. K. Halliday, *Explorations in the Functions of Language* (London: Edward Arnold, 1973).
6. Mark Twain, *The Complete Humorous Sketches and Tales of Mark Twain*, Charles Neider, ed. (New York: Doubleday, 1961) pp. 507–8.
7. See, for example, Williams, pp. 343–48.

8. With many thanks to Jim Quinn and his *American Tongue and Cheek* (New York: Pantheon, 1981).
9. "Business Is Bound to Change," Mobil Oil advertisement, *Chicago Tribune*, January 5, 1977.
10. Fromkin and Rodman, p. 319.
11. See Edward Sapir, *Culture, Language, and Personality* (Berkeley: University of California Press, 1949).
12. Einar Haugen, "The Curse of Babel," in Einar Haugen and Morton Bloomfield, *Language as a Human Problem* (New York: W.W. Norton, 1974), p. 41.
13. Leonard Bloomfield (1961), cited in Dwight Bolinger, *Aspects of Language* (New York: Harcourt, Brace and World, 1968), p. 176.
14. Paul Postal, "Language Differences and Prescriptivism," in Roger D. Abrahams and Rudolph C. Troike, eds., *Language and Cultural Diversity in American Education* (Englewood Cliffs, N.J.: Prentice-Hall, 1972), p. 116.

5 *Matters of Taste*

1. Newman, *Strictly Speaking*, p. 49.
2. Edwin Newman, *A Civil Tongue* (Indianapolis: Bobbs-Merrill, 1976), p. 35.
3. Newman, *Strictly Speaking*, p. 47.
4. Ibid., p. 19.
5. Newman, *A Civil Tongue*, p. 56.
6. Newman, *Strictly Speaking*, p. 50.
7. Newman, *A Civil Tongue*, p. 17.
8. Newman, *Strictly Speaking*, p. 39.
9. Ibid., p. 37.
10. Newman, *A Civil Tongue*, p. 18.
11. Ibid., p. 26.
12. Newman, *Strictly Speaking*, p. 43.
13. Ibid., p. 60.
14. Newman, *A Civil Tongue*, pp. 45–47.
15. Newman, *Strictly Speaking*, pp. 52–53.
16. Ibid., p. 49.
17. Ibid., pp. 63–70.
18. Ibid., p. 140.
19. Newman, *A Civil Tongue*, p. 19.
20. Newman, *Strictly Speaking*, p. 220.
21. Ibid., p. 94.
22. Giamatti, p. 18.

23. William Safire, *On Language* (New York: Times Books, 1980), p. 288.

24. Simon, p. 194.

25. Safire, pp. 300, 104.

26. Richard Mitchell, "John Calloway Interviews," *Chicago*, January 22, 1980.

27. Mitchell, p. 143.

28. Mitchell, pp. 71, 40, 62, 76.

29. Simon, pp. 14, 60, 150, 45–46.

30. Tibbets and Tibbets, pp. 15, 13.

31. Simon, p. 46.

32. Simon, pp. 16, 3–4, 46–47.

33. Morris Bishop, "Good Usage, Bad Usage, and Usage," in the *American Heritage Dictionary* (Boston: American Heritage Publishing Company, 1969), p. xxiii.

34. *American Heritage Dictionary*, pp. vi, x–xii.

35. See Creswell, appendix 1.

36. Ibid.

37. Creswell, pp. 150, 180.

38. Creswell, appendix 1.

39. Mitchell, p. 79.

40. Mitchell, pp. 103, 140, 136, 134, 119.

41. Ibid., p. 130.

42. Mitchell, pp. 81, 86, 84–85, 148.

43. Tibbets and Tibbets, pp. 77, 115–19, 50.

44. Ibid., pp. 108–110, 121, 118–19.

45. "Why Johnny Can't Write," editorial, *Chicago Daily News*, December 27, 1975.

46. The typos are in Gene I. Maerhoff, "Writing Test for College Urged," *New York Times*, January 25, 1976, pp. 1, 21.

47. Advertisement, *New York Times*, May 1, 1977, p. 27.

48. I have by now received three separate mailings concerning this SPECIAL OFFER, postmarked Hicksville, N.Y.

49. "The Decline of Literacy," *Change*, November 1976, p. 31.

50. Committee on the use of English, "Report on the Status of Student Writing in the College," mimeographed (Champaign: University of Illinois, August 10, 1976), appendix C, pp. 4–5, 16.

51. Ibid., pp. 2, 5, 6, 10, 28, 39–40.

52. Ibid. For example, see pp. 16, 19, 22, 24, 26.

53. Simon, p. 65.

54. Simon, pp. 197–98, 211, 101, 169.

55. Ibid., pp. 177, 210, 21.

6 Tests and Measurements

1. It is routinely noted that the verbal section of the ACT test is similar to the corresponding part of the SAT. Though the score declines may be parallel, the test content is not: ACT casts all of its language questions in reading passages that students are asked to proofread for errors, and oddly enough, the ACT calls for considerable skill in punctuation—an ability altogether unmeasured by the SATs.

2. "Test Scores Dip as Standards Skid," *Chicago Tribune*, August 24, 1977.

3. Gerald W. Bracey, "The SAT, College Admissions and the Concept of Talent: Unexamined Myths, Unexplained Perceptions, Needed Explorations" *Phi Delta Kappan*, November 1980, p. 197.

4. *Guide to the Admissions Testing Program* (New York: College Entrance Examination Board, 1977), p. 8.

5. Several of these sample questions have appeared in popular press articles about the SAT score decline and may be familiar to afficianados of testing debates.

6. See *On Further Examination*, pp. 2–6.

7. William H. Angoff, "Distinctions between Aptitude and Achievement Tests," *College Board News*, September 1976, p. 3.

8. See any recent edition of the College Board's *Guide to the Admissions Testing Program*, under the heading: "Interpreting College Board Scores." For another view of test error, see Allan Nairn, *The Reign of ETS: The Corporation That Makes Up Minds* (Washington: Center For the Study of Responsive Law, 1980), pp. 55–160.

9. Steven Brill, "The Secrecy Behind the College Boards," *New York Magazine*, October 7, 1974, p. 68.

10. Narin, pp. 59–66, 71–72.

11. Ibid., p. 73.

12. Brill, p. 74.

13. Nairn, pp. 69, 80.

14. Ibid., p. 201.

15. *Report of the Commission on Tests* (New York: College Entrance Examination Board, 1970).

16. Nairn, pp. 109–35.

17. College Entrance Examination Board, *Guide to the Admissions Testing Program*, p. 25.

18. *About the S.A.T.*, pamphlet distributed to all prospective testees by the College Entrance Examination Board, 1977–78 edition.

19. Nairn, pp. 520–24.

20. *On Further Examination*, pp. 10–13.

21. Ibid., pp. 18–30.

22. Betty Washington, "Studies KO'd by TV; Kids Down for Count," *Chicago Daily News*, August 24, 1977.

23. *On Further Examination*, pp. 1, 19, 24, 26.

24. Ibid., pp. 7–9. It seems worth noting that this early section of the report is titled "An Unchanging Standard" and that its initial subheading reads: "As it was in the beginning." The reverence of these headlines suggests the almost religious quality of the panel's belief in the purity of the tests.

25. Ibid., pp. 18–19. See also Annegret Harnischfeger and David E. Wiley, "Achievement Test Score Declines," in Arthur J. Newman, ed., *In Defense of the American Public School* (Cambridge, Mass.: Schenckman, 1978), pp. 86–103.

26. Professor Roger Farr of Indiana University has made a particular effort to collect and publicize the many studies which contradict the prevalent sense of crisis. He has been generally ignored.

27. Roger Farr, "What Does Research Show?" *Today's Education*, November–December 1978, pp. 33–36.

28. Ibid., p. 34.

29. Roger Farr, "The Teaching and Learning of Basic Academic Skills in Schools" (New York: Harcourt Brace Jovanovich, 1979), pp. 5–6.

30. "Blast Your Critics with Education's Good News," *American School Board Journal*, June 1980, pp. 19–22.

31. *On Further Examination*, p. 16.

32. "Writing Mechanics, 1969–1974," *National Assessment of Educational Progress*, October 1975, pp. 1–2.

33. "Why Johnny Can't Write," pp. 58, 59, 61, 64.

34. Ibid., p. 60.

35. "Society Key to Writing Decline," *NAEP Newsletter*, National Assessment of Education Progress, February 1976, p. 3.

36. *Writing Achievement 1969–1979: Results From the Third National Writing Assessment*, vol. 1, 17-year-olds (National Assessment of Educational Progress, December 1980), p. 51.

37. Ibid., pp. 2, 4.

38. Ibid., pp. 2, 49.

39. Ibid., pp. 48–50.

40. Ibid., pp. 2, 14.

41. See, for example Harold Hodgkinson, "What's Right with Education," *Phi Delta Kappan*, November 1979, pp. 159–62

42. *Focus: The Concern for Writing*, vol. 5 (Princeton, N.J.: Educational Testing Service, 1978), p. i.

43. Ibid., pp. 1–7.

44. Ibid., pp. 8–16.
45. Nairn, pp. 32, 48, 51.

7 Jive

1. J. Mitchell Morse, "The Shuffling Speech of Slavery: Black English," *College English,* March 1973, pp. 834–43.
2. Mitchell, pp. 162, 163, 157–58, 164.
3. Ibid., pp. 162, 163, 164, 158–59.
4. Ibid., pp. 160, 161.
5. Ibid., pp. 160, 165.
6. Simon, pp. 167, 165, 29, 147.
7. Ibid., p. 212.
8. Newman, *Strictly Speaking,* pp. 28, 30.
9. Ibid., pp. 22, 99–100.
10. Andy Rooney, "Everyone Should Speak English," *Chicago Tribune,* March 8, 1981.
11. Bayard Rustin, "Won't They Ever Learn?" *New York Times,* August 1, 1971. Rustin's article appeared in the column paid for by the American Federation of Teachers and normally written by Albert Shanker, who was "on a short vacation" that Sunday.
12. NAACP, cited by Rustin.
13. Roy Wilkins, cited in Karen Shender, "Black English: It's Worth the Effort," *Learning,* January 1975, p. 24
14. Benjamin H. Alexander, "Black English: A Modern Version of Paternalism," *Chronicle of Higher Education,* May 27, 1980, p. 21.
15. Quinn, p. 150.
16. Carl Rowan, cited in Quinn, p. 150.
17. One of many such studies is Nancy Hewett, "Reactions of Prospective English Teachers Toward Speakers of a Non-Standard Dialect," *Language Learning,* December 1971, pp. 205–12.
18. J. L. Dillard, *Black English* (New York: Random House, 1972).
19. Walter Loban, "Problems in Oral English," Research Report no. 5 (Champaign, Ill.: National Council of Teachers of English, 1966), pp. 53–55.
20. Clarence Major, *A Dictionary of Afro-American Slang* (New York: International Publishers, 1971).
21. Bob Greene, "Jive Cuts it Only on the Street, Not in World," *Chicago Tribune,* December 3, 1979.

22. Robbins Burling, *English in Black and White* (New York: Holt, Rinehart and Winston, 1973), pp. 29–47.

23. See Dillard, pp. 73–138.

24. Ibid.

25. Simon, p. 212.

26. The theory was introduced in volumes 9 and 10 (1958–59) of the *British Journal of Sociology*. I quote here from a later, revised version appearing in Frederick Williams, ed., *Language and Poverty* (Chicago: Markham, 1971), pp. 28–29.

27. Bernstein, pp. 32, 37.

28. Marjorie Smiley, "Research and Its Implications," in Arno Jewett, Joseph Mersand, and Doris V. Gunderson, eds., *Improving English Skills of Culturally Different Youth* (Washington: U.S. Department of Health, Education, and Welfare, 1964), p. 40.

29. Ellis G. Olim, "Maternal Language Styles and Cognitive Development of Children," in Williams, p. 212.

30. Rosemary Green Wilson, "The Philadelphia Reading Program for Disadvantaged Youth," in Jewett, Mersand, and Gunderson, p. 135.

31. NCTE Task Force on Teaching English to the Disadvantaged, *Language Programs for the Disadvantaged* (Champaign, Ill.: National Council of Teachers of English, 1965), pp. 42, 196, 224, 223, 233–34.

32. Ibid. pp. 96, 137.

33. For example, see Raven I. McDavid, "Dialectology and the Teaching of Reading," *Reading Teacher*, vol. 18, no. 3 (1964); William A. Stewart, "Continuity and Change in American Negro Dialects," *Florida Foreign Language Reporter*, spring 1968; Roger W. Shuy, "A Linguistic Background for Developing Beginning Reading Materials for Black Children," in Joan C. Baratz and Roger W. Shuy, eds., *Teaching Black Children to Read* (Washington, D.C.: Center for Applied Linguistics, 1969).

34. This article, as well as much of Labov's other related research, can be found in *Language in the Inner City* (Philadelphia: University of Pennsylvania Press, 1972).

35. The Students' Right to Their Own Language," *College Composition and Communication*, Special issue (1974).

36. Simon, pp. 164–66.

37. Ruth I. Golden, "Ways to Improve Oral Communication of Culturally Different Youth," in Jewett, Mersand, and Gunderson, pp. 100–109.

38. Jean Osborn, "Teaching a Teaching Language to Disadvantaged Children," ERIC document ED-015-021, 1968.

39. "Standard Speech Development Program: 1968 Report," Pittsburgh Public Schools, ERIC document ED-025-056, 1969.
40. Richard Rystrom, "The Effects of Standard Dialect Training on Negro First-Graders Learning to Read," research report (Washington, D.C.: U.S. Office of Education, 1968).
41. *Curriculum Guide for the Language Arts, 4–6* (Chicago: Board of Education, n.d.), pp. 96–105.
42. Paul D. Weener, "The Influence of Dialect Differences in the Immediate Recall of Verbal Messages," ERIC document ED-026-199, 1968.
43. Kenneth S. Goodman, "Dialect Barriers to Reading Comprehension," in Baratz and Shuy, pp. 14–15.
44. Sidney Bergquist, "Delano-Sargent-Welch Research Report" (Evanston, Ill.: Northwestern University, 1972).
45. *Psycholinguistic Reading Series*, Mildred Gladney and Lloyd Leaverton, eds. (Chicago: Board of Education, 1968).
46. Ibid.
47. Ibid.

8 Politics and the Arwellian Language

1. George de Lama, "'English-only' Worries Easing in Miami," *Chicago Tribune*, March 8, 1981.
2. Newman, *Strictly Speaking*, p. 17.
3. Mitchell, p. 92.
4. George Orwell, *1984* (New York: Harcourt, Brace, 1949).
5. George Orwell, "Politics and the English Language," in Paul A. Eschholz, Alfred F. Rosa, and Virginia P. Clark, eds., *Language Awareness* (New York: St. Martin's, 1974), pp. 22–34.
6. Schlesinger, "Politics and the American Language," p. 553.
7. Eschholz, Rosa, and Clark, p. 22.
8. Orwell, in Eschholz, Rosa, and Clark, p. 22.
9. Ibid., pp. 22–23.
10. Ibid., pp. 23–24.
11. Ibid., pp. 24–28.
12. Ibid., p. 29.
13. Ibid., pp. 30–31.
14. Schlesinger, "Politics and the English Language," p. 553.
15. Postman, pp. 66–69.

16. Orwell, pp. 31, 32, 33.
17. Haig Bosmajian, *The Language of Oppression* (Washington, D.C.: Public Affairs Press, 1974), pp. 13–14.
18. Ibid., pp. 11, 26–27.
19. Ibid., pp. 23, 20, 31.
20. Ibid., pp. 21, 14.
21. Ibid., pp. 16–17.
22. Ibid., pp. 14–15.
23. Ibid., p. 11.
24. Schlesinger, "Politics and the English Language," pp. 558–59. The "health of the social order" quotation comes from his "Watergate and the Corruption of Language," *Today's Education*, September-October 1974, p. 27.
25. Schlesinger, "Politics and the English Language," pp. 554–55.
26. Ibid., pp. 556–57.
27. Ibid., p. 559.
28. Ibid., pp. 561–62.
29. Orwell, p. 33.
30. Postman, pp. 241–42.
31. Giamatti, pp. 17–19.
32. Ibid., pp. 17–18.
33. Ibid., p. 18.
34. Ibid., pp. 18, 19.
35. Ibid., p. 19.
36. Ibid., pp. 17, 18.
37. Ibid., p. 19.
38. Ibid., pp. 18, 19.
39. Ibid., p. 19.
40. Ibid.
41. *English Journal*, April 1975.
42. Fadiman and Howard, p. 32.
42. Stephen Judy, "Unfinished Business," *English Journal*, January 1980, pp. 7–8. Also pp. 11, 16.
44. Giamatti, p. 17.
45. Ibid., p. 19.

9   *Welcome to Bonehead English*

1. "Why Johnny Can't Write," *Newsweek*, December 8, 1975, pp. 58–63.

2. "Why Johnny Can't Write—And What's Being Done," *U.S. News and World Report*, March 16, 1981, pp. 47–48.

3. Ibid., p. 47.

4. Ibid., p. 48.

5. Ibid.

6. See chapter 3 for details and documentation.

7. Shelby Grantham, "Johnny Can't Write? Who Cares?" *Dartmouth Alumni Magazine*, January 1977, pp. 20–22.

8. Ibid., p. 20.

9. Thomas Wheeler, "The American Way of Testing," *New York Times Magazine*, September 2, 1979, p. 40.

10. Muriel Harris, "Contradictory Perceptions of Rules for Writing," *College Composition and Communication*, May 1979, pp. 218–20.

11. Ibid., p. 220.

12. "Minimum Competency in Writing: What does it Mean?" flyer, Cincinnati Public Schools, 1980.

13. Ibid.

14. Ibid.

15. Ibid.

16. Cited in Markoutsas.

17. Bob Schenet, "Why Can't Big Johnny Write?" *Chicago Daily News*, November 5, 1975, p. 5.

18. Phyllis Zagano, "I Can't Teech Comp No More," *Chronicle of Higher Education*, March 1, 1976.

19. Mitchell, pp. 156–57.

20. Tibbets and Tibbets, p. 85.

21. Zagano.

22. Hank de Zutter, "Essay Question: Why Can't Joe College Read or Write?" *Chicago Tribune*, February 14, 1978.

23. Mary Vaiana Taylor, "The Folklore of Usage," *College English*, April 1974, pp. 764–68.

24. Ibid., p. 766.

25. Michael Hirsley, "Convoluted Prose Tangles Teachers in Web of Words," *Chicago Tribune*, March 8, 1980.

26. Ibid.

27. Robert Klein, "Mindover Matter," Brut Records, 1974.

28. Educational Testing Service has distributed these sample essays in several publications, including the *College Board News*, April 1978.

29. Ibid.

30. Mike Rose, "Sophisticated, Ineffective Books: The Dismantling of Process in Composition Texts," *Composition and Communication*, February 1981, p. 66.

31. Malcolm Cowley, ed., *Writers at Work: The "Paris Review" Interviews* (New York: Viking Press, 1958–).

32. Robert A. Gundlach, *The Composing Process in the Teaching of Writing: A Study of an Idea and Its Uses* (Ph.D. diss., Northwestern University, 1977).

33. John C. Hodges and Mary E. Whitten, *Harbrace College Handbook* (New York: Harcourt Brace Jovanovich, 1977), pp. 331–50.

34. Ibid., p. 335.

35. Holt, Rinehart and Winston has also announced a fourth edition of its introductory grammar text, which includes "an additional section on diminutives and phonesthemes."

36. See, for example, Elizabeth F. Haynes, "Using Research in Preparing to Teach Writing," *English Journal*, January 1978, pp. 82–88. This useful article summarizes and gives helpful bibliographies of research dating back as far as forty-five years.

37. G. M. Wilson, "Locating the Language Errors of Children" *Elementary School Journal*, vol. 21 (1920), p. 290.

38. Tibbets and Tibbets, pp. 62, 52, 55.

39. Ibid., p. 81.

40. Ibid., pp. 126–59.

41. S. A. Barney, J. E. Hunter, and B. L. Packer, *Writing Prose* (New Haven: Yale University, 1975), p. 17.

42. Ibid., p. 10, introduction.

43. Ibid., pp. 2–6.

44. Ibid., pp. 15, 16, 5.

45. Ibid., pp. 9, 10.

46. Ibid., p. 5.

47. Norman L. Trusty, "How to Prepare Research Papers : A Logical System," *Off to College* (Montgomery, Ala: Guidance Research Group, 1980) pp. 50–52.

48. Ibid., pp. 51–52.

49. Jack Mabley, " 'Grammer' Relief A Phone Call Away," *Chicago Tribune*, April 13, 1981.

50. Ibid.

51. Fadiman, p. 37.

52. Ibid., pp. 1, 10.

Bibliography

In the process of compiling this bibliography, I have been reminded that about a dozen special books have been particularly important to the preparation of this volume. It strikes me as interesting that of these thirteen treasured sources, each of which seems vitally connected to the heart of the book, only five are mentioned directly in the text. Only two or three of these titles, in fact, play a major documentary role. These books, in other words, seem to constitute what a linguist might call my "deep bibliography"; books whose influence upon my message lies far below the surface, but which are in a true sense the core of the matter. On the basis of this bibliolinguistic theory, I have set these peculiar and admired titles apart at the head of the list, and have included a few comments about each.

Robbins Burling. *English in Black and White*. New York: Holt, Rinehart and Winston. 1973. A clear explanation and description of Black English written by a linguistic anthropologist with a sense of humor and a profound respect for diversity in human behavior. The fact that this book is so *thin* is a reminder of how slight are the differences between standard and Black English.

James Britton. *Language and Learning*. Coral Gables: University of Miami Press, 1970. Britton has had an enormous influence on the thinking of people involved in teaching writing. Sometimes I think that we are mostly working, after thir-

teen years, to understand and apply the wisdom contained in this book. Unfortunately, while Britton's terminology has entered general academic use, his
deep personal appreciation of students and their language has not been so widely emulated.

Alan Chase. *The Legacy of Malthus.* New York: Alfred A Knopf, 1977. The history
of scientific attempts to justify racism and support extremist politics, from
phrenology to IQ testing. An enormous book, overdocumented really, but all the
sickening detail is assembled with such righteous enthusiasm by Alan Chase that
one cannot resist a single digression. If there ever was an effective angry book,
this is it.

Stephen N. Judy. *The ABCs of Literacy.* New York: Oxford University Press, 1980.
Judy, who at this writing is president-elect of the National Council of Teachers
of English, has made substantial contributions to the English teaching profession. Under his editorship, the *English Journal* resisted the most irrational pressures of the literacy crisis, and occasionally fired off rejoinders (see chapter 8).
On his own, Judy has written a number of very useful books, each of which
models the historical and linguistic awareness so necessary to effective English
teaching.

William Labov. *Language in the Inner City: Studies in the Black English Vernacular.* Philadelphia: University of Pennsylvania Press, 1972. Includes Labov's
important and much-reprinted article, "The Logic of Nonstandard English,"
which demonstrated to a doubting academic community that black children
actually had speech skills equal to their white age-mates. It seems ludicrous,
looking back, that anyone should have to write such an article—or that it could
have been as controversial as it was.

Richard L. Larson, ed. *Children and Writing in the Elementary School.* New York:
Oxford University Press, 1975. This collection has strong short pieces by James
Britton, James Moffet, Herbert Kohl, and others, but I appreciate it most for
Wallace Douglas's "On Value in Children's Writing." Here Douglas displays a
few samples of student writing and proceeds to show, with his own particular
brand of leisurely ruthlessness, how the teaching of writing is perverted by
schools. Honors students are trained to produce empty, high-falutin', me-
chanically perfect tripe; low-track kids are either ignored or red-penciled,
though amidst their error-strewn prose can be found some of the best writing
done in schools. Powerful and saddening; vintage Douglas.

Donald M. Murray. *A Writer Teaches Writing.* Boston: Houghton Mifflin, 1968.
For the past four summers, I have been using Murray as a text in summer
institutes for writing teachers. It is consistently the most popular of the five or six
books assigned. At first, I was annoyed by Murray's persistent habit of giving a
numbered list for everything: The Writer's Seven Skills, The Ten Myths About

Teaching Writing, etc. But I have gradually come to forgive Murray's dogmatism and schematism, in view of the fact that the contents of his tidy lists made so much sense. And also because he wrote a very helpful book about teaching writing in 1968, long before a "literacy crisis" was announced.

Alan Nairn. *The Reign of E.T.S.: The Corporation That Makes Up Minds.* Washington: Center for the Study of Responsive Law, 1980. More commonly known as the Nader Report on the ETS, this homemade offprint volume spends 554 angry pages ripping up the testers. In a sense, it's overkill; but then, the evidence of arrogance, myopia, and prejudice is so plentiful that it would have been too much to ask for Nairn to remain calm. Of course, the ETS has issued sober rebuttals to many of the book's accusations.

Richard Ohmann, *English in America.* New York: Oxford University Press, 1976. A highly personal interpretation of the job of English teaching by a radical Marxist professor who served for many years as editor of *College English.* Ohmann is of the belief that the literacy crisis is not just an illusion, but a hoax. He explains our recent problems with language in terms of the outcomes which the ruling classes want from the educational system they control. Myself, I've never been all that impressed with the manipulative efficiency of the ruling classes, but I do wonder about the emptiness and limitedness of what goes on in some college English classes. At least Ohmann has *an* answer.

Evelyn Pitcher, and Ernst Prelinger, *Children Tell Stories.* New York: International Universities Press, 1963. Oral fantasy narratives of children aged two to five, delicately collected by two psychologists, who reproduce the samples and then subject them to an essentially Freudian interpretation. The stories make wonderful reading; they are violent, inventive, ritualistic, and transparently self-revealing tales. The Freudian translations are less fun to read, though anyone skeptical of analytic psychology may be stumped by the staggering evidence here.

Neil Postman. *Crazy Talk, Stupid Talk.* New York: Delacorte, 1976. A delightfully entertaining review of the ways in which human beings deceive themselves and each other. I disagree with some of Postman's explanations, but almost never with his descriptions. Though he has recently been attacked for leaving the liberal political fold, Postman has done more than anyone else to bring the insights of linguistics into education, and ought to be appreciated for this effort.

Jim Quinn. *American Tongue and Cheek.* New York: Pantheon, 1981. A very funny "populist guide" to American English and rebuke of the language critics. Quinn had the patience to look up practically every currently debated usage in the *Oxford English Dictionary,* thereby providing himself with much ammunition to hurl at Simon et al. A kindred spirit.

General Bibliography

Benjamin H. Alexander. "Black English: A Modern Version of Paternalism." *Chronicle of Higher Education*, May 27, 1980.

William H. Angoff. "Distinctions Between Aptitude and Achievement Tests." *College Board News*, September 1976.

Joan C. Baratz, and Roger W. Shuy, eds. *Teaching Black Children to Read*. Washington: Center for Applied Linguistics, 1969.

S. A. Barney, J. E. Hunter, and B. L. Packer. *Writing Prose*. New Haven: Yale University, 1975.

Sidney Bergquist. "Delano-Sargent-Welch Research Report." Evanston, Ill.: Northwestern University, 1972.

Basil Bernstein. "Language and Social Class." *British Journal of Sociology*, II, 1960.

Morris Bishop. "Good Usage, Bad Usage, and Usage." In *American Heritage Dictionary*. Boston: American Heritage Publishing Company, 1969.

Sissela Bok. *Lying: Moral Choice in Public and Private Life*. New York: Vintage, 1979.

Dwight Bolinger. *Aspects of Language*. New York: Harcourt, Brace, and World, 1968.

Haig Bosmajian. *The Language of Oppression*. Washington: Public Affairs Press, 1974.

"Blast Your Critics with Education's Good News." *American School Board Journal*, June 1980.

Gerald W. Bracey. "The SAT, College Admissions and the Concept of Talent: Unexamined Myths, Unexplained Perceptions, Needed Explorations." *Phi Delta Kappan*, November 1980.

Steven Brill. "The Secrecy Behind the College Boards." *New York Magazine*, October 7, 1974.

Douglas Bush. "Polluting Our Language." *American Scholar*, Spring 1972.

"Can't Anyone Here Speak English?" *Time*, August 25, 1975.

"College Essays: Freshmen Ain't So Good, Mostly," *Los Angeles Times*, November 3, 1974.

E. S. Cox. "English in American Schools." In *Addresses and Proceedings of the NEA Session of the Year 1885*. New York: National Education Association, 1886.

William A. Craigie, ed. *The Critique of Pure English*. Oxford: Clarendon Press, 1946.

Thomas Creswell. *Usage in Dictionaries and Dictionaries of Usage.* University, Ala.: American Dialect Society, 1975.

Curriculum Guide for the Language Arts, 4–6. Chicago Board of Education, n.d.

Harvey A. Daniels. *"Bi-Dialectalism: A Policy Analysis."* Ph. D. dissertation, Northwestern University, 1973.

————. "For Latinos, Flames Fan Linguistic Prejudice." *Chicago Tribune,* January 9, 1977.

————. "Is There a Decline in Literacy?" *English Journal,* September, 1976.

————. "Literacy and the Popular Press: Fear and Loathing at the *Chicago Tribune." ETC: A Review of General Semantics,* September 1978.

"The Decline of Literacy." *Change,* November 1976.

George de Lama. "'English-only' Worries Easing in Miami," *Chicago Tribune,* March 8, 1981.

Hank de Zutter. "Essay Question: Why Can't Joe College Read or Write?" *Chicago Tribune,* February 14, 1978.

J. L. Dillard. *Black English.* New York: Random House, 1972.

————. *All-American English.* New York: Vintage, 1976.

Glendon Drake. "The Source of American Linguistic Prescriptivism." Paper read at the Linguistic Society of America convention, 1975.

Edith Efron. "The 'New Illiteracy': Blaming it on TV Skirts Real Issues." *TV Guide,* October 11–17, 1975.

Clifton Fadiman, and James Howard. *Empty Pages: A Search for Writing Competence in School and Society.* Belmont, Calif.: Fearon Pitman, 1979.

Roger Farr. "The Teaching and Learning of Basic Academic Skills in Schools." New York: Harcourt Brace Jovanovich, 1979.

————. "What Does Research Show?" *Today's Education,* November–December 1978.

Focus: The Concern for Writing. Educational Testing Service, 1980.

Victoria Fromkin, and Robert Rodman. *An Introduction to Language.* New York: Holt, Rinehart and Winston, 1978.

Richard Gambino. "Watergate Lingo: A Language of Non-Responsibility." In *Doublespeak: Language for Sale,* edited by William Sparke, and Beatrice Taines. New York: Harper's College Press, 1975.

A. Bartlett Giamatti. "Sentimentality." *Yale Alumni Magazine,* January 1976.

"Good English." *Nation,* June 27, 1934.

Shelby Grantham. "Johnny Can't Write? Who Cares?" *Dartmouth Alumni*

Magazine, January 1977.

"Guide to the Admissions Testing Program." College Entrance Examination Board, 1977.

Robert A. Gundlach. *"The Composing Process in the Teaching of Writing: A Study of an Idea and Its Uses."* Ph.D. dissertation, Northwestern University, 1977.

M. A. K. Halliday. *Explorations in the Functions of Language.* London: Edward Arnold, 1973.

Annegret Harnischfeger, and David E. Wiley. "Achievement Test Score Declines." *In Defense of the American Public School,* edited by Arthur J. Newman. Cambridge, Mass.: Schenckman, 1978.

Einar Haugen. "The Curse of Babel." In *Language as a Human Problem,* edited by Einar Haugen and Morton Bloomfield. New York: W. W. Norton, 1974.

Elizabeth F. Haynes. "Using Research in Preparing to Teach Writing." *English Journal,* January 1978.

Shirley Brice Heath. "Standard English: Biography of a Symbol." In *Standards and Dialects in English,* edited by Timothy Shopen, and Joseph Williams. Cambridge, Mass.: Winthrop, 1981.

Nancy Hewett. "Reactions of Prospective English Teachers Toward Speakers of a Non-Standard Dialect." *Language Learning,* 21, no. 2.

Adams Sherman Hill. "English in the Schools." *Harper's Monthly Magazine,* June 1885.

Michael Hirsley. "Convoluted Prose Tangles Teachers in Web of Words." *Chicago Tribune,* March 8, 1980.

John C. Hodges and Mary E. Whitten. *Harbrace College Handbook.* New York: Harcourt, Brace Jovanovich, 1977.

Harold Hodgkinson. "What's Right with Education." *Phi Delta Kappan,* November 1979.

Donald Janson. "The Grammarian Stalks Rapists of English Language." *Chicago Tribune,* September 6, 1978.

Arno Jewett, Joseph Mersand, and Doris V. Gunderson, eds. *Improving English Skills of Culturally Different Youth.* Washington: U.S. Department of Health, Education, and Welfare, 1964.

Samuel Johnson. *Preface to the Dictionary,* In *Essays on Language and Usage,* edited by Leonard F. Dean and Kenneth G. Wilson. New York: Oxford University Press, 1963.

Richard Foster Jones. *The Triumph of the English Language.* Stanford: Stanford University Press, 1966.

Martin Joos. *The Five Clocks.* New York: Harcourt, Brace and World, 1962.

Stephen Judy. "Unfinished Business. *English Journal,* January 1980.

————. "Composition and Rhetoric in American Secondary Schools: 1840–1900." *English Journal,* April 1979.

Robert Klein. "Mind Over Matter." Brut Records, 1974.

Ann Landers. "Dear Walter: How Do You Say 'Library'?" *Chicago Sun-Times,* April 24, 1978.

Language Programs for the Disadvantaged, NCTE Task Force on Teaching English to the Disadvantaged. Champaign, Ill.: National Council of Teachers of English, 1965.

Walter Loban. "Problems in Oral English: NCTE Research Report Number Five." Champaign, Ill. National Council of Teachers of English, 1966.

Richard Lloyd-Jones. "Is Writing Worse Nowadays?" *University of Iowa Spectator,* April 1976.

John Locke. *Some Thoughts Concerning Education.* In *The Educational Writings of John Locke,* edited by James L. Axtell. Cambridge: Cambridge University Press, 1968.

Thomas R. Lounsbury. "Is English Becoming Corrupt?" *Harper's Monthly Magazine,* December 1903.

————. "The Correct Use of Words." Harper's Monthly Magazine, June 1908.

Jack Mabley. "'Grammer' Relief A Phone Call Away." *Chicago Tribune,* April 13, 1981.

Raven I. McDavid, ed. *An Examination of the Attitudes of the NCTE Toward Language.* Champaign.: National Council of Teachers of English, 1965.

Dwight MacDonald. "The String Untuned." In *Dictionaries and THAT Dictionary,* edited by James Sledd and Wilma R. Ebbit. Chicago: Scott, Foresman, 1962.

Melvin Maddocks. "Glassboro, N.J.: A Voice Crying in the Wilderness. *Time,* January 29, 1979.

Gene I. Maerhoff. "Fight on Illiteracy Found to Lag Badly." *New York Times,* September 9, 1979.

————. "Writing Test for College Urged." *New York Times,* January 25, 1976.

Clarence Major. *A Dictionary of Afro-American Slang.* New York: International Publishers, 1971.

Elaine Markoutsas. "Good English? It's Foreign to Many." *Chicago Tribune*, January 4, 1976.

George Perkins Marsh. *Lectures on the English Language*. New York: Charles Scribner's Sons, 1884.

Joseph Mersand. *Attitudes Toward English Teaching*. Philadelphia: Chilton, 1961.

Richard Mitchell. *Less Than Words Can Say*. Boston: Little, Brown, 1979.

J. Mitchell Morse, "The Shuffling Speech of Slavery: Black English." *College English*, March 1973.

"Minimum Competency in Writing: What Does it Mean?" Cincinnati Public Schools, 1980.

Edwin Newman. *A Civil Tongue*. Indianapolis: Bobbs—Merrill, 1966.

——. *Strictly Speaking*. New York: Warner Books, 1974.

On Further Examination: Report of the Advisory Panel on the Scholastic Aptitude Test Score Decline. New York: The College Board, 1977.

George Orwell. *1984*. New York: Harcourt, Brace, 1949.

——. "Politics and the English Language." In *Language Awareness*, edited by Paul A. Eschholz, Alfred F. Rosa, and Virginia P. Clark. New York: St. Martin's Press, 1974.

Jean Osborne. "Teaching a Teaching Language to Disadvantaged Children." ERIC document ED-027-056.

Katherine Anne Porter. Cited in Richard Locke, "Jewish American Fiction." *New York Times Book Review*, July 10, 1977.

Paul Postal. "Language Differences and Prescriptivism." In *Language and Cultural Diversity in American Education*, edited by Roger D. Abrahams and Rudolph C. Troike. Englewood Cliffs, N.J.: Prentice-Hall, 1972.

Neil Postman. *Crazy Talk, Stupid Talk*. New York: Delacorte, 1976.

Psycholinguistic Reading Series. Chicago Board of Education, 1968.

Report of the Commission on Tests. New York: College Entrance Examination Board, 1970.

"Report on the Status of Student Writing in the College." Committee on the use of English, University of Illinois at Champaign, August 10, 1976.

Andy Rooney. "Everyone Should Speak English." *Chicago Tribune*, March 8, 1981.

Mike Rose. "Sophisticated, Ineffective Books: The Dismantling of Process in Composition Texts." *College Composition and Communication*, February 1981.

Shelly Ross. "TV Running Children's Language. "*National Enquirer*, undated clipping, 1976.

Richard Rystrom. "The Effects of Standard Dialect Training on Negro First-Graders Learning to Read." U.S. Office of Education Research Report, 1970.

William Safire. *On Language*. New York: Times Books, 1980.

Edward Sapir. *Culture, Language, and Personality*. Berkeley: University of California Press, 1949.

Bob Schenet. "Why Can't Big Johnny Write?" *Chicago Daily News*, November 5, 1975.

Israel Schenker. "Words." *New York Times News Service*, February 24, 1977.

Arthur Schlesinger. "Politics and the American Language." *American Scholar*, Autumn 1974.

————. "Watergate and the Corruption of Language." *Today's Education*, September–October 1974.

Walter Simmons. "Danger—Functional Illiteracy Increasing." *Tuesday Magazine*, October 1976.

William M. Smail, ed. *Quintillian on Education*. Oxford: Clarendon Press, 1938.

M. W. Smith. "Methods of Study in English." *Journal of Proceedings and Addresses, NEA Session of the Year 1889*.

"Society Key to Writing Decline." *NAEP Newsletter*, National Assessment of Educational Progress, February 1976.

Jean Stafford. "Plight of the American Language." *Saturday Review World*, December 4, 1973.

"Standard Speech Development Program." Pittsburgh Public Schools, ERIC document ED-027-056.

"Students' Right to their Own Language." Special issue of *College Composition and Communication*. National Council of Teachers of English, 1974.

Mary Vaiana Taylor. "The Folklore of Usage." *College English*, April 1974.

"Test Scores Dip as Standards Skid." *Chicago Tribune*, August 24, 1977.

Arn Tibbets and Charlene Tibbets. *What's Happening to American English?* New York: Charles Scribner's Sons, 1978.

Norman L. Trusty. "How to Prepare Research Papers: A Logical System." *Off to College*, 1980.

Mark Twain. *The Complete Humorous Sketches and Tales of Mark Twain*. Edited by Charles Neider. New York: Doubleday,1961.

Nicholas Walshe. "The . . . Uh . . . Hangout Thing." *National Review*, December 20, 1974.

Betty Washington. "Studies KO'd by TV: Kids Down for Count." *Chicago Daily News,* August 24, 1977.

"Watch Your Language." *New York Times,* editorial, July 10, 1972.

Thomas Wheeler. "The American Way of Testing." *New York Times Magazine,* September 2, 1979.

Richard Grant White. *Words and Their Uses.* New York: Sheldon and Company, 1870.

_____. *Every-Day English.* Boston: Houghton Mifflin, 1880.

"Why Johnny Can't Write." *Newsweek,* December 8, 1975.

"Why Johnny Can't Write—And What's Being Done." *U.S. News and World Report,* March 16, 1981.

Frederick Williams, ed. *Language and Poverty.* Chicago: Markham, 1971.

G.M. Wilson. "Locating the Language Errors of Children." *Elementary School Journal,* vol. 21, 1920.

Writers at Work: The Paris Review Interviews. New York: Viking Press, 1958–

Writing Achievement 1969–1979: Results From the Third National Writing Assessment, Volume 1—17-Year-Olds. National Assessment of Educational Progress, December 1980.

Writing Mechanics, 1969–1974. National Assessment of Educational Progress, October 1975.

Phyllis Zagano. "I Can't Teech Comp No More." *Chronicle of Higher Education,* March 1, 1976.

Index